The relationship between intellectual life and institutionalism is the grand theme of Jack Goody's new book. His focus is on the development of the discipline of social anthropology in Britain through its key practitioners and how far its concerns interact with the political and ideological debate of the interwar years. As such this is a study of the different ideological and intellectual approaches adopted by the emerging subject of social anthropology and how far these views were incorporated into and defined by the structures and institutions in which they developed. But it is also an analysis of how far the subject was created by its own response to the key issues of the time: colonialism – specifically Africa – anti-Semitism and communism. Goody's approach is characteristically personal: Malinowski dominates the discussion, as well as Fortes, Radcliffe-Brown and Evans-Pritchard, and his own experience, gathered over a varied and wide-ranging life of fieldwork informs the conclusion of the book and the 'whither anthropology?' questions raised by the discussion.

THE EXPANSIVE MOMENT

THE EXPANSIVE MOMENT

*The rise of social anthropology
in Britain and Africa 1918–1970*

JACK GOODY

University of Cambridge

CAMBRIDGE
UNIVERSITY PRESS

Published by the Press Syndicate of the University of Cambridge
The Pitt Building, Trumpington Street, Cambridge CB2 IRP
40 West 20th Street, New York, NY 10011–4211, USA
10 Stamford Road, Oakleigh, Melbourne 3166, Australia

First published 1995

Printed in Great Britain at the University Press, Cambridge

A catalogue record for this book is available from the British Library

Library of Congress cataloguing in publication data
Goody, Jack.
The expansive moment : the rise of social anthropology in Britain
and Africa, 1918–1970 / Jack Goody.
p.   cm.
Includes bibliographical references.
ISBN 0 521 45048 9 (hardback). – ISBN 0 521 45666 5 (pbk.)
1. Ethnology – Great Britain – History.
2. Ethnology – Africa – History.
I. Title.
GN308.3.G7G66   1995
306′.0941–dc20   94–35663   CIP

ISBN 0 521 45048 9 hardback
ISBN 0 521 45666 5 paperback

Contents

.

Introduction

Why would one want to read or write a book about a small group of academics, whose fate might interest only practitioners in the same field? Partly because it illustrates the growth and expansion of an area of enquiry and University teaching and research which has had some influence on neighbouring fields. Partly because the accounts which are emerging of that group seem to overlook some crucial aspects of the social and intellectual situation of the 1930s and post-war period. Following an approach current in much intellectual, sociological and cultural history, they assume a homogeneity of interest between intellectuals and the government which neglects internal contradictions and oppositions. Equally intellectual positions were more differentiated, more argued about than such approaches allow, often holding within themselves the clues to the next development. That seems true not only within the group of scholars involved but also of their sponsors, whether these were foundations or governments. In looking at this situation I hope to throw light on the discussion about the relationships of these scholars to the powers that be, which I see as much more differentiated, less homogeneous, than some recent commentators.[1]

As a professional field of enquiry, social anthropology emerged at the beginning of the twentieth century, though it had many earlier progenitors. This book presents an account of the period when this subject came of age in Britain, largely under the auspices of Bronislaw Malinowski, the Polish professor teaching at the London School of Economics (LSE). There he attracted a group of scholars who had already had considerable experience in other fields, who came to form the core around which the major teaching departments in the country were formed, and who founded a tight professional organisation of trained, research-orientated personnel, the Association of Social Anthropologists (ASA), in 1946. Their research consisted mainly of work done in British territories in Africa during the late 1920s and the 1930s, carried out under the auspices of the International African Institute which published much of their results. Although Malinowski was not an Africanist, his personal reputation for fieldwork based on observation and his association with the LSE enabled that Institute to attract money from a philanthropic body in the United States which was interested in the contemporary situation in Africa. This was the Laura Spelman Rockefeller Memorial which contributed significantly to the growth of the social sciences in Britain and had selected the LSE as a centre of excellence worthy of support as early as 1924, at which time it developed a fellowship programme in North America through the newly formed Social Science Research Council (SSRC) – which it had encouraged and financed – as well as in Europe and later Australia.[2]

This then is an account of the interactions of a group of scholars, with many of whom I later worked, and of the research they undertook. Inevitably it concentrates upon my own teachers, Meyer Fortes and E. E. Evans-Pritchard, and in particular on contributions made by research in West Africa where I did my own fieldwork. At the end it becomes frankly autobiographical.

How did I get into this enquiry?

The unfolding of an anthropologist's career, like that of many an academic, can be described in terms of the progression: from the seminar, to the field, to the study and to the class, although one phase does not replace another. One attends seminars as a graduate student and again later on, but in a different capacity and with different intentions, when other professional activities – writing-up or teaching – dominate one's life. For many, probably most, possibly all, academics, writing and teaching themselves gradually take a less important place than administration and politics, that is, than the participation in committees, than the round of learned societies, than the support of one candidate or one issue as against another, and than the multitude of other tasks that tend to overwhelm the pursuits that are normally identified with the profession. Distracting as these are, they form the institutional setting of teaching and research in the context of which takes place a continual hunt for funds and personnel. It is this institutional context of intellectual activity which comes out so clearly in the minutes of meetings and, increasingly over time, in the personal letters of the teachers themselves. It is the relationship between this body of material and their contributions to knowledge in the shape of reviews, papers and books, that lies at the centre of my interest. What I have to offer consists of two parts. The first is an account of the emergence of an academic discipline in this country, largely from the perspective of one of the participants, Meyer Fortes, and to a lesser extent, Evans-Pritchard. The second part is an attempt arising out of an invitation from Claude Tardits to lecture on the subject of 'What did we do?' to a seminar on African anthropology at the 5ème Section de l'Ecole Pratique des Hautes Etudes in Paris in the spring of 1988.

It is often claimed that British social anthropology was the child of colonialism. Its work was carried out mainly within the colonial empire – Malinowski in New Guinea, Radcliffe-Brown in the Andamans, Firth in New Zealand, Tikopia and Malaysia, Evans-Pritchard in the Sudan, Fortes in the Gold Coast, Richards, Gluckman and Schapera in British East and South African territories, Leach in Burma. But the further implication of the claim is that since research had to be carried with the approval and support of these regimes, it influenced both its empirical direction and its theoretical underpinning.[3]

By examining a selection of documents, I want to suggest that these implications need modifying, firstly with regard to the financial base, secondly with regard to the approval of colonial governments, and finally with regard to the supposed homogeneity of the empirical and theoretical approaches. On the individual level, the participants came from differing national, social and ideological backgrounds, though many were influenced by contemporary interests in the ideas of Marx, the rise of Fascism in Europe and the ending of colonial empires. At a social level, the standard claims fail to take account of the contradictions, the conflicts and the diversity of perspective that one finds in any social formation, and specifically in the relations between research worker and the support agencies (whether government or not), and the role of human agency in interpreting, enacting or generating these conflicts. Anthropologists of the 1930s understood this well and they knew, as some have told me, that the situation was yet more complicated than the documents reveal.[4] Nevertheless it seemed to me worthwhile to sketch out the position as it appeared to me from what I had read, even if it confirmed earlier worries about the conclusions one can draw from such textual material.

I have to add that I did not deliberately intend to get involved in this subject at all. In other words, my interest in anthropology has not been in the history of the discipline as such, although I have touched upon the development of some specific intellectual topics. In other words, my interest in history has usually had to do with some problem I was working on, an enterprise in which boundaries have to be breached rather than defined. How then did I come to write these pages?

As a member of the post-war generation of anthropologists, I did not know the two founders of the subject in Britain, A. R. Radcliffe-Brown and B. Malinowski, though I once met the former, and attended his very anthropological funeral; like most funerals of academics, and unlike their weddings and certainly their births, it consisted of colleagues rather than kin. But I did become acquainted with their pupils and colleagues, with Alison Davis, Evans-Pritchard, Firth, Forde, Hogbin, Kaberry, Mair, Mead, Talcott Parsons, Richards, Schapera, Srinivas, Stanner, Lloyd Warner, and with Fortes and Leach I worked closely over many years.

The historical background of social anthropology in early twentieth-century Britain may appear to be a well-worn topic discussed in the works of Jarvie (1964), A. Kuper (1973), Langham (1981), Lombard (1972), Stocking (1983, 1984, 1985) and Kuklick (1991) on the general issues, and of Douglas (1980) on Evans-Pritchard, of Firth (1957) and Panoff (1972) on Malinowski, and of others on particular aspects. I myself took up the topic partly to share the results of some archival research which I undertook when I became interested in a personal file on Fortes in the Ghana archives which related to the difficulties he had in getting to the field and the view taken of his proposal by senior colonial officers; it had been destroyed by the shredders in London, and Fortes told me he did not want to look at it. After his death I was asked to write an extended obituary for the *Proceedings of the British Academy*. I spent some time in the archives of the London School of Economics (before realising that Stocking had looked at many of these) as well as those of the International African Institute since I wanted to produce something substantial, given that these obituaries constitute one of the fullest sources that we have of immediate biographical and bibliographic data, and in some cases of intellectual achievement, especially those on A. R. Radcliffe-Brown and M. Gluckman by R. Firth, C. D. Forde by M. Fortes and E. E. Evans-Pritchard by J. A. Barnes.

For the obituary of Fortes, then, I decided to look at some of the archival materials, including the Public Record Office, and I had access to some of the papers of Meyer Fortes. These pages are a by-product of those enquiries but they originally took shape when I became dissatisfied with some comments on the conservative nature of an undifferentiated British 'structural–functional' anthropology with regard to colonial rule. These came mainly from Americans and Russians whose anthropologists have rarely given much effective support to self-government for the aboriginal peoples of their own immense, internal, empires, contenting themselves with limited ameliorative measures a good deal less radical than those proposed by 'colonial' anthropologists, many of whom supported freedom movements.

But I think of the result as 'notes towards' or a 'personal account' because there are other things I want to write, rather than a full-blown history. Only certain lines are followed up; I am aware there are other documentary sources, close to me, that I have not used. I am also aware of the limitations of the material. While my own background knowledge provides me with anecdotes of the past and residues in the present, I have concentrated upon the documents at my disposal. The results make one realise the limitations of a history based upon written materials, especially letters to close friends. I do not believe one can reconstruct Malinowski's persona from his letters, which express extreme attitudes to Reds and Jews, for example. Yet his behaviour to the outside world regarding Fortes and Kirchhoff, who were both, was exemplary. Equally Evans-Pritchard's letters to Fortes contain the most intolerant, reactionary statements and while he was never a political progressive in any sense, his life was marked by close friendships with two left-leaning Jews. The authors of the letters seem at times to be deliberately striking an extreme attitude as a kind of *épouvantail*, a sick joke, a shocker, to which the other is meant to respond, 'Oh B. M.!', 'Oh E. P.!'

In looking for materials, I have had much help from individuals and institutions, especially the International African Institute. But the attitude of universities and their members towards their own archives worries me. A considerable proportion of their members gain their living by archival research. Through the Public Record Office the Government provides them with excellent facilities to examine most records after a period of thirty years. When I went to the London School of Economics and asked the then Director if I could see the administrative records dating from over fifty years before, I was not allowed direct access, which seems to be one of the perks of the job and provides the basic data for their own histories of the School. I returned to my own university and made a similar request to see the archives, and was told, 'As it is you, there is no problem.' But there is one. Even if universities were not effectively public institutions, they have a collective interest in promoting 'openness', glasnost as we have come to call it, freedom of information. Large numbers of academics live on bits of paper written by other people. There is no excuse for not making records available on the same basis as the government does, that is, thirty years after they have been written, and I hope such access will be a future condition of grants that are made to the universities by the central authorities.

I have wondered about the propriety of using personal correspondence, especially of people I have known, since it seemed like a breach of confidence. Some of this is distasteful enough to lead some readers to want to leave it out. But I have used nothing, except for a few personal observations of my own, that does not appear in a public archive, nothing which is not available, now or in the near future, to other students. So it would be a mistake to bowdlerise their contents by selecting some extracts and deliberately avoiding others, although I do not exclude the possibility of unconscious selection. What I have done is to try and place such remarks in a wider context of understanding, the *verstehen* of the anthropologist. In any case I have not been concerned with aspects of their personal life except in so far as I considered that this affected 'the history of social anthropology'. By this I mean not only the intellectual history but their relations with organisations and colleagues, as these influenced the course of events and the situation in which I and others found ourselves. For in many ways the reader can regard this as 'une recherche du temps perdu'.

I have left untapped a large number of records of this period, partly because they were not always on open shelf, partly because I had limited intentions. But the documents are many. Some have been collected through the efforts of Raymond Firth who in 1974 wrote round to persuade his colleagues of that period to deposit their papers at the London School of Economics. That library contains those of Malinowski, Firth, Richards and Nadel. The Fortes papers are in the University Library at Cambridge. Radcliffe-Brown and Evans-Pritchard appear to have left nothing, or rather to have destroyed all that was in their hands.

CHAPTER I

The economic and organisational basis of British social anthropology in its formative period, 1930–1939: social reform in the colonies

The role of foundations in the social sciences and parallel activities has been the subject of considerable debate. How far were they the tools of capitalism? Were the social policies of the Rockefeller Foundation 'essential cogs in the production and reproduction of cultural hegemony'?[1] The Gramscian argument, espoused by Fisher, places its emphasis on the 'critical-conflict' perspective in the process of knowledge change in which causes are sought in the economy, class, ideology and hegemony. This perspective succeeds in giving to an interesting and informative paper a top-heavy superstructure which does not do justice to the subtlety of the situation, nor yet to Fisher's own analysis. At that level the interpretation has come under attack from Bulmer (1984) and from Karl and Katz (1987). For the attempt to see the social policies as cogs in the reproduction of cultural hegemony overplays the extent of interlocking of family and foundation on the one hand and underestimates the degree of autonomy of structures and actors on the other. As this case history shows there was more conflict, contradiction, disagreement and independence than is often allowed. That conclusion seems even more true of the argument that British social anthropologists as a whole were 'tools of colonialism' since both their interests and those of the foundation that funded them (not to speak of a large part of the British population) rarely coincided with those of colonial governments.

Anthropology, 'the study of man', is a term that goes back to Aristotle and has usually meant the study of the other, the 'primitive' other at that. Its beginnings are lost in the interest that any people has about its neighbours but it emerged as a specific field only in the post-Darwinian era when it was closely associated with the study of the early, undocumented past of mankind (prehistory) and with its physical constitution (physical anthropology, human biology). It became established as a separate field only in the latter part of the century. Sir

7

Edward Tylor, author of *Primitive Culture* (1871), first lectured in anthropology in Oxford in 1883 when he was appointed keeper of the University Museum. In the following year, the Pitt Rivers Museum was founded and Tylor was made Reader in Anthropology, with responsibility for lecturing on subjects held in the museum. He later became the first Professor of Anthropology in Britain and in 1905 a Diploma in Anthropology was established, the first course offered in a British university. Social anthropology itself was singled out by the appointment of R. R. Marrett as Reader in 1910 and a department was set up in 1914.

The other great name associated with that of Tylor was Sir James Frazer of Cambridge, author of *The Golden Bough* (1892), who was appointed as first Professor of Social Anthropology at Liverpool in 1907 but remained there for only one term. Teaching was developed in Cambridge and London, largely for the purpose of training cadets for the Colonial Service. In 1904 the University of Cambridge established a Board of Anthropological Studies which was to offer teaching in 'prehistoric and historic anthropology, ethnology (including sociology and comparative religion), physical anthropology, and psychological anthropology'.[2] However, a vigorous graduate programme was established only after the First World War under Bronislaw Malinowski at the London School of Economics. That was where most of the action took place during the thirties, not at the ancient universities. His intellectual status, his energy, his enthusiasm and his ability to raise funds resulted in a great expansion of field research. He was able to do this because of his connection with the London School of Economics and through them with the Laura Spelman Rockefeller Memorial which provided the large bulk of the funds.

From the 1930s to the 1960s social anthropology in Britain was marked by a commitment to periods of long and intensive fieldwork, much of it carried out in Africa. Even when the investigator was interested in one aspect more than others, the object was to grasp how social action (behaviour and norms) interacted, how to comprehend the existing community or 'society' as a whole. As such it tended to set aside the comparative and historical dimensions and to focus on the ethnographic present.

That orientation arose partly from a dissatisfaction with the results of earlier anthropology, which was now seen as engaging in doubtful reconstructions of the past and in the global comparison based upon inadequate ethnographic fieldwork. But it also coincided with a massive increase of funding that enabled research workers to be trained and to make intensive enquiries, as well as the arrival on the scene of highly motivated scholars. Under the inspiration of the Polish anthropologist, Bronislaw Malinowski, they formed a small group that experienced the usual friendships and enmities, but which on the intellectual level gave consideration to a number of related problems which they managed to advance and clarify by reference to field observations and to social theory.

On a theoretical level their orientation turned around the notion of 'functionalism' which some rejected or modified in favour of a more 'structural' approach. Both those approaches had their origin in the work of nineteenth-century reformers, Comte and Spencer and above all in that of the French socialist thinker, Emile Durkheim. Radcliffe-Brown had lectured on sociology in Cambridge in 1908 (as the classicist Jane Harrison attests); Malinowski encouraged his graduate students to read *Année sociologique*.[3] That influence represented the important shift in British anthropology. But these new anthropologists were more concerned with concrete problems of matrilineal systems, lineage organisation, the developmental cycle, witchcraft, the nature and settlement of disputes and so forth. Current American interpretations of the development of anthropology sometimes find this approach consistent with the interests of colonial authorities, of whom the anthropologists were their pensioners if not their prisoners, even their unconscious mouthpieces. My reading of the evidence derived from archives and from personal contacts suggests that such a view needs to be heavily qualified. Firstly it neglects the motivation, origin and background of most anthropologists (many from overseas), as well as the leftward, sometimes Marxist, leanings of university life at that time, especially at the London School of Economics where Malinowski taught. Secondly, it overlooks the fact that the major source of funding lay in an American foundation with reformist rather than imperial interests. Thirdly, these two factors heightened the suspicions of administrators in the colonies towards academic research, even if those in London were more open to enquiry in the social sciences.

In the period after the Second World War, the sources of funds shifted and much research was then undertaken under the auspices of the newly founded Colonial Social Science Research Council, at a period when India and Burma had already achieved independence and when that goal had appeared on the horizon of colonial dependencies throughout the world, in other words in the twilight of colonial rule.

The funds were distributed by a body consisting largely of academics who were under little or no pressure from the authorities, according to priorities sketched out in the reports of senior anthropologists. The recipients of the grants included students from the USA, the Indian subcontinent, from China as well as from Britain and other Commonwealth countries. The subsequent spread of the teaching of anthropology in universities gradually weakened the small-group atmosphere generated by these scholars, who had spent their earlier years in research rather than in undergraduate teaching. A diversity of interests in more historical and comparative topics (including the comparative, symbolic studies of Lévi-Strauss) began to manifest themselves. New perspectives were opened up in the work of those who constituted the third and fourth generations. But at the same time something was lost when the field became so diffuse, when the audience consisted of undergraduates rather than colleagues, when the focus on common problems (as distinct from philosophical trends) tended to disappear. That is the background to the story I present in the chapters that follow. My account dwells primarily on Africa. That is not simply the result of a personal quirk: it was the continent where the bulk of the research took place, partly because of the earlier grants by the Rockefeller philanthropies to the International African Institute and the later ones by the Colonial Social Science Research Council. If I concentrate unashamedly on work in that continent, I do not mean to underrate the importance of the research carried out in India (especially by M. N. Srinivas), in Burma (by E. R. Leach), in the Pacific (by Firth, Fortune and others) and in other parts of the globe by anthropologists associated with the British 'school'.

The development of social anthropology in Britain obviously had much to do with the position of the country as a colonial power, as was the case in Russia, in the USA and in France. In that country professional field research was of little significance until the thirties when funds became available to train and finance anthropologists. But those funds came largely from outside, as did the anthropologists themselves. Neither the givers nor the bulk of the recipients were primarily interested in propping up colonial empires. For Africa, the Colonial Office was concerned with the problems of ruling a large empire. While, unlike India, the movement to independence in that continent did not achieve much momentum until after the Second World War, with its promises of a new dispensation, many politicians, backed by a significant segment of the population, were interested not only in reform but in a gradual movement towards independence. It was with the more extreme of these elements that most anthropologists in Britain were identified.

At that time the main impetus, or at least the means, for the growth of fieldwork and of the subject more generally was dependent on the activities of the Laura Spelman Rockefeller Memorial set up in 1918 in memory of the wife of John D. Rockefeller, Snr. The Memorial was established partly to take care of 'the more dangerous social concerns' which had been excluded from the scope of the Rockefeller Foundation ever since the McKenzie King affair of 1914–15 when it had been heavily criticised for mixing research and business interests. Some seven years later Beardsley Ruml, who had taken a doctorate in psychology at Chicago, was appointed Director.[4] That appointment represented a change from social welfare to social science and public administration, as well as to professional specialisation among foundation staff. Within two years he had transformed 'an unremarkable charity into a major vehicle for funding basic social science', much of it in Britain.[5] Social studies were to be converted to academic social science.

The Memorial was one of four groups sharing in the 450 million dollars accumulated by the founder, which in 1928 became the Division of Social Sciences in the Rockefeller Foundation. During the course of the 1920s the Memorial broadened its aims to comprise support of higher learning, including overseas, and to promote human welfare. The profound importance of this relatively small foundation for the development of American social science has been examined by Martin Bulmer and others;[6] it had a similar influence in Britain and other parts of the English-speaking world.

The social sciences were not the only academic field in Britain to gain from the largesse of the Rockefeller philanthropies. The Rockefeller Foundation played a major role in the development of 'scientific medicine' in this country, that is, in the integration of medical schools, hospitals and universities, in the encouragement of units in research and teaching and in the establishment of chairs in specialist fields.[7] These enormous benefactions, especially to the London School of Hygiene and Tropical Medicine and to University College, were made under a policy developed by Wickliffe Rose who administered the projects in the medical field and who had decided that the best way to develop a field of knowledge was to identify and strengthen centres of excellence, providing fellowships to bring other scholars to study there.[8] Fellowship programmes attached to these centres were key

developments in academic philanthropy in America following the First
World War.

Initially established to support the kind of social welfare projects in
which Mrs Rockefeller had been personally interested, the Memorial
was reoriented towards the social sciences when Beardsley Ruml was
appointed director in 1922. Ruml had been a graduate student in
psychology at Chicago between 1915 and 1917 where the social sciences
had already become well established under the sociologists W. I.
Thomas, Robert Park (after 1914) and Albion W. Small; it was Small's
vision of 'group study as opposed to departmental study or individual
study', elaborated in conjunction with the political scientist, Charles
Merriam, and the economist, Leon Marshall, that stimulated Ruml's
policy for the Foundation. Within a year or so of his appointment he
approached the trustees with a view to investing in the social sciences
(which meant 'sociology, ethnology, anthropology and psychology, and
certain aspects of economics, history, political economy and biology') in
order to provide a scientific basis for social welfare.

In the following year, 1923, the three Chicago departments of
political science, of sociology and anthropology, and of political
economy presented to the trustees of the Foundation a plan which
aimed to make fundamental contributions to the methods and
achievements of the social sciences through a study of the problems of
the local community. Approval of the plan meant that Park, Burgess
and their associates could undertake 'maps of urban growth, through
the mapping of local community areas, studies of the distribution of
juvenile delinquency, juvenile gangs, family disorganisation and
divorce, and detailed investigations of homeless men, hotel life,
rooming-house keepers and the Lower North Side', as well as a great
deal of other work. The resulting publications included those minor
classics, Thrasher's *The Gang*, Zorbaugh's *Gold Coast and the Slum*,
Cressey's *Taxi Dance Hall* and Louis Wirth's *The Ghetto*.

Under the stimulation of Ruml the philanthropy of the Memorial
was not limited to Chicago, nor yet to the United States. Together with
his friend Merriam, Ruml encouraged the founding of the Social
Science Research Council in America. While through Rockefeller
largesse this body awarded fellowships rather than grants, it became a
kind of forerunner for such councils in other parts of the world. In
England the first such body was significantly the Colonial Social
Science Research Council, founded in 1944 under the enlightened
secretaryship of Sally Chilver; the Social Science Research Council was

only established by the Labour Government in 1965 under the Directorship of Michael (now Lord) Young, and in 1984 its name was changed under direct pressure from the Conservative government to the Economic and Social Research Council – the only one in the English-speaking world to exclude the phrase 'social science'.[9] One of Ruml's first moves as Director of the Memorial was to commission a report on the social sciences in America by L. K. Frank, which concluded that very few enquiries employed 'scientific research involving actual experimentation and investigation' and that there was barely any provision 'for training in scientific methods'.[10] Between 1923 and 1929, when the Memorial became part of the main Rockefeller Foundation, Ruml distributed $21 million for fundamental work in the social sciences. In Britain the main beneficiary was the London School of Economics which under Beveridge's direction received $2 million between 1923 and 1939.[11] Beveridge and Ruml had met in September 1923 and got on well together. Both agreed that the social sciences were too abstract and required more emphasis on empirical observation. As a result of their discussions the School became one of the five major beneficiaries of the Foundation's generosity, which financed the Library, buildings, professorships, research projects and visits to the United States.[12] It was under these auspices that the dynamic Professor of Anthropology at the School, Bronislaw Malinowski, was invited to visit America at the same time as Radcliffe-Brown who was about to move from Cape Town to Sydney to take up the Chair in Anthropology founded in 1926 with Rockefeller support. Malinowski too established friendly relations with the Foundation personnel and approached them independently for help. For example, he appealed to them in 1930 when the Sydney Chair in Anthropology seemed to be threatened by Radcliffe-Brown's impending departure for Chicago and the possible withdrawal of national funds; Malinowski was keen to see that chair filled by a former student, Raymond Firth, who later succeeded him at the London School of Economics.[13] But his major contribution in attracting funds was to that School and to the newly formed International African Institute.

The London School of Economics was already central in the institutional development of British social anthropology. Although the first full-time appointment was not made there until 1913, a course in 'ethnology' had been given in 1904–5 by A. C. Haddon of Cambridge, and was thought likely to interest 'civil servants destined for the tropical portions of the empire' together with missionaries.[14] A similar development took place in Cambridge, beginning in 1906 with instruction arranged for prospective Indian civil servants and in 1908 for those going to work in the Sudan. In his London teaching, Haddon was followed by Radcliffe-Brown who had been elected to a fellowship at Trinity College, Cambridge, on his return from the Andaman Islands. Charles Seligman, a medical doctor who had accompanied the Torres Straits expedition – one of the first attempts at professional anthropological research in Britain, organised by A. C. Haddon, originally a zoologist – succeeded him in 1910 and he received a permanent appointment in 1913 as part-time Professor of Anthropology. In May 1923 Malinowski, who had been giving lectures there since his return from the Trobriands, was elected Reader in Social Anthropology, a title which he himself had suggested, partly to distinguish the School from University College where proposals had been made for a Readership in Cultural Anthropology, and partly because ' "social" will also indicate that our interest is mainly sociological'.[15] That post itself was made possible by the Rockefeller funding.

Cambridge also acquired a Readership (in Ethnology) when A. C. Haddon was appointed in 1909 – he had been made a lecturer in 1900; but there was no Chair until the William Wyse Professorship was established in 1932 by a friend of J. G. Frazer and filled first by T. C. Hodson, then by J. H. Hutton (both formerly of the Indian Civil Service) and then by a student of Malinowski, Meyer Fortes. The Chair in Social Anthropology at Oxford (Tylor had previously held a professorship in general anthropology) was initially held by Radcliffe-Brown from 1937 until he retired in 1946, again to be followed by another student from the London School, E. E. Evans-Pritchard. Radcliffe-Brown had previously held the first Chair of Social Anthropology in Cape Town in 1921, and five years later he moved to Sydney which with the help of Rockefeller money he made the base for research personnel from America and Great Britain who were working in Australia and the Pacific. In addition he founded the journal *Oceania*.[16] It was not accidental that he moved from Sydney to Chicago, the cradle of Rockefeller generosity to the social sciences (where he was pushed partly because of the threat to funds) nor that the move should lead Malinowski to worry about the influence he might wield in those quarters where he was so well placed. However, in Sydney it was a pupil of Malinowski, Raymond Firth, who took over his responsibilities (but not his Chair).

It was at the London School of Economics, in the late twenties, that Malinowski proclaimed anthropology in Britain, his anthropology, to be the one kind that mattered. That anthropology was based on extensive fieldwork, preferably with one tribe or people, and in this he saw the key to the development of the social sciences and to their contribution to practical life. Indeed it was his success in convincing the Rockefeller philanthropies of the value of his approach that was an important constituent in the opening up of anthropological research in Britain. Before that its history had been essentially linear, a pedigree rather than a branching genealogy, a descent line rather than a ramifying lineage. One man handed over to the next. Even Malinowski's pupils were few and far between in the twenties. He started his famous seminar soon after he took up his appointment as Reader in 1923. At first it consisted of Evans-Pritchard (who had studied history at Oxford), of Ashley Montague (whose main work was on the biological side), of Ursula Grant-Duff (the daughter of Lord Avebury, an important figure in the earlier history of British anthropology), of Raymond Firth (who had studied economics in New Zealand), and of Barbara Freire-Marresco (or Mrs Aitken, who worked among the Tewa of Hano in the south-west of the USA). When Hortense Powdermaker, a trade-union organiser from America, arrived there in 1925 and eventually wrote a study of Hollywood as well as of the Copper Belt of Zambia, there were only three graduate students in anthropology: she herself, Evans-Pritchard and Firth, followed the next year by Isaac Schapera who had worked under Radcliffe-Brown at Cape Town. As we have seen, Evans-Pritchard, who did fieldwork among the Nuer and the Azande of the Sudan, was to fill the Chair at Oxford. Firth carried out research among the Maori (before going to London), in Malaya and above all on the Pacific island of Tikopia, prior to becoming the successor to Malinowski in London. Schapera worked extensively among the black population of Southern Africa and he too became a professor at the School. However, Powdermaker was soon joined by others who were to become well-known in British anthropology, Audrey Richards, a natural scientist from Cambridge who was to work among the Bemba of Zambia, Edith Clarke from Jamaica, and by Jack Driberg (a former colonial officer), Camilla Wedgwood, and Gordon and Elizabeth Brown of Canada, who carried out fieldwork in East Africa, Melanesia and East Africa respectively.

Several of these students were in receipt of grants or fellowships from the Rockefeller Memorial, which in 1929 had opened the way for anthropologists to apply. Clarke, Mair and Richards fall into this category. But the great development came with the establishment of the Fellowship programme of the International African Institute in 1931, a programme that was also called upon to provide grants for Richards, the Browns and Clarke, though never for Evans-Pritchard or Driberg, who by that time had come to oppose Malinowski, an opposition that led the former to seek a strong link with Radcliffe-Brown.

Of course, the Rockefeller Memorial was not the only source of funds for anthropological research. Malinowski himself had received a grant to work in New Guinea from Dr Robert Mond; Gregory Bateson was supported for his enquiries in New Guinea by a Research Fellowship at St John's College, Cambridge, as well as by other grants; Edmund Leach carried out his initial work among the Kurds using his own funds; during the war Firth was supported in Malaysia by a grant from the Leverhulme Foundation; Radcliffe-Brown held an Anthony Wilkin Studentship from Cambridge; for his work among the Azande Evans-Pritchard obtained grants from the Royal Society and the Government of the Sudan. Nevertheless, Rockefeller money made grants available through the Australian National Research Council (of which Radcliffe-Brown and later Firth were secretaries of the relevant committee) as well as through the International African Institute. Meanwhile the British government did very little. Although the Universities of Oxford, Cambridge and London produced and to some extent trained most of the personnel that staffed the colonies, which (as in Paris) was a major part of the justification for teaching the subject of anthropology at those institutions, very little money was provided for ethnographic research. It is true that there were some government anthropologists in the colonial service: Rattray in Ghana (Gold Coast) and Meek in Nigeria. They were men who had started their careers as administrators and then had become involved in studying the lives of the people.[17] Apart from the awards to Seligman and later to Evans-Pritchard from the government of the Anglo-Egyptian Sudan, there was little support for outside ethnographic research in British territories. Even in India, where much work was done, it was largely carried out by administrative officers.[18] Nor did missionary societies make much contribution outside their own ranks, while the great capitalist concerns that were making money out of Africa were equally sparing of their finances. Although each of these interests was represented on the Executive Committee of the International African

Institute, its research funds came not from Britain at all but from America. Anthropology on the continent of Europe had a yet harder struggle for independent funds and one recalls the great efforts Griaule had to undertake in France, putting on a circus, promoting fights, in order to raise funds for his expeditions.

By 1937 the situation in British Africa had begun to change with the establishment of the Rhodes–Livingstone Institute in Northern Rhodesia (Zambia) with the aid of government and private contributions.[19] Nevertheless the Rockefeller philanthropies played the dominant part in financing research. The greater largesse of America was partly due to the huge accumulations of the early 'robber barons', partly to the nature of tax laws and partly to the higher propensity for charitable giving; indeed the three are very closely intertwined. As a result of this generosity, anthropologists could look forward to several years on a well-financed grant to carry out research, which was undoubtedly a factor in attracting senior research workers to come and join with Malinowski in London.

The inauguration of the International African Institute had followed from a meeting at the School of Oriental Studies in September 1925 (before 'African' had been added to the title of that School) as the result of a series of consultations among academic, missionary, educational and administrative interests. It was founded the following year with the help of a grant of £1,000 a year for five years from the Laura Spelman Rockefeller Memorial. Towards the end of that period the Institute thought of applying for additional funds, but it was intimated to them that the Rockefeller Foundation, whose Social Science Division the Memorial had now become, considered that there was too much administration and not enough research. A substantial programme was then submitted to the Foundation for Fellowships and grants. As a result the Institute received an award of £10,000 a year for five years from 1931 and established a special bureau to deal with these matters.

The key figure behind the new Institute was Dr J. H. Oldham, a missionary, educationalist and administrator who was committed to the acquisition and diffusion of scientific knowledge (in the widest sense) about Africa with a view to social amelioration. Oldham, once described as 'that arch intriguer for good', had been involved as early as 1912 in the attempt to apply the Tuskegee policy concerning the non-academic training of southern American Negroes to the continent of Africa. From 1908 to 1910 he had been secretary of the World

Missionary Conference at Edinburgh and from 1910 to 1921 he was secretary of its Continuation Committee. Besides being secretary of the International Missionary Council he also edited the *International Review of Missions* which became 'the quasi-official journal of the Protestant missionary societies in Great Britain from its inception in 1912'.[20]

Oldham was a key figure in the group searching for elements of a uniform educational policy for Africa and in 1923 was associated with the founding of the British Advisory Committee on Native Education in Tropical Africa, which adopted the Tuskegee policy emphasising vocational rather than literary education, described by a critic as 'the surest way to achieve the formation of a malleable and docile African worker'.[21] It was in this context that Hanns Vischer, the chairman of the Committee, an ex-colonial officer and later secretary of the International African Institute, was sent on a three-week study tour of the American South.

This enterprise had already received assistance from the Laura Spelman Rockefeller Memorial which became the main support of the International African Institute. But the aims were obviously very different. Moreover the criticisms levelled at the attempt to make African education more sensitive to rural life are partly misdirected. It was not a choice between agricultural and literary education with the aim of excluding the African from the latter. The missionary societies set up many secondary schools along British lines which were directed towards the academic side and which achieved some remarkable results. But anyone who has sat through watered-down versions of a similar curriculum in a rural African school, most of whose pupils will have to return to agriculture for decades to come (and hoe agriculture at that), must wonder about the appropriateness of much that was included from European urban models. In any case academic and practical courses are not alternative paths but complementary ones, whose nature and mix must be related to the society at large. Certainly in West Africa secondary and higher education made great strides, though this has often been more in the individual's than in the nation's interest, since it has provided students with the ability to sell their labour abroad for higher rewards than the country itself can afford. The argument is much more shaded than has been allowed but certainly, like most missionaries, Oldham's interest in African education was not confined to the encouragement of the practical. The International African Institute, for example, was devoted to the cultural and to research.

Oldham and Malinowski became close friends and developed an intimate working relationship, with Malinowski often complaining about the way things were going (usually with humour) and Oldham replying in a soothing, diplomatic tone and always depending upon his friend's academic judgement, to the exclusion, it should be said, of other voices such as those of the Directors from the Continent, the linguist and ethnologist Diedrich Westermann of Germany and the administrator and ethnologist Henri Labouret of France, as well as of other council members such as Seligman who had considerable African experience. Seligman, who was Malinowski's fellow Professor at the London School of Economics, had not only been a member of A. C. Haddon's expedition to the Torres Straits in 1898, but had also carried out work in the Anglo-Egyptian Sudan and it was under his supervision that Evans-Pritchard was working.

Plans for the Fellowship scheme began to crystallise in the latter part of 1930. In September of that year Malinowski wrote to Oldham from his Italian home reporting on a meeting with Van Sickle, Paris representative of the Rockefeller Foundation, referring to 'our plan' and to 'the London group'.[22] Oldham replied congratulating Malinowski: 'If this venture meets with success it will owe more to you than to anybody else.'[23] Earlier that year he had thanked Malinowski for agreeing to act as secretary to the group, remarking that this was especially important because of Seligman, who was at once an Africanist and a representative of the Royal Anthropological Institute on the Council. Malinowski was determined to set aside any influence he had, regarding him as an antiquarian ethnologist.

So Malinowski's influence was dominant. In June 1931 Hanns Vischer, the ex-colonial officer who was Secretary-General of the Institute, wrote thanking him for the help he had given Oldham in preparing the Rockefeller proposal, and declaring that 'anthropology for us is social anthropology after the manner in which you teach it'.[24] No wonder then that Malinowski, who became the holder of a Chair specifically entitled Social Anthropology (as Frazer's had been in Liverpool), found it difficult to get on with his former patron, Seligman, the part-time Professor of Ethnology. For he needed to be alone in charge, the sole prophet of the new science of man. Malinowski admitted to a 'one-sided sociological interest', a development that Seligman opposed.[25] Indeed he complained to Oldham that Seligman had attacked him at the University Board of Studies, insisting that students who wanted to study social anthropology should also work on prehistory, physical anthropology, archaeology and the distribution of man, the whole range of the post-Darwinian field of studies.[26]

How was it that Malinowski achieved this dominant position in the African Institute when he had done no work in that continent? As early as 1927 Oldham wrote to Malinowski about the latter's approaches to Rockefeller, and in 1929 he visited the USA and entered into negotiations with the Foundation.[27] Some twenty-seven months later their correspondence contained a specific reference to the fact that Malinowski had approached Ruml and his deputy (and successor as head of the Social Science Division from 1929), Dean Day, about the Institute.[28] A few days later Malinowski sent Day a memorandum about the possibility of research in Africa, following up discussions they had had in the spring of 1929. He pointed out the parallel to the Foundation's existing work in the Pacific, carried out under the supervision of Radcliffe-Brown, and reminded him that in Autumn 1929 the Foundation had extended its Fellowship scheme, first intended to bring young scholars to the United States, to include the possibility of anthropological fieldwork.[29]

The incorporation of the Laura Spelman Memorial into the main Rockefeller foundation in 1929 had shifted the focus of its support from academic institutions to the 'promotion of the welfare of mankind and not for scattered projects in basic science'.[30] Support grew for the anthropology of the contemporary world. As Head of the Social Science Division, Day became fed up with what he saw as the lack of co-operation from anthropologists in the States, and this perception inclined him to look to the Institute for scientific co-operation.[31] This was not only a personal matter, but rather a positive attraction to Malinowski's 'functional' anthropology in contrast to the antiquarian studies prevalent elsewhere, combined with the prospect of the access to Africa that the Institute could provide through its relation with the colonial authorities. The terms are Malinowski's, but it is clear that he convinced the social scientists manning the Rockefeller Foundation whose intellectual and practical predilections already leant towards a sociological approach. Functionalism and fieldwork meant an interest in the functioning rather than the historical, the quick rather than the dead, the present rather than the past. The Foundation was interested in what was happening now, in what could be learned by observation in actual situations, in the kind of fieldworking functionalism that Malinowski was advocating.

The memorandum on policy, which was to form the basis of the research programme of the Institute, was drafted by the Directors in September 1931, the major part being played by Oldham who was the Administrative Director. Westermann's contribution was entirely rewritten by Audrey Richards, who consulted Malinowski by letter at every stage, for he remained at his Italian home until the 10th Executive Council meeting of the Institute, held in Paris on 14 and 15 October of that year.

At the time the policy document was being prepared, Radcliffe-Brown was in England and was consulted by Oldham who duly reported to Malinowski that 'Radcliffe-Brown has come on the scene and will be an important factor.'[32] Malinowski's views were clear cut. While he respected Radcliffe-Brown's work, he did not want anything to do with him personally. At first he remained silent; 'On Radcliffe-Brown I shall say nothing.'[33] But three months later he wrote from Toulon, saying, 'if Radcliffe-Brown got into England, it would be a damn bad job for our Institute as well as for everybody else'. The struggle for the control of resources was clear to one and all.[34]

When the memorandum for the research grant to be submitted to the Rockefeller Foundation had been prepared, it was then submitted to Radcliffe-Brown and Malinowski for comments. Their reactions were different. On the contents of the policy document Radcliffe-Brown commented, firstly, that it should have more focus, and secondly, that it should avoid involving anthropologists in value judgements about policy.[35] He wrote:

I think it would be better if the Institute's investigations all dealt with the subject in a purely scientific way, confining themselves to the precise observation of what is taking place and not concerning themselves with what is good and bad in the original society or in the changes that it is undergoing, nor with the practical problems. The task of the investigator should be to obtain exact knowledge, impartially presented, in such a form that it can be immediately utilised by those who are actually concerned with native government and education.[36]

For Malinowski, the first suggestion ran contrary to the particular holistic approach he espoused, while the second was incompatible with his practical orientation. He replied, saying: 'There is no doubt we are all aiming at the same thing, that is, a thoroughgoing study of several tribes from the point of view of contact with European culture, the ensuing changes and the possibilities of controlling these changes.'[37] That was Rockefeller's aim. While he agreed with Radcliffe-Brown's substantive comments he could not accept his view about the study of social change. He remarked that: 'I think the Institute's investigators should be as fully aware of practical problems and of the "good" and "bad" in the original society and in the changes, as is possible.' In a letter written on the following day he recommends the work of Audrey Richards who, with Gordon-Brown, is 'the best of my Lieutenants', since she has shown how to do 'practical anthropology in the field'. The emphasis on practicality seemed to be encouraged by the known interests of the Foundation. At this point the funds were calling at least part of the tune.

The fact that Malinowski was living at such a distance from London meant that he could not exercise any direct control over the text, but his students on the drafting committee regularly reported back to him, as did Dorothy Brackett (the Administrative Secretary), Oldham and Westermann. Immediately after the meeting of that committee Richards sent him an account which revealed the full extent of the split that had already developed in social anthropology in Britain. She explained that while 'the FAITHFUL have the field to themselves', during the course of the discussion she came to realise that a larger plan was at stake. 'Gordon and I immediately guessed at Radcliffe-Brown's snaffling up the anthropological part of this sum in his American trip' if the Institute's policy is not formed straight away. She hoped his advice will not be taken 'on general principles' (though it is largely in agreement with Malinowski's) and 'hearing that E.-P. is making up to him' (R.-B.), began to see possibilities of future strife.[38] While the composition of the 'faithful' was not absolutely fixed and while there were important cross-cutting ties, the expression was used by those both in and out of the group.[39] Radcliffe-Brown certainly constituted a bogeyman for Malinowski too, for about the same time he wrote to Hall at the Rockefeller Foundation of a meeting which was 'mainly about future anthropology plans, above all about a man named Radcliffe-Brown, who wants to open a big anthropological centre at the School of Oriental Studies', which was one of the rival possibilities.[40]

Evans-Pritchard had already crossed swords with Malinowski as early as 1925. The latter had suggested to Firth that he come to London from Sydney, where he had succeeded Radcliffe-Brown as acting head, to take up the position of director of the research programme of the International African Institute.[41] 'Naturally', remarked Malinowski, 'I hope to retain my influence.' When this appointment proved impossible because of Firth's lack of African experience, he wrote again urging him to apply for a Fellowship. About other possible applicants he was less keen:

as to the claims of such people as J. H. Driberg and E. Evans-Pritchard, both of them are not very popular with anybody who knows them, and it would be quite useless for me to try pushing them into any position which requires loyalty and decent cooperation with other people . . . As to Evans-Pritchard, I have definitely stipulated to Seligman, that if Evans-Pritchard gets a permanent post at the L.S.E., I would write tendering my resignation.

The particular complaint that occasioned this comment appeared to be that Driberg, with Evans-Pritchard's knowledge, had corresponded with one Rentoul of Papua (now Papua-New Guinea) behind Malinowski's back, in order to be able to query his statements about the Trobrianders' lack of knowledge of a connection between intercourse and procreation. Rentoul was a magistrate who served on the Trobriands after Malinowski's day.

Later that year, on hearing that Evans-Pritchard and Driberg were to be encouraged to work 'really hard for the Institute' (like Malinowski himself, who had done so 'in an entirely disinterested way'), Malinowski remarked: 'The real trouble about some of our younger colleagues is that . . . they are incapable of honest and disinterested service.'[42] Richards spoke in even stronger terms, telling Malinowski in September that she had written 'a gloomy letter to Elsie [her sister] about the whole crew', but cheered up on realising that 'E.-P. can't speak about anyone without sneering, friend or foe alike'. At this point she had recently been to hear Radcliffe-Brown give a talk in London on education in Melanesia, the content of which she approved. Indeed Radcliffe-Brown himself made a favourable impression, and Richards wrote to Malinowski that he 'himself was quite decent about your work – merely disagreed with it, and thought himself the more eminent of the two! Which is just what we think of his work.'[43]

The conflict over the policy document is interesting for a number of wider issues. One aspect of ideas, especially in the less obviously accumulating fields of knowledge, is their role in relating people one to another. From this standpoint Malinowski and Radcliffe-Brown are often linked together in the so-called structural-functional school. The term was not Malinowski's, for he insisted on a 'functional' approach, and saw Radcliffe-Brown as part of the same school, though an erratic member who had more links with antiquarian predecessors. With his interest in Spencer (as well of course as in Durkheim), Radcliffe-Brown was more concerned to lay emphasis on 'structure', and it was in the emphasis on this concept (or rather on 'social structure') that the group of people with whom he later worked at Oxford distinguished themselves.

The intellectual character of the discrepancies between Malinowski and Radcliffe-Brown seems of a fairly minor kind compared with their convergences, and compared with the alternative trends in American and European anthropology at the time. When Radcliffe-Brown left Sydney in 1931 he wrote a very friendly letter to Malinowski, speaking of 'our common aim'.[44] In the previous October Malinowski had written to the Rockefeller Foundation saying that Radcliffe-Brown was 'one of the best anthropologists and also an excellent organiser', although adding that he could not get on with the university.[45] The difficulties between them arose partly out of the dominant role played by Malinowski in Britain and the concurrent attempt of some of his students to align themselves with an alternative focus of academic power and intellectual achievement. Thus the constellation, Seligman, Evans-Pritchard, Radcliffe-Brown, became somewhat opposed to that of Malinowski, Richards and in a sense Firth, though cross-cutting ties were always present. Intellectually the work of Evans-Pritchard was certainly closer to the sociological approach of the Malinowski group than to the eclecticism of Seligman. Firth in particular had close relations with Evans-Pritchard, though the latter was often critical of his attitudes towards authority; Evans-Pritchard's close friend and colleague, Meyer Fortes, probably had more respect for Firth's work than did his colleague, as he had for that of Nadel and Forde. Nevertheless an opposition existed and an appreciation of it is significant for the intellectual history of anthropologists like Fortes whose ties of friendship were with Evans-Pritchard but whose financial resources depended upon Malinowski. Moreover, it also had something to do with the different emphasis of teaching at the two most important formative departments in Britain in the early fifties, the London School of Economics and Oxford, as well as with the growing strength of Cambridge in the later part of the decade. Here I want to emphasise neither the priority of the intellectual dispute, nor the intellectual consequences of the opposition, but rather the organisational aspects of the quarrel.

The divergence between these two groups had a history going back to the 1920s. At the London School of Economics Malinowski had to work with Seligman, the supervisor of Evans-Pritchard's work in

Africa, but his correspondence in the early thirties displays some hostility towards Seligman, more towards Radcliffe-Brown and most of all towards Evans-Pritchard. The split took a territorial form with separate High Courts being held in summer at Seligman's home at Toot Baldon and at Malinowski's residence at Sopra Bolzano, to which their respective friends were invited. One can exaggerate the division. For Evans-Pritchard and Schapera stayed at Bolzano, while Firth and Richards went to Toot Baldon. There was also of course interchange on the intellectual level. Gluckman attended Malinowski's seminars while Firth went to stay with Radcliffe-Brown and Evans-Pritchard at All Souls, Oxford. Firth remarks that 'despite the intellectual differences which separated Seligman from Malinowski in later years over general versus social anthropology, there was much coming and going between them'.[46] Nevertheless a cleavage existed and one continuing focus was the struggle for resources.

Both Malinowski and Radcliffe-Brown received strong support from the Rockefeller Foundation. But an element in the opposition between the two was control of posts, students and monetary grants. While at Sydney Radcliffe-Brown built up anthropological research in the Pacific, and at Chicago, in the Americas, largely on Rockefeller money; Malinowski was to do the same at the London School of Economics for Africa, a continent in which he had no personal experience before making an extended trip at the Foundation's expense. I do not wish to imply that there was no theoretical basis for the opposition between the two men and their respective 'adherents', although that has been much exaggerated. But institutional affiliation (which creates or imposes its own loyalties, though in no automatic fashion) and conflicts over resources were factors of considerable importance in any intellectual history – or rather history of intellectuals – that looks at the development of British social anthropology. At the same time there were a number of cross-cutting ties, especially among their students. What is remarkable is the degree of coherence at the level of professional activity and approach to the subject of those trained by Malinowski and Radcliffe-Brown. That was the great strength of the subject at the time.

CHAPTER 2

Training for the field: the sorcerer's apprentices

Once the Rockefeller Foundation had agreed to sponsor the Fellowship scheme, which started in July 1931, the Institute had to look round for possible recipients. It was here that Malinowski exercised his patronage and made his influence felt. While he had at first no official position with the Institute, his relations with the Foundation, his friendship with Oldham, the missionary administrator of the scheme, and his participation in meetings of the Africa group, which brought him into contact with the influential colonial administrator, Lord Lugard, and others, made his co-operation essential for the fulfilment of the programme, including the training of the participants.

In recruiting Fellows Malinowski naturally thought first of his own students, while the Directors of the Institute also played a part. But it was the Bureau, formed to administer the grants, that carried out the interviews and made recommendations to the Council of the Institute. The initial selection included a number of people with whom Malinowski had worked and approved of. 'What then with Gordon Brown, Fortes, Audrey Richards, Margery Perham and Kirchkoff [*sic*], we have got quite a good set of young people.'[1] Additional Rockefeller Fellowships had been previously awarded to Lucy Mair, who was Lecturer in Colonial Administration (and whose mother was secretary of the School, under the Director, Beveridge) and Edith Clarke, a well-connected student of Jamaican background, who was about to go to the Gold Coast. All except Kirchhoff, who had already been employed by Rockefeller and was recommended by Westermann, Director of the Institute, were 'students' of Malinowski, though Gordon Brown was at Toronto, Audrey Richards teaching and Fortes had not yet studied anthropology.

The Fellows later appointed by the Institute were drawn from a much wider range and made up a remarkable collection. So many foreigners were included in the first Fellowships that Kitteridge expressed the hope that 'you will have enough English students to balance the group'.[2] Although many of them had little previous experience of anthropology they were to form much of the core of the teaching of African studies for the next thirty and more years. The seventeen full-time Fellows were Fortes (South Africa), Hofstra (Holland), Kirchhoff (Germany), Nadel (Austria), together with the two Kriges (South Africa), Lucy Mair (Britain), Margery Perham (Britain), Margaret Read (Britain), Monica Wilson (Britain), Matthews (a Masuto), another German, G. K. Wagner, another Austrian, the missionary, Father Schumacher (who worked in Ruanda), two French-women, T. Rivière, the niece of G. H. Rivière, and Germaine Tillion, who worked in North Africa and was later interned in a concentration camp, and two linguists, Father Crazzolora (Italy) and J. Lukas (Germany).[3] Grants were made, among others, to Jomo Kenyatta of Kenya (later the leader of the independence struggle) and to Fadipe from Yorubaland, so that they could work at the London School of Economics. Indeed a number of the other Fellows were asked to come to London to work under Malinowski. As a result of his endeavours, the Institute, combined with the London School of Economics, became 'a factory of really competent anthropologists and sociologists'.[4] The list of students attending Malinowski's seminars at the School in the session 1932–3 consisted mainly of Africanists, all of whom produced valuable studies: H. Beemer (later Kuper), M. Fortes, M. Lecoeur, S. F. Nadel, S. Hofstra, M. Read, G. Wilson, M. Perham, L. Mair, A. Richards and potentially P. Kirchhoff, a total of twenty-four which included 'Mr and Mrs Davis' (the distinguished Black American, Alison Davis), occasionally the sociologist, Talcott Parsons, and others.[5] Not all the members of the seminar were aiming to work in Africa; his students, Fei and Hsu, followed at the School by Tien Jukung, were important in extending social anthropology to China. But as the result of the benefactions of the Rockefeller Foundation much of the research of the School was directed to that continent, to the study of which the majority of the Fellows contributed important monographs. There can rarely have been a more effective use of funds in the history of research in the social sciences.

The programme was very much in line with the aims of the Rockefeller Memorial and later the Foundation to encourage co-operative groups on a more systematic and empirical basis, at the same time as breaking down old subject divisions.[6] Day, for example, was wary of 'many of the prescriptions of capitalistic individualism'.[7] That programme was to establish centres of excellence, to which they would bring advanced students by offering them fellowships to 'receive training in scientific methods and be allowed the freedom to conduct their own research'.[8] That policy, outlined in Ruml's memorandum submitted to the Memorial in 1922 and in the Frank Report, was aimed at consolidating and professionalising the academic social sciences, which is exactly what happened with British social anthropology, although the contradiction was, as Fisher points out, that the process itself involves erecting new disciplinary barriers.

The letter Malinowski addressed to Oldham about prospective students reminded him that he had already spoken about 'the South African Ukrainian Jew named Fortes. He is perhaps for sheer brilliancy and real capacity and intelligence the best pupil I have ever had.' He had come with glowing recommendations from Flügel, the psycho-analyst at University College, but since he was judged not to be dogmatically committed to that approach, he was acceptable. 'I want you ...', he wrote to Oldham, 'to take him into your little fold.' Meanwhile Malinowski said he was arranging for him to go to the States to work with Radcliffe-Brown for a session, probably at Fortes' insistence, after which he would return to spend the academic year 1932–3 at the London School of Economics. 'Don't be put off', he told Oldham, 'by his manners ... which are South African, nor by his ideas, which are a little Eastern European ghetto.' The significance of these remarks was brought out later when it came to considering Fortes' proposal for fieldwork, in his difficulties in getting into the Gold Coast, as well as in his ambiguous position, situated between Malinowski and Radcliffe-Brown. While Malinowski's comments may appear full of prejudice, given his style of writing they cannot be altogether taken as evidence of anti-Semitism on his part. It would be wrong to read his verbal statements in a way that one would those of a more reserved character. In writing to the Social Science Research Council (US) about Frank Meyer, one of the founders of the October Club in Oxford and a member of his seminar, he remarks that 'His drawbacks are that he is a Jew and has strong leanings towards the left.'[9] He says virtually the same of Fortes and others, including Evans-Pritchard at that period. At the same time he is equally uncomplimentary about French and Germans, insisting on his stance as a Polish nobleman but affecting the extreme attitudes of a true Anglo-Saxon that 'wogs begin at Calais'. I say 'affecting' because it appears in some ways as a mask, for it certainly does not prevent him from devoting his teaching time as well as a great deal of extra-mural support to Jews and Reds, clearly numbering them among his best friends. He also spoke six European languages fluently and always remained a foreigner in England. The written word has always to be understood in relation to the personality and social systems of the actor, but in Malinowski's case this was a relationship of great complexity.

Fortes had attended South African College School, Cape Town, between 1918 and 1922, and moved to the University of Cape Town in 1923, remaining there until 1927. He took the BA with distinction in 1925, obtaining the Noble Scholarship for the best graduate of the year, and passed the MA in 1926, when he received the highest post-graduate scholarship of the year. He came to London in 1927, registered for a PhD and worked under Professor Spearman at University College. His future wife, Sonia, came to London to be married in 1928 and he took his PhD in 1930. He was awarded the Ratan Tata Research Studentship at the London School of Economics in that year and continued to be attached, now to the School rather than University College, as a part-time student for a further PhD.

His preliminary application for a Rockefeller Fellowship in December 1931 gave as his referees the mathematician, Professor Lancelot Hogben, whom he had known personally since 1927, the psychiatrist, Dr Emanuel Miller (since 1928), and the sociologist, Professor Morris Ginsberg, whom he had met intermittently since the same year and who had introduced him to Miller. The application was supported in a lukewarm fashion by the psychologist, Professor Bartlett at Cambridge, whom he had just met, as well as by Radcliffe-Brown and by Seligman, both of whom he had encountered through Evans-Pritchard. But the strongest recommendation came from Evans-Pritchard himself who described him as 'a first-class man' with 'a quite exceptional critical ability', who was especially keen on the study of culture contact. A knowledge of Evans-Pritchard's views on the subject makes it seem that the latter remark was made very much tongue in cheek, aimed to please the providers of funds, although that interest was certainly strong not only for Fortes but others of his South African contemporaries, such as Schapera and Gluckman.

Owing to Fortes' position in relation to Malinowski and Radcliffe-Brown, there was a tug-of-war about where he would study. Radcliffe-Brown wrote from Chicago in support of his application in February 1932, saying that he had already made two attempts to get Fortes to come to Chicago; one failed because the university did not have the money, the other because the normal Rockefeller awards were not available to South Africans. Radcliffe-Brown claimed to have formed a high opinion of Fortes based on interviews and because the psychologist, Reyburn, at the University of Cape Town where Radcliffe-Brown himself had taught, regarded him as his best student, but thought he needed further training before doing fieldwork in Africa, possibly at Johannesburg with Hoernlé (a former student of Radcliffe-Brown).

As it turned out, the plan to go to Chicago did not work out and Fortes had to remain with Malinowski in London, which was where the Fellowships were based. His first research proposal, two quarto pages in length, was sent to Malinowski, who had already talked to Noel Hall of the Rockefeller Foundation about the possibility of getting a Fellowship for him, although the psychologist, Flügel, was his official nominator.[10] The proposal began: 'My object is to study the primitive child, in the setting of his family and community, by observational methods which have hitherto been used only with civilised children.' He goes on to state that he has been trying to do a sociological study in the East End of London for the past six months and would like to do comparative work on primitive children using 'the methods of functional anthropology' to solve psychological problems, that means beginning with 'a sociological analysis of the child's domestic, cultural, and community setting, and then proceeding to study the child's behaviour in this setting'. Obviously Fortes had already been influenced by the ideas of Malinowski whom he had met at Flügel's house earlier in 1931, before he ever formally studied with him.[11]

In his final application for a Fellowship, dated March of the following year, Fortes describes his part-time activities as a PhD student at the London School of Economics, as a lecturer at the London County Council Evening Institute from 1929 and as a psychologist at the East London Child Guidance Clinic, attached from 1928 to the Jew's Hospital, the Head of which was Dr Emanuel Miller. Evidence of the debt which Fortes owed to the association with this psychiatrist is provided by the fact that he was later to give the first Emanuel Miller memorial lecture to the Association for Child Psychology and Psychiatry in 1972 under the title of 'The first-born'.

Already in October 1931 the Executive Committee of the International African Institute meeting in Paris had been told of the candidates for Fellowships and Fortes was number one on the list. They were informed that he 'wishes to study anthropology for a year and then go out to Africa to work on the psychology of native children and to make some attempt at standardizing intelligence tests for natives', the subject on which he had worked for his PhD. He was ready to adopt numerical experimental techniques as well as to analyse 'the exact place of individuality'. At this point in his programme emphasis was placed on experimental psychology in an African setting, but that was to change under the influence of functional anthropology and of the social psychological research he had been carrying out in the East End. For, although Fortes' application for an award was accepted, the Institute memorandum he submitted did not greatly please his future teacher. The Institute discussed the memo in February 1932, and found it 'not very lively', as Oldham reported to Malinowski, asking 'Is he past the clever young man stage and ready to do some work?'[12] Malinowski replied from Toulon, telling the Secretary, Dorothy Brackett, whose influence was very strong, that Fortes was making other plans but was not yet ready to go to Africa and should work with him for another full year.[13] In other words Fortes had to stay under the master's tutelage for longer than he expected.

To Oldham Malinowski wrote in stronger terms. He claimed to have known Fortes for three to four years during which time 'he has improved greatly', but he is still 'impossible'. 'I know that politically he is wrong-headed, I know that he has started as an absolutely impossibly arrogant South African Jew; I know he has improved and is damnably clever. But I don't know whether he can work and produce ...'[14] About Fortes' memorandum he was even more scathing; 'I regard it as preposterous – any clever journalist could write 200 such memoranda over the weekend. In his memorandum, that is, there is no single concrete and founded statement, only promises and good intentions, and even these pretty badly expressed.' The next sentence indicates a more immediate source of his concern. 'He has been rather rude and impertinent but it is better he works here with me than go to R.B.' Clearly this was part of the problem for both men. Fortes wanted to work with Radcliffe-Brown for at least part of the time, influenced no doubt by Evans-Pritchard. In the end he had to stay in London. Malinowski arranged for him, Nadel and Wilson to get 'special coaching' from Audrey Richards and he had apparently extracted a promise from Fortes to work with him for a year, that is, 1932–3.[15] In March 1932 Fortes wrote saying that he had already spent a year on 'sociological studies', indicating his impatience to get on with research or else to get away from Malinowski, possibly both. But Malinowski held the purse-strings and said he could not recommend him for a

Fellowship unless he kept his promise.[16] Malinowski persuaded
Oldham to press the Foundation to allow Fortes to study in Britain,
since he could then learn the languages (he was later in touch with
Westermann at Berlin about learning Twi) and could get in contact
with Edwin Smith, Rattray and others, who had worked in the Gold
Coast.[17] Those purse-strings opened wider when Kirchhoff, another
Fellow, was prevented from going to Africa. For it was on the same day
that Oldham wrote to Malinowski saying: 'Now that we have lost
Kirchhoff I should be glad to go ahead with Fortes.'[18] As will become
clear, the reasons for the sudden vacancy were central to the history of
Fortes' research. The recommendation for a fellowship for Fortes was
put before the Executive Council in July 1932. For this meeting another
memorandum was submitted, dated 26 March 1932, which begins
'Somewhere in his well-known article on Anthropology in the
Encyclopaedia Britannica, Professor Malinowski remarks ...' The
obeisance, as Evans-Pritchard saw it, paid off, though Fortes was
genuinely attracted to Malinowski's work. Meanwhile it was announced
at the meeting that Fortes, described as 'a brilliant psychologist' with
'excellent recommendations', had just been given a ten-month Fellowship by the Rockefeller Foundation to study in London (an exception,
as South Africans were not included in their normal schemes) on
condition that the International African Institute subsequently awarded
him a fellowship for field research, which in turn they did.

    Other Fellows were elected at the same time. In each case the
condition of receiving their grant was that they received a training in
anthropology under Malinowski since his links with the International
African Institute were so close. The three Fellows, Fortes, Nadel and
Hofstra, the first two of whom became known as the Mandarins, were
actually to be given instruction in anthropology under both Malinowski
and Seligman, though the latter seems to have been a formal addition.
All three already had PhDs, Fortes in psychology, Nadel in the same
(Vienna 1925, specialising in music) and Hofstra in anthropology. All
three intended to work in West Africa, Fortes with his wife Sonia, who
had been a fellow-student in Cape Town, where she had come from
the Soviet Union. Eventually Fortes, Nadel and their wives set sail to
West Africa on the same ship in December 1933, while Hofstra went to
Sierra Leone in the following month.

    Malinowski regarded supervision as an exclusive relationship; it was
a task he could not share with anyone else. In June 1932 he sent a
memorandum to the Rockefeller Foundation entitled 'On the exclusive

supervision of fieldwork by one teacher'. The immediate cause was the fact that Lucy Mair, who was in Africa on a ten-month field trip, had been receiving advice from her mother (the Secretary of the School), from Beveridge (the Director) and from Coatman (who later wrote supporting Fortes' entry to the Gold Coast). In the field Malinowski objected to her moving about from one group to another, a practice of which he strongly disapproved in Seligman's students.[19] He objected even more strongly to interference from others. He wrote to Mrs Mair protesting that she had sent a cable to her daughter using his name and calling her back six weeks before the anticipated end of her research; 'fieldwork', he insisted, 'is not a sinecure nor a form of exotic entertainment'.[20]

What did his pre-fieldwork training consist of? Writing to Hofstra, who was about to join him, Malinowski said, 'I would like you to become acquainted with the work of the French sociological school of Durkheim.'[21] That advice would have sounded more characteristic had it come from Radcliffe-Brown since the work of the French school appears to have made less impact on Malinowski's writings. Nevertheless Fortes also characterised himself as pursuing 'sociological studies' when working with him, and this was certainly one way in which his teacher characterised his own work. However, for Malinowski training consisted principally of participation in his seminars which were usually based on an analysis of fieldwork, either his own or that of other participants.

So their formal activity consisted mainly of going to his lively seminars which were attended by colleagues, students and a number of visitors. In these they had to present their plans and later their findings before a critical audience of peers. It was a kind of collective apprenticeship, the form of which was later copied at Oxford under Evans-Pritchard, then at Manchester and Cambridge under Gluckman and Fortes respectively. The discussion often centred upon the collection of data in the context of social action and its analysis in the framework of the social system as a whole. Usually it did not finish in the classroom but continued afterwards in a café or pub. In addition students were encouraged to read sociological theory, the ethnographic literature on the area to be studied and to acquire whatever necessary language skills were available.

They were also taught to present their data not only verbally but in the form of analytic tables, such as are scattered through the numerous studies of his students. This technique can lead to unnecessary formalisations, even the tabulation of absurdities, but tables were also useful ways of summarising field data, of pointing to gaps in the record and of leading generatively to new perspectives.

In addition they were taught 'field methods', though it has to be said that most of these bordered on the simple-minded. Audrey Richards has described how Malinowski recommended using different coloured pencils for notes on different topics. While such techniques are of limited use, they do help to keep track of the multifarious material that the observers were asked to record in their field notebooks. The holistic approach that Malinowski advocated meant taking notes on the whole range of human interaction; that was implied in methodological functionalism. It entailed examining the interrelations between the different aspects of social life, between politics and religion, between family and the economy. All this had to be carried out by one research worker and possibly an assistant, so that much emphasis was placed on systematic methods; that tendency was especially noticeable among those who later worked with Gluckman at the Rhodes–Livingstone Institute. The result was a series of excellent ethnographic accounts of African societies, to which most of his students made substantial contributions.

Malinowski was often critical about his new students, though he appreciated their efforts. Of Fortes and his wife he wrote to Oldham that 'they are keeping up to expectations which, as you know, were fairly high'. Nadel he regarded as very capable and brilliant, 'but not without some rather difficult continental mannerisms i.e. argumentative, running into unproductive abstract discussions'.[22]

When Fortes, Nadel and Hofstra came under Malinowski's direction for the academic year 1932–3, they had been asked to work together on the study of culture contact and to elaborate the necessary techniques. The choice of topic was of course dictated by the Rockefeller Foundation. While that topic had little influence on their main research, it did lead to a number of publications on the subject. However, at the end of the period of training the Directors asked them to submit a joint memorandum on Schemes of Research, plus individual statements on the proposal for 'practical anthropology', all of which were put before the Bureau of the International African Institute at a meeting held after the three Fellows had already left for West Africa.[23]

The documents, which are given in Appendix 1, make interesting reading because they testify to the strong influence that Malinowski (and others at his seminars) had on these proposals, as well as to the strength of 'functionalist paradigms' at a purely theoretical level. However much of what they absorbed was not so much functionalism as usually defined but rather a formalising, systematising approach to social facts, together with the need for a continuing attempt to relate institutions to one another, at the level of individual action, of the group and of the domain or sub-system.

It is also interesting to look at the changing nature of the individual research proposals under the influence of Malinowski's teaching and, later on, the changing nature of the research itself as field circumstances impinge upon plans, interests and ideas. Fortes' first proposal, as presented to the meeting of the Executive Council of the Institute, was basically psychological, though certainly not psychoanalytical, partly aimed at the development of cross-cultural intelligence tests, a subject on which he had already been influenced by Malinowski. Nadel's first proposal, presented to the London meeting of the Executive Council in July 1932, centred upon music – he had already worked on archives of recordings in Vienna, where he was born, as well as in Berlin, where he was then living, apparently unable to continue his work in anti-Semitic Austria. His research was to be in 'African ethnography and fieldwork, in order to increase ethnographically and practically the knowledge of music'.

In keeping with the emphasis on group work, the three Fellows produced a joint memorandum at the end of their training period, followed by three separate statements; Fortes' was entitled 'Sketch of a plan for the study of the African Family', Nadel's was a 'Scheme for the investigation of religious institutions', and Hofstra worked out a 'Scheme for a study of secret societies'. The joint memorandum given in Appendix 1 was subdivided into three sections, (1) Classification of social facts, (2) Function and relation of institutions, (3) Problems of psychological factors. It ends by noting that 'the best practical means of presenting the concrete application of the points of view elaborated above are diagrammatic schemes as suggested by Professor Malinowski in his Seminar'. In Fortes' own memorandum he talks of 'basic needs', a Malinowskian formulation of one aspect of his approach, and goes on to point to the role of the ancestor cult in social cohesion; Edith Clarke, another student of Malinowski, wrote in similar terms of Asante ancestor worship contributing to social solidarity, a theme taken up by Fortes in his first paper on fishing magic. Fortes then speaks of 'sentiments of respect for authority in the family', of the importance of the 'ritual of family life' (e.g. funerals), as well as of the necessity of looking at the family along the 'time co-ordinate', biographically. In more general terms he perceived the links between the personality system and the social system (to employ Parsons' terms) as in need of exploration. In other words, a number of ideas which he developed later on were already being sketched out, the role of familial cults, of the developmental cycle, of domestic authority, of the interlocking nature of sociological and psychological enquiry.

The memorandum contained an acknowledgement of the help of Malinowski but that proved not to be sufficient for their teacher. He immediately expressed an objection to Oldham, though he waited before bringing it up with the students themselves. The joint document, which he had been sent as a member of Council, 'is in a way a fake, or more exactly a partial plagiarism. It is really more a summary of my teaching which the three fellows received over the last eighteen months.'[25] That complaint is itself an indication of how much his students had 'learnt' from him.

When the three Research Fellows had established themselves in the field, they sent back regular reports. Malinowski wanted them monthly but Fortes' first statement was dated three months after he had got to the field,[26] and the second was four months later. Nadel did not report until 5 May and he was regarded as the best fieldworker.[27] Hofstra on the other hand suffered from ill health and his performance left something to be desired.

All three returned for a period in 1935. During this time they again attended Malinowski's seminar. The session began by laying out the elements of social organisation.[28] 'Tradition, culture, society, mean the same thing', it was proclaimed, so stick to 'culture'. Culture consisted of the following elements arranged in a specific way:

Education
Government – war – political organisation
Language
Economics – crafts
Material culture
Religion – magic
Social organisation
Law – morality – custom

Later on in the session Fortes made a contribution on 'The culture scheme and the fieldworker', taking funerals as his case material and being more concerned to differentiate tradition, culture and society rather than to lump them together.[29] At this time Malinowski was trying to elaborate in a more explicit fashion his 'functional theory' (of culture) which he began to oppose directly to the functionalism of Durkheim.[30] His approach (or 'theory') was characterised by three factors:

(a) the elaboration of 'a sort of inventory of the elements of culture',
(b) a belief in the 'wholeness of culture', none of the elements receiving any special emphasis,
(c) and the idea of 'fieldwork as experimental testing of a theoretical approach'.

Only perhaps in the context of the highly fragmented amateur ethnographies of earlier times would remarks of this level of generality have much to offer the budding anthropologist and it is difficult now to see what could have been borrowed by sophisticated social scientists. Nevertheless Malinowski felt that in writing up their initial proposals for the field, Fortes, Nadel and Hofstra had plagiarised him, as he had pointed out to Oldham in 1934. Two years later he returned to the matter and wrote to Fortes asking that the Fellows once again insert the original acknowledgement to his seminar which had been included in the joint document circulated to the International African Institute, because he now wanted to publish some of the ideas. He even enclosed a draft of what he wanted.[31] This may well be the occasion referred to by Meyer Fortes when he told me that Malinowski had once asked him to acknowledge in writing that all his ideas were borrowed from him.[32] At another time Fortes referred to the contributions made by students to Malinowski's writing up, as well as to his research generally. There does seem to have been a considerable *quid pro quo*. While no-one would attribute most of Fortes' ideas to his teacher, the research documents that were prepared by the three as a result of their year's work differ considerably from the original proposals they had submitted and bear very strong marks of Malinowski's teaching, partly in their functional vocabulary and the desire to see things working in an interlocking way (as they appear in fieldwork), but more especially in the sociological questions they were asking and in the degree of formalisation of the results, rather than on the more superficial level of 'elements', of socio-cultural phenomena. They tried to look, as Fortes would later say, at systematic relationships. In his own account of his training, which he called 'An anthropologist's apprenticeship', he described his encounter with Malinowski whose 'catalytic virtuosity kept the seminar at a high pitch'.[33] While he later said that they were not impressed with his claims for functionalism, 'all agreed that it represented a revolution in fieldwork method'. But an important element of Malinowski's theoretical influence lay at a different level, in encouraging the examination of more concrete problems. For example, since the Trobriands were matrilineal he became interested in the general attributes of such systems, both at the societal and interpersonal levels. It is not accidental that two of those who worked with him – Richards among the Bemba, Fortes among the Ashanti – made very substantial contributions to the study of such societies not only of the organisation of that type of kin group and to the concomitant problems of residence, ownership and marriage, but to the interpersonal tensions that marked particular kinds of matrilineal system.

Malinowski's ability to gather round him a group of students lay partly in his profound commitment to the subject and to the intensity of his belief in the value of field research. Intellectually he clearly played a great part in redirecting the research of Fortes, Nadel and many others. But it was also the case that he held the purse-strings in his own hands through his friendship with Oldham at the Institute and through his contacts with the Rockefeller Foundation; in both quarters his reputation was high, not least because he displayed an interest in 'practical anthropology' as distinct from the purely academic variety.

It was also practical in the further sense that his correspondence shows him to have been at the centre of numerous manœuvres to place people in jobs. In June 1933 he wrote to the Rockefeller Foundation of his deep conviction that the future of linguistics lay 'in the study of meaning connected with the study of phonetics' and asked for a lectureship for J. R. Firth, described as 'the coming man'. He placed much emphasis on linguistics, partly because fieldwork required the learning of a language but also because he was interested in theoretical aspects of language and wrote an important appendix to *The Meaning of Meaning* (1923) by those key figures in interwar intellectual life in Britain, C. K. Ogden and I. A. Richards; the interest in meaning was intrinsic to his field studies. At the same time as he wrote on behalf of Firth he requested a post for Audrey Richards.[34] In the following year, 1934, he wrote to the Rockefeller asking for money to go to see his students in Africa as well as for Reo Fortune, whom he had backed for the proposed Chair of Sociology at Cambridge;[35] Fortune was attending his seminars at the time and had asked Malinowski to write an introduction to his valuable ethnographic study, *The Sorcerers of Dobu* (1932).

But Malinowski's major interest was in practical anthropology of another kind, which, while offering help to colonial governments as well as to the governed, inevitably led to a series of conflicts. The research programme meant recruiting intellectuals from various countries whose views on society were in many cases strongly influenced by the political climate of Europe in the early thirties, by the economic depression, by the rise of Fascism and by the growth of communism. These were the people he required to carry out the programme of practical anthropology elaborated in conjunction with the Rockefeller Foundation. Much has been made in recent years of the role of British anthropologists working under colonial regimes, supported by a conservative social theory known as structural-functionalism. Some of this criticism has emanated from members or supporters of the two major world powers, European in origin, that have managed to subdue and incorporate, temporarily at least, the native populations of the areas in Russia and North America into which they expanded. But the attempt to show structural-functionalism as the necessary ideology of the colonial regimes and anthropologists as their instruments comes up against a number of difficulties when we look at the actual history of the participants, for in many cases their attitudes and roles were very different from what these holistic assumptions would predict. That is because such pronouncements ignore the internal contradictions of colonial rule as well as the relative autonomy (however limited) of fields of knowledge. Both before and after the Second World War a number of anthropologists were excluded from or had great problems in getting access to the colonies, while most others were concerned not so much to support colonial rule as to modify or even abolish it. One clear example is the case of Meyer Fortes who faced considerable difficulties in getting into what was then the Protectorate of the Northern Territories of the Gold Coast, now part of the independent nation of Ghana.

The problem of entry into colonial territories had already arisen with missionaries and even with traders but never with academics. In anglophone West Africa professional anthropology began with the appointment of existing members of the colonial service as government anthropologists. There were few of these: R. S. Rattray who worked among the Asante of Ghana, Meek among the Ibo of Nigeria – figures who were the rough equivalents of Tauxier in the Côte d'Ivoire and H. Labouret in what is now Burkina Faso. In both France and Britain, colonial officers received some training in anthropology, Cambridge

providing teaching from 1906 and starting a Diploma in 1908 with such
professional courses very much in mind. Mauss gave similar instruction
in Paris. So that apart from those of the specialists like Rattray, a
number of contributions were made by other district officers like
Cardinall in his works on the Gold Coast, especially when, as the result
of the extension of the system of indirect rule, they were expected to
write essays on aspects of the social organisation of local peoples. These
appeared in the early 1930s and often constitute useful pieces of
ethnographic research, many of which were deposited with the Royal
Anthropological Institute in London. But it has to be said that there
was little in the anglophone areas comparable to the kind of historical,
linguistic and ethnographic survey contained in say Delafosse's 'Haute-
Sénégal-Niger' (1912) or Clozel's volume on the customary law of the
Côte d'Ivoire (1902). One might suggest that this was a matter of scale,
with France dominating West Africa. But early German research in
Togo and the Cameroons displays a similarly high quality; from the
end of the nineteenth century, the journals of the *Deutscheschutzgebiet* are
full of interesting papers by Herr Doktor this and that. These people
often carried out their research with a notebook in one hand and a
machine-gun in the other, for their colonial procedures were usually
more aggressive than those of the dominant colonial powers –
necessarily so, from one point of view, for they felt that they had to
carve out for themselves by force a *Lebensraum* since their rivals had
long established bases in the region from which they could operate in a
more leisurely fashion. What was the reason for this relative backwardness of scholarly research in British West Africa? The conven-
tional answer is that the area meant less to the metropolitan country
than in the case of France or Germany. The best British administrators,
those with the best degrees from Oxbridge, as well as the weight of
overseas scholarly interest, were directed to the Jewel in the Crown,
India, rather than to the less glamorous Dark Continent. The first two
William Wyse Professors at Cambridge had been members of the
Indian Civil Service associated with the census; census taking and
ethnography went hand in hand as in Cardinall's work in the 1931
Gold Coast Census. It is also the case, in my view, that the Durkheim
school in France provided a better basis for such activities than did the
contributions of Tylor and Frazer, Perry and Elliot Smith, which were
largely concerned with speculations concerning early developments in
the history of mankind – not a useless activity by any means but of less
relevance in increasing the knowledge of the contemporary 'natives'.

There were of course others such as W. H. R. Rivers who contributed both theoretically, in *Kinship and Social Organisation*, published in 1914, and ethnographically in his work on the Todas of South India, not to speak of the later work of Malinowski, who published *The Argonauts of the Western Pacific* in 1922 and Radcliffe-Brown whose study, *The Andaman Islanders*, appeared in the same year, as well as the work of Charles and Brenda Seligman. But while Paris saw the early embodiment of Durkheimian sociology into the training of future commandants, London had little influence on Oxbridge where the majority of colonial officers were educated. It was only with the dominance of Malinowski that the situation changed, when he started to train career anthropologists rather than colonial officers. The outlook for British professional anthropology in West Africa was profoundly altered in December 1932 when Fortes and Nadel set sail in the same boat for the Guinea Coast.

The local government was not altogether prepared. Rattray has been described as the Gold Coast's 'first government anthropologist', of whom it has been said that his appointment established an official anthropological orientation that persisted long after his retirement in 1931.[36] Rattray's official position had come about because of his long-standing interest in African languages and cultures, which made it possible for him to move within the administration and to become an 'anthropologist' later in life. But far from establishing an official orientation, this administration, like others in Africa, was heavily split in its attitude to the subject. Field officers did not encourage outside research in the social sciences, at least until the period after the Second World War when both the climate of opinion and the views of the junior personnel had greatly changed. Nor were colonial governments very interested in outside research, preferring to get it done by their own staff. That was not necessarily the view of the Colonial Office, which was directly responsible to Parliament and more sensitive to public opinion. But it made for difficulties for academic research, which was exactly why the Rockefeller Foundation thought that the International African Institute could be a valuable intermediary. That turned out to be so, even if they were not always successful.

CHAPTER 3

Making it to the field as a Jew and a Red

The position of anthropologists in relation to foundations, to other sources of funding and to the colonial authorities is brought out very forcefully in the story of Fortes' efforts to get to the field and carry out his research. Even with the collaboration of the International African Institute with the Rockefeller philanthropies on the one hand and the Colonial Office on the other, there were many difficulties in undertaking fieldwork, about whose merits opinions differed.

The Rockefeller plan called for the study of culture contact. The scheme was intended to be relevant to current issues, not to concern itself with antiquarian matters. Malinowski later wrote that they 'had been training young men and women in practical anthropology'.[1] An internal memo of March 1938 sums up the intention of the scheme as it had been conceived seven years previously.

After careful consideration the Council of the Institute decided to direct the research to be undertaken towards a better understanding of those aspects of native society making for social cohesion, the economics of communal life, the ways in which African society is being disrupted by the invasion of western ideas and economic forces, and the resulting changes in African institutions and behaviour. Thus the research would be concentrated on problems of most direct concern to colonial governments, educators and others engaged in practical tasks in Africa.

So conditions were laid down that had some influence on subsequent research, but nevertheless the results were not altogether as planned. The Rockefeller Foundation was interested in the effects of culture contact, specifically on native peoples. It was also interested in group projects. It was specifically the wishes (and the funds) of the Rockefeller Foundation that accounted for the attempt to get all the Fellows of the International African Institute to consider this topic, even though that was rarely their main interest. The result was a special number of the journal, *Africa*, devoted to the subject, the focus of a debate between

Malinowski, Fortes and later Gluckman. The latter objected to Malinowski's vision of cultures coming into contact like thunderclouds, preferring to look at the situation in terms of social relationships that partially cross-cut, say, the black and white division in South Africa, as exemplified in Gluckman's analysis of a social situation in Zululand (1958). But the differences lay not simply at the level of theory but also of what one might call morality. Here the main protagonist, Evans-Pritchard, was a romantic as well as a scholar and held his main object to be to get to know and analyse the simpler societies for their own sake. Getting involved in culture contact meant not only neglecting the scholarly task but also having to deal with colonial governments; with them, he used to say, you should only sup with a long spoon, as with the devil. In practice Evans-Pritchard had himself worked closely with the Sudanese government, from whom he received funds as well as favours, though he saw himself as independent. He certainly held ambivalent attitudes, on this as on many other issues.[2] But in my experience his advice to students was unambiguous. Keep right away from the administration.

It hardly needs pointing out that in Africa during the colonial period this advice was as impractical as it is now; the fieldworker is forced to put himself in the hands of some network or other, at least for part of the time. But his insistence on independence did mean that students were encouraged to choose topics in which they themselves rather than the administration were interested. It also meant, less happily, that they often avoided including the District Commissioner in their analysis, say, of the Samo or the Mossi, the Tallensi or the Asante. They kept away too for many years from a direct confrontation with the problems of dramatic social change. That avoidance persisted longer in Britain than in France, where many scholars worked with ORSTOM, a government agency; others like Tardits studied the urban situation in Porto Novo. Such enquiries received little or no encouragement after the war either from Evans-Pritchard at Oxford or from Fortes at Cambridge.

It was much the same with the Institute's Fellows. While their initial proposals referred to social change, few (except perhaps A. I. Richards) paid much attention to the topic, although in South Africa anthropologists like Schapera and Monica Wilson were inevitably forced to discuss the question. The avoidance in Britain was due not only to Evans-Pritchard's objections, nor to the sometimes rather sloppy theoretical approach of Malinowski, but to the fact the independent conditions under which the fellows worked permitted them to follow their own ethnographic interests. In almost every case this freedom led to a concentration on gaining a deeper knowledge of native society rather than to following the lines laid down for the study of 'culture contact'.

The extensive programme of field research demanded the co-operation of the colonial authorities in Africa, the prospect of which had been one of the reasons for the establishment of the Rockefeller project in London. It also demanded the recruitment of a group of first-class students drawn from different nationalities (including South Africans, who were excluded from the ordinary Rockefeller Fellow-ships). Grounds for conflict were built into the scheme, both in the form of potential opposition between colonial government and the intellectuals of the period, and because the latter were being financed to carry out practical anthropology when their interests as intellectuals lay elsewhere, in more 'academic' or 'theoretical' directions.

The first problem of a group of intellectuals of the 1930s carrying out fieldwork in African colonies was brought to a climax in the case of Paul Kirchhoff. He had come to London for some weeks of study preparatory to going to the field but was eventually told by the Colonial Office that he could not have permission to work in Nyasaland. As a consequence his Institute award was terminated. It was the problem of Kirchhoff that made difficulties for Fortes' entry into Ghana.

Kirchhoff had spent a short while working with Malinowski in 1926, had subsequently been employed by the Rockefeller Foundation in South America for two years and was recommended to the Interna-tional African Institute by one of its Directors, Diedrich Westermann. He had left Berlin at the beginning of the Hitler regime under which he had been involved in left-wing political activity, but he was strongly supported by members of the Foundation and encouraged to become an Africanist. On coming to London in 1931, he made an excellent impression on his colleagues, as Audrey Richards reported to Malinowski when he was living at Toulon.[3] At first he wanted to go to Basutoland (now Lesotho). Oldham had practical reasons against this choice and suggested he should go to Northern Rhodesia (now Zambia) because of the mining interests. But Malinowski did not approve because Richards was already working there. So Kirchhoff applied to go to Nyasaland (now Malawi) and, since he was judged to be experienced, arrangements went ahead for him to leave right away without the period of training which the others had to undergo.

A few days before he set sail for Africa 'some intelligence service or other' sent a report to the Colonial Office (who had been very helpful up to that point) and he was refused permission to go into any British territory. 'The indictment against him was that he had something to do with communistic views or perhaps propaganda.'[4] Oldham duly reported to Malinowski telling him that his colleague at the Institute, Major H. Vischer, had seen the information. According to Oldham, the Colonial Office had acted properly, for Kirchhoff had kept something back. Moreover, his wife was also involved in what was 'more than a philosophical commitment to Communism, or mere political associations'.[5] Despite the fact that Kirchhoff obtained a certificate of good behaviour from the German police, the Colonial Office refused to consider the matter: 'We know from himself that both here and in Germany he has been mixed up with communism.' However the government claimed to know more.[6] The Institute was therefore not in a position to do what it wanted, as the Secretary, Dorothy Brackett, pointed out, 'without the goodwill of Government'.[7] So it had to cancel his contract and look for money to enable him to return to Berlin, although it would clearly have been unwise for him to do so.[8]

The case of Kirchhoff was worrying to Malinowski not because he disapproved of the Colonial Office vetoing the entry of an active communist, but because the reasons were not made public. He compared the situation with his own in the Trobriands where rumours about him flew around during the First World War. In addition to 'victimisation' he was worried about the repercussions of this action on his research programme, since he was well aware of the leftist inclinations of others of his students.

Take the case of Fortes for instance, I know the boy is or imagines himself to be a Communist and pro-Bolshevik. I have been advising him for some time to look up to the Institute as his future alma mater. But now I have to warn you [he wrote to Oldham] and shall also have to warn him some sort of definite understanding will have to be arrived at with the Colonial Office as to the way in which they will deal with us, and as to the definite conditions which we shall have to impose on our candidates before we accept them.[9]

He demanded clarity, but in fact he went much further.

Despite his disapproval of Kirchhoff's beliefs Malinowski did his best to help him, prompted by Audrey Richards whom Oldham had placed in charge of the newcomer. Richards organised anthropologists in his support and actively looked for another post he could fill. She wrote to T. T. Barnard at the University of Cape Town to see if it would be possible for him to work there. Barnard replied that the university would accept him if she could get the Institute to re-vote the funds they had withdrawn. In this way they could try to get the Colonial Office off the hook. In an attached note, Barnard comments that Richards seemed 'unduly impressed with the powers of the Colonial Office. But they will of course have to be squared.' As things turned out, Richards' fears about its influence were fully justified.[10]

At the same time Malinowski was writing to the linguistic anthropologist, Edward Sapir, at Yale as well as to Raymond Firth in Australia about the possibility of an Oceania Fellowship at Sydney. Firth had inherited Radcliffe-Brown's position as Secretary of the Social Science Committee of the Australian National Research Council. In fact Malinowski wrote two letters on the subject of Kirchhoff on the same day, one official, one personal.[11] In this he claimed, 'The whole [communist] theory is a canard', a view that was apparently based on Seligman's assertion to him a few days before that Kirchhoff 'is not a member of the Communist party, or was not when I last saw him'.[12]

At first there seemed some hope for Kirchhoff in Australia and in September Malinowski reported to the Rockefeller Foundation from Toulon that he would receive a generous allowance for fieldwork.[13] But on his return to London shortly afterwards, he was met by Audrey Richards 'who has been in charge of Kirchhoff's affairs'. She told him a cable had been received from the Chairman of the Australian Research Council withdrawing the award, since the Australian Government had informed the Council that they had been warned about Kirchhoff by the British authorities.[14] Malinowski's reaction was strong. 'I shall set everybody I can in motion, and either discover that Kirchhoff is really a criminal communist, or find something for him.' Indeed he had already spoken to someone 'in touch with the C.I.D.' When the papers came from Australia, he sent them to his friend Oldham for advice, 'feeling rather uncomfortable about the surreptitiousness of the whole affair'.[15]

Malinowski had supported Kirchhoff from the beginning. He thought it 'unlikely that he should be a Bolshevik agent of a dangerous type; more likely he might have been a little silly once or twice, or perhaps convivial'.[16] He even wrote to Kirchhoff saying, 'I cannot believe that a man of your common sense could be a Bolshevik agent.'[17] He later concluded that it was all 'an official error ... probably backed up by one of the political heads of the Colonial Office, who is an extreme diehard conservative as well as notoriously a fool (I mean, of course, Sir Philip Cunliffe-Lister)' whom he already suspected of further victimisation, preventing Kirchhoff from going to Australia.[18] The tentacles of the Colonial Office spread very wide and Kirchhoff eventually had to move right outside their range.

Malinowski had become heavily involved in the affair. Kirchhoff was staying in his London home while he was away, being supported by a group of anthropologists, although he also received a grant of $600 from the Rockefeller Foundation.[19] He was awarded a grant-in-aid to enable him to join the seminar group the following year.[20] However, by the beginning of 1933 Malinowski notes that Kirchhoff has largely dropped out of the group of research students as 'his linguistic interests seem to make functional anthropology of little interest to him'.[21] In May 1933 he reports Kirchhoff going to Ireland to see about fieldwork in connection with the Harvard Sociological Study of County Clare under Lloyd Warner (who had worked with Radcliffe-Brown in Australia), since he could no longer return to Germany.[22] The following year, 1934, Evans-Pritchard met him in Paris where he had a job at the Trocadero Museum, and concluded ' it was not so bad from that point of view'.[23]

Kirchhoff was certainly involved in left-wing politics as his history both before and after this incident attests. But the immediate point is that his case showed the political colours and the solidarity of the anthropologists at the London School of Economics, as well as the difficulties some of them had with the Colonial Office, and especially with the individual colonial governments, in getting to the field. That was especially true in the case of Meyer Fortes.

To some extent Fortes benefited from Kirchhoff's disappearance from the scene, since it created a vacancy in the Fellowship programme. At the same time the precedent caused him serious difficulties. He had sent his proposal to Malinowski in July 1931 and submitted an application to the Institute at the end of December. On January 1932, Oldham wrote to Malinowski asking him for a letter about Fortes including comments on the memorandum he had submitted, saying at the same time that a decision on the grant had been postponed. It was just then that the Kirchhoff affair blew up.

Malinowski replied on 5 February, mentioning Fortes' pro-Bolshevik leanings, and on the 16th Oldham again wrote for a recommendation, asking that he make no mention of that subject since the matter was best raised in conversation (for he had invited Fortes to dinner) and in any case the Colonial Office had 'not heard anything to his disadvantage'.[24] Oldham was satisfied with the results of his enquiries and observations and his conclusions appear to have been accepted by Malinowski who on 3 March wrote about Fortes saying, 'I am far less tolerant of any communistic ideas and propaganda than you are, indeed I feel very strongly about it.' Had he had any strong objections he would have raised them at this stage.[25] So Fortes' name was put forward to the Council in July and he received an award for the preliminary year, though on other grounds there was still a measure of uncertainty about his subsequent research, since as late as September Malinowski writes that 'We have been dangling that bait before Fortes for twelve months.'[26]

Meanwhile, as early as March of that year Fortes had been getting impatient, wanting to get off to the field. Writing from Toulon, Malinowski reminds him that they had agreed to work together for the year 1932–3 and he could not recommend him for one of the Fellowships of the International African Institute to carry out fieldwork unless he fulfilled his side of the bargain. Fortes replied immediately, referring to 'another misunderstanding between us' but after pointing out that he had already spent a year 'in sociological studies', he agreed to wait until December 1933. There was already tension between the benefactor (or patron) and the recipient (or client).

At an early stage Oldham wrote to the Governor of the Gold Coast, Sir Ransford Slater, outlining the proposal for Fortes to work there and in February 1932 he received a reply that was 'generally favourable to the project'.[27] When he returned to England in June 1932 Oldham arranged for Fortes to meet both Slater who had been the Governor since 1927, as well as his successor, Shenton Thomas. Slater was impressed by Fortes' 'youth, keenness, common sense and readiness to accept suggestions' as well as by his research project. Another virtue in his eyes was that, 'though South African born, he evidently does not hold the common South African attitude towards the native, which makes him suitable for the Gold Coast'. In writing about this interview, Slater recommended that a start be made on the formal approach to the Colonial Office so that they could make any enquiries they might deem desirable. As a result Oldham wrote at once to the Secretary of

State for the Colonies, W. C. Bottomley. The reason for this caution was that the very first Fellow to be appointed by the Institute had been Kirchhoff, who was to have worked in the British Protectorate of Nyasaland of which Shenton Thomas had unfortunately been Governor at the time. Because of the protests that followed his exclusion from Africa, especially on the part of the London School of Economics, the Colonial Office was in some trouble and the Institute had therefore become 'more than ordinarily careful in regard to the selection of our candidates'.[28]

When Oldham asked Bottomley to ensure he was safe in proceeding with Fortes, investigations were made 'in the authoritative quarters'. Since no black marks had been recorded he was told that 'Fortes was all right'[29] and it was arranged that the applicant should have tea with the new Governor at his club. However, at roughly the same time, Vischer, the Secretary-General of the Institute, informed the Colonial Office that at one of its recent meetings they had been told that Fortes 'made a special point of telling his fellow students at the London School of Economics that he was a communist', gilding the lily by pointing out that he was married to 'a Russian lady'. Shenton Thomas was given this information just after his interview with Fortes and so made no further report, thinking the whole matter was closed. The source of Vischer's information on Fortes is unclear, but it may well have arisen out of remarks Malinowski made to Oldham in the light of the Kirchhoff affair. These Vischer would have duly reported, being 'in the pay of the Colonial Office'; he had earlier worked in West Africa as a Colonial Officer and continued to be their man. However this may be, the project now bristled with difficulties. Knowing nothing of these complications, Oldham thought the coast was clear and in March 1933 formally applied to the Colonial Office on behalf of Fortes for permission to undertake 'sociological research'. At the same time he wrote to Shenton Thomas as Governor of the Gold Coast asking that the application be favourably received, for although Fortes might be 'somewhat lacking in personal charm', he was a man of quite unusual ability, of sound judgement, and one whose work would be of interest to the government as well as being an original contribution to sociology. He reminded Thomas that he had met Fortes in London earlier in the year. The response was explosive. Shenton Thomas expressed his objections in a handwritten comment to his assistant on Oldham's letter about Fortes' entry which reads: 'You had better keep this in the D.C.'s cupboard. Fortes struck me as a particularly nasty type of Jew!'[30] He replied in more measured terms to Oldham[31] but made it clear that the 'handicap', to which Oldham referred, would prevent him getting on with Europeans and natives alike. At the same time the Governor wrote to Fiddian at the Colonial Office reminding him that he had spoken about Fortes' communistic views. But his objections went further than the overtly political. 'I don't want him whether communist or not.'[32] This letter crossed with one from Creasey at the Colonial Office forwarding the formal application from the Institute and reminding the Governor that Creasey had told him the previous summer of the report of Fortes' communistic tendencies and of his reply that 'no one who was even suspected of communist views should be allowed to visit the Gold Coast'.[33] However, as further enquiries had provided no support for the rumour, the Secretary of State had agreed to his going on condition that 'fresh enquiries would be made' towards the time of his departure ('October or November next') and that 'even if the result of these further enquiries was satisfactory, Dr Fortes could only go on the distinct understanding that if he were suspected of subversive activities, he would be promptly expelled from the Colony'. The future enquiries were to include Mrs Fortes who is, 'we understand, a Russian lady'. The source of the allegations pointed directly to Vischer.

After going to see the Colonial Office, Oldham replied at length to the Governor's letter, explaining how, in January of the previous year, he had requested Bottomley at the Colonial Office to make enquiries about Fortes and had been told that these were 'entirely satisfactory'.[34] Only some months later did Bottomley indicate that he had 'some less favourable information' (presumably that supplied by Vischer) but agreed that in view of the assurances he had received, 'if nothing further occurred no difficulties would be raised'. It was as a result of these queries that Oldham took his own steps to satisfy himself. He had Fortes and his wife to stay three times, as well as meeting him at Lord Lugard's. 'I have had many hours of intimate conversation with him and I am certain that communism has no attractions for him. He has, in fact, an intellectual contempt for its principles. His interest is wholly scientific and I can imagine nothing more remote from his purpose than to instil political ideas in the mind of the natives ... I have been extremely impressed by the accounts of what he has been doing in the East End and by his understanding and appreciation of work of the church and of social agencies.'[35] If Fortes had any association with communism, it was as a devil's advocate; meanwhile Fortes was 'in all respects admirable and harmless'.[36] Oldham was quite convinced that Fortes was in the clear.

A few days after Oldham had written, Bottomley himself wrote to the Governor explaining the position. He was worried about the possible repercussions of a refusal to allow the project to go forward, since it was he rather than the Governor who had to face the people and the politicians at home. 'If Fortes was refused admission, there would be a much worse storm, especially at the London School of Economics, than in the case of Kirchhoff [when] the Secretary of State himself had a good deal of trouble over the affair and I know that my stock went down completely in various quarters for obstructiveness.'[37] It was not only apprehension about the protests from the London School of Economics which Malinowski, but principally Richards, had encouraged, but that evidence about Fortes' subversive activities was lacking. Bottomley had arranged for further enquiries to be made and the Colonial Office was told that 'as far as can be ascertained, Fortes takes no part in any subversive propaganda, neither can it be established that he belongs to the Communist Party'. Even at this late stage Oldham was asked to make further enquiries, which he did from Malinowski and Coatman at the London School of Economics. Coatman had had a career in the Indian police and was connected with the Criminal Investigation Department, so his voice carried much weight. He replied that Fortes was 'a man of sensible and balanced views, very easy to get on with, quick to see the humorous side of things, and altogether very much a man to my liking'.[38] Malinowski generously concentrated upon his 'exceptional intellectual gifts'. 'He is an original thinker, an extremely able constructive critic ... he is going to make an exceptionally good field-worker' because he is 'an excellent mixer'. The only qualification he has is that Fortes is still 'very self-conscious' and did not at first make a convincing impression on the Council of the International African Institute. At the end of this long succession of enquiries, the 'wail' from Oldham, as Shenton Thomas called it, did the trick and permission was given for Fortes to go to the Gold Coast to carry out his research.[39] It was not only the wail from Oldham but the fear of an outcry from senior members of a metropolitan university.

Oldham and Malinowski successfully prevented Fortes' views, which were presumably known to Malinowski better than anyone else, from becoming an issue. He told Fortes where his future lay and indicated what he needed to do to ensure it. Fortes did not rock the boat. In fact

he got on well with many members of the administration of the Gold
Coast after his arrival there. It is true that when he had returned to
England and was about to make a second visit in 1935, the Chief
Commissioner of the Northern Territories called for a report, saying
that 'he should not be encouraged to resume his studies in the
Northern Territories until the value of his work *in its bearings on
administrative questions* has been appraised'.[40] Once again the Colonial
Office, in the person of Creasey, took a more liberal attitude than the
local administrators: 'we can hardly close the Northern Territories to
any form of scientific investigation because we are not satisfied that it
would be directly useful to the political administration of the place'. In
fact Fortes did pay some attention to administrative matters. His first
Tallensi paper on marriage laws was published by the Government
Printer in Accra and he clearly had a hand in Kerr's memorandum on
local government among the Frafra, in which category the Tallensi
were included. Kerr was the local District Commissioner working at
Bolgatanga, and Fortes got on well with him and with the Agricultural
Officer, Lynn. During the period of his return to London, when he
attended Malinowski's seminars, evidence of an ambiguous kind came
along of his 'utility' to the authorities in the Gold Coast. For in
November he was written to at length by Canon H. M. Grace, the new
Principal of Achimota College, in very flattering terms, asking him to
join the staff. An anthropologist's help was needed to deal construc-
tively with the restless spirits of the students who found themselves
between two worlds. Fortes was very receptive to this suggestion both
from the 'practical' and from the 'scientific' point of view. As he was
still a Fellow of the International African Institute, he sent them a copy
of this letter, pointing out that such a post would make it possible for
him to pursue the Institute's interests in changing African cultures. But
a copy of the letter was duly despatched by Vischer (again) to the
Colonial Office and hence to Sir Arnold Hodson, the acting Governor
of the Gold Coast. Hodson became very worried, not so much at the
invitation to Fortes as at the tone of Grace's letter. He objected to the
statements that 'this country is in a precarious position in regard to its
future political life' and blamed the bad reputation the Gold Coast had
got on the local press as well as on policy statements to the effect that
we are training Africans to take over the administrative structure.
However the question of the appropriateness of an anthropologist for
such a position, and of Fortes in particular, was inevitably raised.
Hodson consulted his advisors. The Head of the Education Depart-

ment thought that Grace was quite right to be worried about the future and hoped the Government would make a clear statement about its policy, for example, regarding Africans filling 'European' jobs. But he did not think an anthropologist would do the job. Nor did the acting Governor, certainly not in the case of Fortes.[41]

Hodson apparently based his judgement on the earlier correspondence in the file about Fortes and thought him unsuitable for the post. 'He is a South African and married to a Russian wife, and from all accounts has an unprepossessing appearance and no charm of manner.'[42] An additional source of information was Hugh Thomas, younger brother of the Governor, Shenton Thomas, who was now Secretary for Native Affairs and had known of Fortes in the North. When approached by Hodson he, like the Director of Education, was not unsympathetic to Grace's complaint about training people for a fictitious future, nor was he against anthropologists, holding them to be 'a valuable asset in any backward country'. Of Fortes he knew little, except that he was 'a very extreme anthropologist'.[43] By this he meant something quite different from his brother. Far from being over-interested in changing local society, Fortes was criticised for wanting to maintain it – the classic dilemma of the anthropologist, the contradiction of the progressive preservationist, the radical conserver. For 'he would prefer to let the races remain in their natural state. For instance he deprecates the introduction of coinage into the N.T.s [Northern Territories] when the system of barter would be equally beneficial to the native. In fact it does exist in some spots in the N.T.s and that is Fortes' objection, that we are trying to alter it.'

On the same day that he replied to Bottomley at the Colonial Office, the acting Governor sent off a secret telegram to the Chief Commissioner of the Northern Territories asking for information about Fortes' political views, his social, personal qualifications and the value of the work he was doing. The reply was interesting and showed how correct Oldham had been, or alternatively how Fortes' supposed views had been changed by his experiences. His present views were found to be 'more in accord [with] Government policy' while the administrative officers 'like him personally [and] consider his social qualities up to average [while he] has shown readiness [to] give advice when asked and [there is] no reason to think [the] advice unsound or prejudiced'. He added that he had published one article in *Africa*. Much the same assessment was implied in the report of Hugh Thomas, who saw Fortes at the time of the next meeting of the Council of

Achimota School when he spent a month there after leaving England on 18 March 1936. This visit to Achimota had been arranged by the Colonial Office in London before it heard of the Governor's initial objections. When he spoke to Thomas of the job, Fortes said he had first to finish the work in the Northern Territories and in any case would not consider the matter at all, 'unless he had Government's full support'.[44] This seemed to settle the question as far as the acting Governor was concerned. Fortes no longer appeared a threat, indeed was viewed as the possible source of sound advice about future developments.

It should be added that Fortes' views were not as much in accord with many aspects of colonial policy in the Gold Coast as his interlocutors supposed. On the other hand he was very much in tune with the movement that saw education as a means to self-government, that backed the shift from 'Trusteeship' to 'Partnership', especially as it was later embodied in the Colonial Development and Welfare Act of 1940. That proposal replaced the 'conservative' *laissez-faire* policy of colonial rule with a commitment to the positive intervention of the state in increasing the pace of social change. He was very much part of the pre-war group of left-wing intellectuals associated with the Fabian Society who influenced the movement towards colonial independence that took place in Britain in the decade and a half following the Second World War, affecting on the one hand the actions of politicians in the metropolis and on the other giving some support to the growing pressure from the subject populations.

Fortes took 'practical' anthropology seriously, as he had done 'practical' psychology in London's East End. But in this context practical anthropology was understood to be a matter of helping people to adapt to social change rather than promoting those changes themselves. That would have been his role at Achimota and it was certainly one that interested him, but it was to be combined with research. As a result of this visit to the College he wrote a 'Memorandum on social research at Achimota: the need for socio-logical research', which was to have an impact not only on his own career but also on further developments in the Gold Coast.

Despite all that political manoeuvring, the Achimota invitation did bear fruit. Fortes carried out a further year of fieldwork and returned to London in mid-August 1937 by way of South Africa.[45] He applied straight away to the International African Institute to prolong his Fellowship for a further year in order to write up his material. But his original project on the family had been shifted, at least formally, in favour of writing up 'that segment of the culture of the Tallensi which is of most immediate concern to people working in the area, officials and others. Its topic will be the social structure: Local and Kinship grouping: political organization: the economic systems: law and family government.' This statement represents exactly what he did in his two major monographs, although the way in which he carried out the project demonstrates more his changing theoretical interest in 'social structure', following the work of Evans-Pritchard and Firth, rather than any strong impulse to communicate to those 'in the area', who would find his work heavy going if not incomprehensible.[46]

At the same time as he made his application to the Institute, Fortes reported that he had been to see Grace, who told him of an unexpected obstacle in his coming to Achimota. However he asked him to co-operate with his Arts Supervisor (Meyerowitz) 'in drawing up a comprehensive scheme for the establishment of an Institute of West African Culture, for research and teaching in West African sociology and arts and crafts', a project that was then being considered by official bodies both in Britain and the Gold Coast.

The memorandum for this project was drawn up later that year by W. B. Mumford of the Colonial Department of the University of London Institute of Education, who proposed to include as chapter III of his report a contribution by Fortes entitled 'Some notes on the formation of a School of Social Studies at Achimota College'. The proposal was for a Museum, a Research Unit, a Teaching Unit and a Service Unit with applied functions; the Teaching Unit would offer courses at different levels including those at the university now planned for Achimota; the other units would involve the training and recruiting of local staff. The emphasis would be on facing the problem of the 'transition mentality'.[47] As things turned out, the project did not get off the ground before war began, in less than two years' time. One way and another Fortes had to seek other means of support. He held a number of temporary jobs while he was writing up his material and planning *African Political Systems* with Evans-Pritchard, a project submitted to the same 16th meeting of the Executive Committee as his application for an extension. At the same time Evans-Pritchard, who for some years had had a job at Oxford where in 1937 Radcliffe-Brown had taken up the first Chair in Social Anthropology (and was about to give his first seminar), wrote to say how much Brown (i.e. Radcliffe-Brown) would like to have him there as well. 'With R.-B., you, and me we would have quite a decent nucleus for a school.'[48] But the hoped-for post at Oxford did not materialise and Fortes had to take a year's appointment at the London School of Economics for 1938–9. Nevertheless the trio was always looking forward to getting together later and in a sense *African Political Systems*, with the Preface by Radcliffe-Brown and the Introduction by Fortes and Evans-Pritchard, is a memorial to their collaboration, hoped-for and later achieved, including as it does contributions by their allies, Max Gluckman and Isaac Schapera.

The Achimota project remained on the books and was revived towards the end of the war. Fortes, who had spent the latter years of the war in Nigeria and Ghana, partly on intelligence work, wrote another memorandum on the proposed Institute in 1943, entitled 'The West African Institute of Arts, Industries and Social Sciences: notes on policy', which refers specifically to Grace's work eight years before and includes the name of Mr Meyerowitz, the Arts Supervisor at Achimota and an important influence on modern artistic developments in West Africa. The plan for this Institute, although still in association with Achimota, was much more ambitious than the previous scheme, a scope clearly influenced by Fortes' wartime participation in Lord Hailey's investigations in Nigeria, where he first went from Oxford before carrying out intelligence work on the border of the Vichy-held territories. It was to be established on a West African basis, and the long-term plans included a comprehensive ethnographic survey, as well as work on local agriculture, political systems, cash crops, new industries and an enquiry preparing the way for a town plan for Accra. Later in the same year, he submitted a memorandum to the Commission on Higher Education in West Africa on setting up a new University of which the Institute would form a part. Its establishment was once again supported by the new Principal of Achimota, the Revd R. A. Stopford, later Bishop of London, who became chairman of the management committee. Further general support came from missionary circles, strongly associated with Achimota, and particularly from the energetic Oldham of the International African Institute. The whole venture now became possible because of the changing policy of the metropolitan government towards colonial development as embodied in the Colonial Development and Welfare Act of 1940, the provision of which supported much post-war research. The Second World War represented a decisive turning point in the history of colonial empires, partly as a result of the coalition government, the war itself and the leftist ideologies that were promoted to support it, partly because of changing public conceptions at home and partly because of greater pressures from below and the concessions needed to secure local support in wartime. Each of the factors had important influences on the development in social anthropology in Britain.

How far was the direction of Fortes' research influenced by the suppliers of funds and the providers of permits? A bow was certainly made to the wishes of the Rockefeller philanthropies for work on 'culture contact', but it was little more than that. A contribution was made to the reorganisation of Tallensi local government, while a paper on marriage was published by the Government Printing Press. Basically the latter were uninterested in his work, in which they saw little value. Of Malinowski's teaching something remained, but basically Fortes' agenda was set in discussions with his peers, and specifically with Evans-Pritchard. The written analysis of his fieldwork owes most to Firth and Evans-Pritchard, but it was also Radcliffe-Brown whom he looked upon as his real guru. That meant setting on one side some of his psychological interests, but they returned later with renewed force. Meanwhile it was undoubtedly his friendship with Evans-Pritchard that led him in a sociological direction.

CHAPTER 4

Personal and intellectual friendships: Fortes and Evans-Pritchard

To see the work of British anthropologists of the 1930s, even in Africa, as being largely under Malinowski's patronage is correct. Most of the early teachers of the post-war period had worked with him. But that does not mean to imply that they were passive followers or that subgroups did not form within the tribe. Such differentiation took place early on, the friendships and animosities leading to a physical separation (Oxford from the LSE) as well as to a theoretical parting of the ways as between Malinowski's functionalism and Radcliffe-Brown's structuralism, which brought the work closer to that of the French sociological school under Durkheim. It was the latter that gradually achieved dominance but only after Malinowski's death in 1942. That is the story behind the next three chapters.[1]

I have outlined the events that led to Fortes shifting his focus of interest from psychology to anthropology. Intellectual concerns had moved him in that direction following his involvement in studies of children and adolescents in a deprived area of the East End at a time of world depression. But symbolically and actually the shift was carried out as a result of his encounter with the anthropologist Malinowski, at the house of the psychologist, Flügel. That led to his meeting other members of the seminar, of whom the most important for him were the later arrivals, Siegfried Nadel who came from Berlin to take up a Fellowship at the Institute, Raymond Firth, who returned from Sydney early in 1933, but above all an anthropologist who was already marginal to the seminar, Edward Evans-Pritchard.

From the very beginning Evans-Pritchard's relation with Fortes was one of intellectual companionship. Long before Fortes had done any fieldwork, Evans-Pritchard recommended him for a position involving starting a Department of Psychology at the University of Cairo, where he himself was teaching at the time. That was in the first letter he sent, before he even knew how to spell Fortes' first name.[2] He also acted as a referee for his application to the Institute, writing:

I consider Fortes to be a first-class man. I am not competent to judge his psychological work, but I have known him for a long time and have discussed anthropological problems and methods with him on a score of occasions. He has in my opinion, a quite exceptional critical ability and is one of the very few people I know who really understand how complex are social data and how inadequate is our present technique for estimating the many social factors which regulate human behaviour. His work in psychology has trained him in a rigorous use of controls in scientific work.[3]

In fact, Evans-Pritchard had not known Fortes for long but he was clearly very impressed by his abilities and continued to rely on Fortes for advice on psychological topics. In 1932 he referred to their discussions on 'the influence which members of a family have on the feelings of one another about people outside the family and about each other' and asked Fortes if Malinowski had ever committed himself to a statement of what he meant by 'extensions'. Evans-Pritchard intended to write an article 'making clear the distinction between behaviour-patterns in R.B.'s sense (the German sense, I think, of social types – submissiveness, entreaty, equality, etc.) and the psychological attitude of one person to another'.[4] Twenty years later, when Fortes was in Cambridge, he wrote:

The Nuer have some outstanding traits, or I think they have, such as intense anal interests (as shown in their obscenities), and oral orientations (taboo on sexes eating together, not on copulating, etc.), thanatophobia (refusal even to discuss death) and so on. Can you tell me of a good P-Analytical book which might discuss the psychic internalisation of such mental traits? I suppose that a Freudian would hold that they form an interconsistent pattern.[5]

A further twenty years on he is asking for a copy of Fortes' paper to the 'Psycho-analists' (*sic*) – that is, 'Totem and taboo'.[6] What is more surprising is his early faith in Fortes' anthropological judgement, though this is perhaps a measure of his separation from his other contemporaries. Even before he went to do fieldwork among the Tallensi, Evans-Pritchard sent Fortes a paper on 'Theory of magic' and asked for criticisms. While Fortes was in the field, he sent him a draft of *Witchcraft, Oracles and Magic*, requesting comments.[7] Part of the Nuer manuscript he left for him and wanted 'as devastating criticism as you can give'.[8] At the same time he referred to the criticisms he had made of Fortes' paper on incest. A chance comment by Fortes brings out the basic contradiction he sees in pastoral society between drinking the milk and preserving the calves.[9] He repeats the problems of working with Nuer 'informants' and explains that one of the difficulties of writing the book is that 'I have not quite made up my mind what I want to show in it – what the plot is going to be – so to speak.'[10]

Just as Evans-Pritchard asked for criticisms of his papers, so did Fortes, sending his first anthropological article on a communal fishing expedition, the theme of which related to Evans-Pritchard's current interests.[11] From Khartoum Evans-Pritchard replied with his forthright comments. Some sections are too involved to understand and should be rewritten in simpler English. The rest is ' "functionalism" with a vengeance. You know my objections to it. One can only establish functions by analysis of many similar situations in different societies and the application of the methods of difference and concomitant variations.' While he accepted that the elements of the communal fishing expedition make a whole (XYZ and not X+Y+Z), how could one be sure that these were not 'mere random variations'?

Also supposing the Government said that at all such expeditions the Union Jack must be flown. It is likely that the Government would then become a participating element in the situation and that the flying of the flag (and ideationally what it stands for) would be so incorporated into the action (and notions relating to) the fishing that it would constitute part of 'a unitary structure the disruption of which entirely alters the significance of any of the constituents'. But would it or not be 'a mere random aggregation' – if not what would constitute a 'mere random aggregation'?

Put finally, my objection to this 'functionalism' is this. What it says is that in a certain society the people do certain things and if they did not do them, their customs would be different from what they are.

Fortes had based his analysis not only on Malinowski but on a certain fashionable holism (the whole is more than the parts) that was in the air, and that in one form or another is intrinsic to many forms of cultural studies.[12] As Evans-Pritchard points out, at a certain level the doctrine is self-evident, at another it requires substantiation in every case – and the difficulties of that are apparent. His no-nonsense attitude was equally apparent in his comments on Fortes' use of the term 'structure'.

I quite agree that the structure of society is evident in any social activity. But when we say this we are saying nothing. For there is no 'structure' outside the activities. They are the 'structure'. Or, if you like it, we create an abstraction called 'social structure' by observing social activities. It is not surprising therefore that we perceive that any social activity bears the stamp of the social structure as a whole e.g. by observation of the part a 'chief' plays in a fishing expedition (among other of his activities) we create the abstraction of 'chieftainship'. It is not surprising therefore to find that a fishing expedition expresses (among other things) social (political) status.[13]

It is clear that Evans-Pritchard's 'empiricism' was not a-theoretical; it arose from what he saw as the poverty of theory or of theoretical concepts. He is interested in those concepts and hypotheses he can use to test against ethnographic data, and draws, 'eclectically', on a series of sources. But the concern with ethnographic data is always present.

When Fortes was working among the Tallensi, Evans-Pritchard not only sent him comments on fieldwork (mostly directed against 'functionalism') but also asked for information for comparative purposes.

Would you mind noticing the attitude of your people towards
    Dogs.
    Fish.
    Chicken and other birds.
Do they eat fish and chicken? Are chicken kept solely or mainly for ritual purposes? etc. If they keep any kind of cattle will you please note carefully the names of the various colours and their distributions and discover their etymology?[14]

There was a great deal of interchange of this kind between the two men, and their friendship, intellectual and personal, was very close. At one time in 1941 Evans-Pritchard tried to persuade Fortes to take a Chair at Johannesburg, although he expected that they would link up again at Oxford later on: he added, 'I can't do without the inspiration of your mind'.[15]

The friendship had its problems, since Evans-Pritchard came from a very different background, especially of class, and he developed very different political views which became more apparent after the war. Even earlier he had shown little sympathy with Gluckman's 'anti-war' attitude, although he did not cease to be on friendly terms. Indeed he prided himself on separating matters of belief from friendship. 'All my friends since I reached 21', he wrote to Fortes, 'have been Jews or Catholics.'[16] In the context of current prejudices, that comment was certainly farther to the left than society as a whole. He knew the views of Fortes, Gluckman and his other friends; he read some Marx, or about Marx, and asked Fortes to send him H. Levy's book, *Philosophy and Marxism* when it appeared, just as he read, or read about, Freud. But while he accepted part of psychoanalysis and started off with leftish views, he later came directly to oppose them. A South African anthropologist wrote to Fortes from Oxford in 1951 complaining that Evans-Pritchard had recently told him that 'in his opinion no left-wing person ought to be allowed anywhere into Africa'. He would exclude from this category all those who had 'made a mistake at the time of the Spanish Civil War and have since atoned for their sins'.[17] Fighting 'patriotically' for the Allied cause presumably cancelled out any earlier commitment to the struggle of the Spanish Republic against Fascism.

The disagreements were also intellectual. When Evans-Pritchard wrote to Fortes about these in the 1950s, he thought that Fortes had got him wrong over 'history'. What he had said was:

(1) that when a people being studied has a history, that this history is relevant, (2) that in comparative studies, especially of social development, the general data of history is relevant and (3), that as things are, Social Anthropology is, in fact, more akin to certain types of historical study than it is to a natural science like chemistry. These statements seem to me to be equally obvious and uncontrovertible. I have nowhere said that I think we should be historians – that would be silly with reference to the study of primitive societies – on the contrary one would like to see historians becoming more sociological.[18]

The propositions now seem unexceptionable, but in the 1930s the question of history in the simpler societies had to be seen in the context of the need for field studies, the paucity of records and especially the earlier addiction to 'conjectural history'. Moreover, the use of historical data is a practical matter of problem and of relevance rather than an abstract one of 'history' versus 'culture'.

Evans-Pritchard's friendship with Fortes had a number of roots. But it stemmed partly from the estrangement of the former from Malinowski and, as he saw it, from the circle of the London School of Economics. That separation was related not simply to intellectual or even personal disputes; many individuals of quite different views managed to survive and even to profit from their contact with the dominating figure of Malinowski: Fortes and Nadel, for example, were two such survivors. In making any assessment of the situation, Evans-Pritchard's background has to be taken into account, since this contributed directly to his independence of action, not least economically. His milieu was upper middle-class, public school (Winchester), Oxford, a private income (at least before the war), the Welsh Guards, Clubland (the Royal Societies Club, London, and the Turf Club, Cairo). That background influenced his approach to life, life as a scholar, life in general, which had a strong romantic element.

This element comes out in his view of fieldwork. He writes early on that he found it

great fun. It enables you to indulge in the most exclusive kind of private property. No gold prospector ever held possession of his metal more exclusively than the anthropologist of the facts he had dug out of a distant tribe. The only drawback is having to write up the notes at the end of it all. Personally I like collecting facts but when I know about a tribe my interest in it ceases and it is pure agony to have to write a book on it – not that I have succeeded in doing so.[19]

Of course he later wrote, wrote well and wrote analytically, which is why his pretension of an extreme empiricism ('I am only an ethnographer', he once said) is certainly false, indeed false modesty; at this very time he was writing articles on Pareto, Levy-Bruhl, Tylor and Frazer, preparatory to including them in a book on the theory of magic. Nevertheless in Egypt he rejoiced in 'desert exploration combined with amateur pre-history. Travel by camel in the Libyan desert has now become a passion with me and I am seldom able to remain in Cairo for long.' His aim was to carry out research among the Galla of Abyssinia (Ethiopia) and he had already resigned his post at Cairo when a research grant seemed to make this possible, since he could not manage to get adequate funds out of the Sudan government.[20] Meanwhile he intended to set out for a long and risky trip in the desert in June. 'If we have no sand storms all ought to be well. If we have sandstorms for two or three days God help us as the camels will not last out. This situation honestly amuses me.'[21] The attitude is at once self-mocking and self-dramatising; at times it approaches self-parody.

With that background, with these attitudes, Evans-Pritchard found his feet when war broke out. When he left Oxford early on to take part in the war and went to the Sudan, he wrote back using the cliché that he was longing 'to have a crack at the Italians'.[22] By October 1940, he had been engaged in operations 'for some time' and welcomed the danger:

I have always felt that to be killed in action would be a very suitable ending to my rather peculiar career. One's life should have a certain form of dramatic sequence; otherwise it is uninteresting to oneself. It is true that the final act would, perhaps, not be appreciated by oneself as audience, but it can be appreciated in the imagination. Anyhow it is pleasant to know that I have no regrets about the past, nothing but pleasure in the present, and no interest in the future.[23]

With a small Anuak force he harassed the Italians, but they did the same to him so that the incoming mail was lost. That setback caused him to work up an extreme but superficial hatred of the enemy. 'Damn, curse and blast the Italians! I am going to kill a lot of them for the loss of my letters, books, and all sorts of necessities.'[24] It was all very much like hunting game, as he readily acknowledged. The excitement is of the same order. 'I have taken like a duck to guerilla warfare, but I am inclined to be so reckless that I get raspberries from my Commander that would win first prize at any horticultural show.' He had difficulties in getting the Italians to fight, 'What is a war for except fighting. I suppose I am 17th century in my ideas of it.'[25]

There is a good deal of mock or perhaps false heroics in Evans-Pritchard's written version of his activities; he is playing a part. In my experience that was not an untypical stance, a matter of bolstering one's courage, taking an exaggerated view of one's own contribution and cursing the enemy for his interruption of one's life. Even those whose participation was more political could easily fall prey to this kind of structuring, but without that element it was yet easier to drop into inflated patriotism, heroics and self-dramatisation, combined with a certain casual insouciance regarding both present and future that was part of a soldier's defences.

He certainly played a very active part in the war. Not only did he serve in the Sudan Defence Force but he was trained in the use of high explosives in Palestine, was attached to the Spears Mission in Syria, returned to the Sudan Defence Force, served as the military governor of the Cyrene District in present-day Libya and then became a liaison officer with the Bedouin of that region, which led to his important work, *The Sanusi of Cyrenaica*. While he was on the Spears Mission he was supposed to liaise with the Free French in Syria, preparing for post-occupational sabotage, should the German forces advance through Turkey. But he had problems with the French support of the Alawi minority (the British supported the orthodox Sunnis) which had led them to overlook the deeds of a religious leader, al-Murshid. Evans-Pritchard quarrelled with the French, claiming that he could not stand by 'watching the poor and weak being plundered by the rich and powerful without making some effort to stop them'. Although it is not clear how local his objections were, he did stand up to al-Murshid, to the French and to his superior officer, as a result of which he was reprimanded for infractions of his written instructions and then returned to his regiment.[26]

It was soon after the beginning of the war that Evans-Pritchard went to the Sudan to offer his services. In order to join the Sudan Defence Force he first became a member of the Sudan Administration, although he protested that he was not doing administration. He was living among the Anuak and hoped to be able to persuade the government to allow him to take a flying column into Italian-occupied Ethiopia. The Governor was initially against starting 'a native war', but Evans-Pritchard later had his way and found himself in his element. 'Borkman was right. In the Victorian age I should have been an explorer. In earlier times a Crusader or buccaneer. I am just beginning to enjoy myself. There is a lot of the non-intellectual in me.'[27] His specific aim was to organise intelligence 'and perhaps a little sabotage', work for which he feels anthropologists are especially cut out. 'Neither of us are under any illusions about the place which anthropology has in the minds of Government officials, but I was a little surprised that they do not easily admit that such activities as intelligence and sabotage are those for which an anthropologist's training benefits him.'[28] The Government's real problem, he felt, lay in being unable to comprehend the segmentary structure of tribal society, which required an application of a central theme of *African Political Systems*, the book that he and Fortes edited in 1940:

they think all the time of the natives who straddle the frontier as being either pro-British or pro-Italian. In fact, I have no doubt that their political cleavages will determine their allegiance. This is what has happened all over Africa. If Section A is for the Government, Section B will support the Italians: not that they have any preference for them but because of a traditional opposition between the sections.

Despite his earlier pronouncements, anthropology had its applied uses.

Romanticism went hand in hand with an anarchistic attitude to authority. Those authorities at Oxford with whom he had to deal became identified with the politicians he sees as having brought about the war:

When this show is over, whatever happens, we must deal with the Chamberlain–Coupland type of politician once and for all. Hitler at least had the merit to kick them clean out. If only they would put the Chamberlain–Halifax–Simon–Hoare group of fifth columnists in prison and leave Mosely and his crowd alone we might win this war. Far from kicking them out

Churchill has added to them the more toad-bellied lilly-livered mugwumps of the labour party. God help England in her greatest trial.[29]

Both the sentiment and the language reflect the kind of right-wing attitudes pervading the usual officers' mess at that time. It sometimes led him to lean towards Fascists like Hitler and Mosely in preference to the active politicians from left and right who were more immediately responsible for his fate. He is scathing about the lack of foresight regarding the war in the Sudan, and pessimistic both about the survival of his interest in anthropology and about the outcome of the war itself: a 'decisive victory' seems 'unlikely'.[30] It was a genre of pessimism widely shared in those quarters, but one that went hand in hand with an irrational optimism. The two were patently inconsistent but they were often held simultaneously, as if to offset both the possibilities of success and failure. However as time goes on he thinks better of anthropology and of what will happen at Oxford after the war.[31] A qualified optimism wins out.

It was perhaps this aspect of his thinking, radical, right-wing, anti-authoritarian, that enabled him to get on with Fortes, a man of distinctly left-wing views. Fortes writes to him of class prejudice at Oxford; Evans-Pritchard replies telling him of factions within the governing class, especially among the wartime administrators, incompetents from England. His solution is not revolutionary but apocalyptic. 'The truth of the matter is that until the war becomes much fiercer and there is "wastage" on a big scale, such maladjustments cannot be got rid of. A really fierce war, like a great river in flood, carries all before it, and then, and then only, does what you can do, rather than what you are, become important.'[32] In this mood of an Old Testament prophet, a violent war was cathartic both for society and for the individual.

One aspect of Evans-Pritchard's radicalism was his love–hate relationship with the United States. He had been invited to Yale before the war, and was on the point of sailing to America when the war broke out. The alternative was South Africa, where his wife came from and about which he rarely had any qualms, although much later in September 1951 he writes from there that he hopes this will be his last visit, 'I have learnt a lot.'[33] After the war he refused to go to a Wenner-Gren conference in the States and advised Fortes to do the same (although he would go if his wife were to be invited). 'Everybody ought to see it once – just to know what a combination of barbarism and decadence is like.'[34] It is possible that this attitude was fuelled by the American support accorded to Malinowski, although it is consistent with a certain British love–hate relationship marked by extreme ambivalence towards the US. Later he was to accept an invitation to spend a year at the Center for Advanced Study in the Behavioral Sciences at Palo Alto, but these inconsistencies are characteristic of such attitudes in general, a resentment of dependency and of a declining status in the world, as well as being typical of Evans-Pritchard himself.

The close friendship between Evans-Pritchard and Fortes was important for them both. It gave them mutual support in their confrontation with others; it provided them with an informal sounding-board for their anthropological ideas and personal problems; it led to a measure of intellectual collaboration in the sphere of publishing as well as in the establishment of the Oxford Department in the post-war period, when its reputation surpassed that of the London School of Economics. It was a friendship between two of the best of a remarkable generation that seems to have been partly created in a segmentary fashion out of their opposition to Malinowski in the thirties, but which had important consequences for anthropology in Britain.

CHAPTER 5

Personal and intellectual animosities: Evans-Pritchard, Malinowski and others

Evans-Pritchard's friendship with Fortes was undoubtedly motivated by the strong intellectual attraction the two men had for one another. But the alliance also very much suited Evans-Pritchard's battle with Malinowski. Part of his dependence on intellectual discussion with Fortes reflects his isolation from the group at the London School of Economics, or '£.S.D.' as he sometimes called it, referring to Malinowski's success in attracting funds for research. Although at times he got on with Firth, he suspected him for his attachment to Malinowski, as well as for what in Evans-Pritchard's view was his social conformism in contrast to his own romantic detachment from the world. Some, like Richards, he never spoke to, at least after an initial friendship. If anything he tended to cleave to the old school, the Seligmans, Balfour, Rattray, Driberg.

He was greatly affected by the death of Seligman, who had helped him start his fieldwork in the Sudan, who had himself led an independent scholarly existence based on inherited wealth and who as a fellow Professor at the School had had a raw deal, as Evans-Pritchard saw it, from Malinowski. He regarded Seligman as much more than a supervisor, rather as a close friend and as a shield against Malinowski. In the context of the production of Seligman's festschrift, the care of which he handed over to Fortes when he left to teach sociology at Cairo in 1932, he wrote that 'he (B.M.) may try and do us all down but I think he fears the Sligses too much'.[1] But Seligman grew tired of the struggle with Malinowski and handed in his resignation. When Evans-Pritchard heard of this move he wrote to say that Seligman had not been 'valiant' enough. 'At one time he could have fought and won; then he was left clinging on to his job on sufference [sic], almost in contempt. It is better that he should retire.'[2] Later on, when he heard of his death, he wrote that:

68

Sligs meant more to me than most things in this world. Apart from personal grief, which I feel strongly, a really great figure in the anthropological world and one of the very few with real scientific interests has gone. His loss and that of Haddon means the end of the Homeric heroes of anthropology. The last who fought on the ringing plains of windy Troy have gone![3]

That is not exactly how the future was to measure the men, unlikely heroes from an intellectual standpoint, but men who struggled to initiate the study of the subject in their universities. Romanticism, personal friendships and antagonisms coloured his vision as well as his prose.

Evans-Pritchard was already in conflict with Malinowski before he met Fortes. The dislike seems to have been instantaneous and mutual.[4] Audrey Richards saw this as the basis for his rapprochement with Radcliffe-Brown, declaring that 'E.P. is making up to him'[5] when Radcliffe-Brown was visiting Europe on his way to Chicago. Evans-Pritchard did spend a good deal of time with him and brought Fortes, whom he had recently met, into the discussions of the nature of the lineage.[6] Later, in 1934, he made an almost deliberate attempt to attach Gluckman to the group, although he was always worried about the 'applied' nature of his research.

Gluckmann, Mrs Hoernlé's pupil from Witwatersrand, was down here [he wrote from Pevensey] for 3 or 4 days last week. He is at Oxford but goes once a week to the School of Economics. I gather from him that they go on in the same old way – only rather worse as it becomes more and more wordy and metaphysical. I think I have thoroughly corrupted him but leave the final stages of dissolution to you. I have commended him to you and suggested he gets in touch with you as soon as you return as he will learn more from you than from anyone else in anthropology today. This is a Christmas bouquet, but I mean it. He seems a decent youth.[7]

Later on, Evans-Pritchard backed Gluckman for a job with the newly formed Rhodes–Livingstone Institute in Northern Rhodesia (now Zambia) where he worked under Godfrey Wilson, a pupil of Malinowski's. When Wilson committed suicide, Richards was appointed Director, a position she never took up, which was then filled by Gluckman. Despite his hostility to some of these activities, Evans-Pritchard continued to hear from him throughout the years, as he did from Fortes and Schapera.

Perhaps the most surprising 'recruit' to this camp was Lucy Mair who lectured in Colonial Studies at the School (and later became a professor) and whose work, very much in the applied sphere, had been originally directed by Malinowski, though with unwanted assistance from others. In a letter to Fortes she agrees that Malinowski 'took possession' of Firth, Richards and herself, and goes on to add that it was a situation 'from which you rescued me';[8] there is no evidence that Evans-Pritchard was in any way concerned.

Evans-Pritchard's dislike of Malinowski, whom he saw as getting his way by 'lying and blustering', was extended to those close to him.[9] The main recipient of his ire was Richards, his conflict with whom led him to make preposterous statements of a phallocratic kind. His letter criticising the notion of function at '£.S.D.' (as he referred to the LSE) continued: 'Women ought not to be allowed to do fieldwork. I have always considered their intrusion undesirable. Audrey's real work was that she started on before doing anthropology – the work of a welfare worker (benevolence can there be combined with interviews and census taking and snippets of daily life (to please subscribers to the Mission)).'[10] Worse was yet to come. When he heard from Fortes about her comments on Oxford, he dismissed her rather than them. 'I feel I am to blame for not having poked her when there was still an opportunity for doing so. That would have settled her.'[11] There was an element of jealousy in his relations with her which these sexist and sexual comments bring out.

These antipathies lived on. Fortes was far from happy when Richards decided to return to Cambridge, where he had been appointed to the Chair, after giving up her post as Director of the East African Institute of Social and Economic Research. That was a natural thing to do, since she was a graduate of Newnham where her friend, Ruth Cohen, sister of the post-war Governor of Uganda, was the Principal. At the time I failed to understand the problem, although it obviously went back to Malinowski days. Again, when I first attended Friday seminars in Oxford in 1949, which were modelled on those of Malinowski in London, I was surprised at the level of animosity against Malinowski displayed by Evans-Pritchard and made a remark in the discussion about the conflict between adjacent generations (I had obviously been reading Radcliffe-Brown, or perhaps Fortes' studies on the Tallensi). In the Institute of Social Anthropology the next morning, Evans-Pritchard took me aside and asked me to come for a walk in the Parks, which were adjacent to the building in which the Institute, associated with Sir E. B. Tylor, was based. He explained that Malinowski had not been a good man (he did not speak about his ideas) – look how he treated Audrey Richards. She had undoubtedly tried to follow the Malinowski line as closely as she could, in her work and in academic affairs; Evans-Pritchard was critical of both sides of her activities. But this comment he levelled against Malinowski, as if to suggest that his treatment of students had been essentially unfair.

At Cambridge Fortes was particularly worried about the successful attempt of Richards to start an African Studies Centre with the help of the Faculty of Economics, especially Kenneth Burrill. Many at Cambridge, by no means only anthropologists, were keenly interested in what was going on in Africa in the period before and after independence. Some anthropologists were even involved in more than 'tribal' studies. So they participated in the seminars she organised in her capacity as Director and as Smuts Reader, while the lectures she gave in the Department on urbanisation and similar experiences had a considerable influence among the students. When I followed Richards first as Director, then as Smuts Reader, Fortes seemed to feel that bonds of loyalty were being stretched by those whom he had unreservedly helped – he had already had similar experiences with Edmund Leach and Stanley Tambiah.

Evans-Pritchard's dislikes, especially in his latter years, were not confined to those close to Malinowski. He resigned from the British Academy when Leach was elected. Although he gave economy as the reason and had 'nothing personal against Leach, even though he is very far from being a scholar', he was 'tired of all the lobbying, jockeying, even cheating'.[12] His opinion was no more favourable to other anthropologists at Cambridge. Of my appointment as Fortes' successor (and I had been a pupil of them both), he wrote: 'I was very sorry to see in the Daily Telegraph today the appointment of your successor in the Chair – a great mistake, in my opinion.'[13] But his comments on Firth and Gluckman, with both of whom he was on overtly friendly terms, are often equally strong. He wrote to Firth: 'I always think of you as being part of a trinity with myself and a personified Anthropology as the other two persons.'[14] He had met him as a member of Malinowski's seminar in October 1924, along with Barbara Freire-Marresco, Ursula Grant-Duff and Ashley Montague (then Ehrenberg). In the summer of 1925 he went to Malinowski's house at Oberbolzen in the Tyrol, joined Firth and visited Malinowski in the evenings. But already, while he was preparing the Azande work, he had had a break with Malinowski and became closely associated with Seligman and Jack Driberg, with whom there was a family connection.[15] On the other hand his remarks to Fortes about Firth's work could be severe. As Richards had earlier commented, 'After all, Evans-Pritchard can't speak about anyone else without sneering, friend or foe alike',[16] which from his letters to Fortes appears to be a reasonable assessment.

As far as personal relations were concerned, Radcliffe-Brown made a rather different impression on Richards. He was 'quite decent about your work', she wrote to Malinowski, '– merely disagreed with it, and thought himself the more eminent of the two! Which is just what we think of *his* work.' For both Malinowski and Richards, Evans-Pritchard fell into a different category, 'I enjoy a scrap with anyone but E.P.', she wrote.[17] The feeling was mutual. Evans-Pritchard's letters are full of scathing comments about Richards, which reach the outrageous level we have seen. However, as with Malinowski, it is not clear that in these personal letters we are necessarily dealing with the 'real' (or at least considered) views of Evans-Pritchard but rather with a particular way of expressing himself (or perhaps of creating a persona) in writing. In personal contact he did not reveal himself, to me or my colleagues, as a man of intense hatreds but rather of the glancing comment.

One of the main lines of Evans-Pritchard's intellectual disagreement with Malinowski turned on the question of the 'utility' of anthropology, of 'practical anthropology' as presented in the proposals of the International African Institute. This was a question on which, as we have seen, Radcliffe-Brown and Malinowski had disagreed in relation to the initial memorandum setting up the Institute's research scheme. Evans-Pritchard was much more vehement on that subject. One reason why he agreed to contribute to Radcliffe-Brown's festschrift was that 'When B.M. led the pack on the bunny-scent of applied anthropology, R.B. was the only one who kept straight.'[18] It is a theme he pursued for many years, 'applied' being placed in the other camp to 'scientific'. He always had serious reservations which he thought were shared by Radcliffe-Brown, Fortes and Schapera. Towards the end of the war he wrote approvingly that Schapera has given up the idea of doing any more 'useful', 'practical' or 'applied' research.[19]

Evans-Pritchard heavily criticised the activities of other of his fellow anthropologists at that time. 'It is very amusing how all these people are engaged in competitive business, to wit, the sale of anthropologists to Governments. "We have the best anthropologists, you want them." Very jealous of each other.'[20] Then a month later he wrote again to Fortes in West Africa.

The racket here is very amusing. It would be more so if it were not disastrous to anthropology. Everyone is advising governments – Raymond, Forde, Audrey, Schapera. No one is doing any real anthropological work – all are clinging to the Colonial Office coach. This deplorable state of affairs is likely to go on, because it shows something deeper than making use of opportunities for helping anthropology. It shows an attitude of mind and is I think fundamentally a moral deterioration. These people will not see that there is an unbridgeable chasm between serious anthropology and Administration Welfare work.[21]

The reference is to the surveys of potential research programmes that were being conducted under the auspices of the Colonial Social Science Research Council by Firth in West Africa, Schapera in East Africa, Leach in Borneo, surveys which laid the loose framework for the research of many post-war students from Britain and America. Far from being 'disastrous' for anthropology, this enterprise was its great support, but his warnings bring out the opposition he had to working with or for governments.

He was also worried about the kind of work being carried out at the Rhodes–Livingstone Institute under the supervision of Gluckman and advises him to choose between staying on and doing administration or taking a teaching job and doing 'science'.[22] Nor did he have much respect for the work being done at the Institute. He describes the enterprise as 'a public menace – cheapening anthropology'.[23] This is a harsh description of the work carried out by J. A. Barnes, Clyde Mitchell, Elizabeth Colson and many others who were later associated with the vigorous group which Gluckman gathered around him at Manchester and who made many contributions to various branches of anthropology and sociology. On this subject his judgement was flawed, as it often was about his colleagues. As we have seen, Audrey Richards, to whom he was never generous, he sees as a welfare worker.[24] Nadel, he assumes, is aiming at some administrative job, partly because in the Sudan he appeared to be modelling himself on the District Commissioner, putting brass buttons on his coat and judging cases.[25] All this, he adds, 'deepens my contempt for him', although he had earlier supported his application for a chair at Johannesburg, partly because he considered he was the only one to defend Fortes when Malinowski had been making 'violent attacks' on him in his seminar.[26] Later on his judgement appears to be confirmed when he sees Nadel tasting the bitter side of administrative activity. As he was 'desperate' to stay in the Sudan, he had to accept a request from the authorities to write a book on the peoples of the Nuba Mountains suitable for District Commissioners to read; 'you can imagine what it is like for a man of his temperament to have to write such a book in Central Africa away from the contact of his fellow anthropologists.'[27] Even at the end of the war he sees Nadel becoming an administrator rather than an academic, another judgement in which he was greatly mistaken.[28]

This rejection of applied work, and even of Government funds, was connected with his dislike of Malinowski, partly because of the way the latter had treated his own patrons, the Seligmans, partly because of his failure to keep to a scholarly programme and partly because of his intervention in practical affairs. In his very first letter to Fortes he pours scorn on Malinowski's claim to be 'largely responsible for a book which has just appeared giving advise [sic] on courtship and marriage to young people contemplating both'.[29] Interestingly it was a contribution of this kind by Fortes to a popular magazine that led to a cooling of relations between him and Evans-Pritchard in the late forties. Not that Fortes made this known. He always displayed the greatest loyalty to Evans-Pritchard, very rarely making adverse comments about him or any other of his colleagues of the 1930s. He usually managed to separate intellectual matters from personal ones. But Evans-Pritchard's case was special and he clearly tried to maintain his ties with 'his elder brother' in anthropology even when this effort presented him with the greatest of difficulties.

Even after he left London, Evans-Pritchard continued to view Malinowski's activities in a poor light. Writing to Fortes from Cairo, he calls him 'a bloody gas-bag' because of his participation in 'the mass-observation bilge', an opinion that was apparently shared by Fortes since Evans-Pritchard says that he is 'Glad to hear that B.M. has reached his nadir.'[30] 'Mass-observation' had been started by the ethnologist, Geoffrey Harrison, and others with the aim of recruiting local personnel to observe their own community, Britain; at this stage Malinowski was willing to popularise social science in ways that others rejected, but he was certainly more in touch with the general intellectual pulse of the society. At another time Evans-Pritchard quotes Kirchhoff's claim that, in a slip of the tongue, Malinowski declared that he was engaged in 'telling South Africa how to take the Natives' land away according to their Customs'.[31]

Part of Evans-Pritchard's objections to applied enquiry, or indeed to any application of anthropology, came from his vision of himself as a detached scholar engaged in pure research, a romantic exploring the unknown world. But he was not consistent in his views. For he was an enthusiastic supporter of an anthropological contribution to the Second World War. He encouraged Fortes to participate in intelligence work in Africa and he himself was a member of the military government in North Africa. Moreover, probably more than any other anthropologist of his generation, he was dependent upon support from official funds, in his case, from the government of the Anglo-Egyptian Sudan. That happened partly because of his very estrangement from Malinowski, but partly too because he was perhaps closer to the traditions of the governing class.

Evans-Pritchard's other great objection to Malinowski was the notion of 'function'. His problem with functionalism was partly empirical. He writes to Fortes:

I am glad your fieldwork experience tallies with my own in that it is apparent to a genuine investigator that the functional theories of behaviour have no relation to facts and are not based on observation and cannot be investigated in the field. They are purely paper inventions. I think that in a few years there will be a big and proper reaction against all this 'balls' and that the more purely descriptive and ethnological work will rank higher than the functional hotch-potch of fact-cum-theory which has nothing to do with the facts.[32]

He gave up using the word altogether, rejecting it even as a field technique.

As for Audrey! well if you meet her again [he wrote to Fortes in 1937] you might tell her that I have not mentioned the word 'function' for the last five years. It always was meaningless to me. You may add that the £.S.D. [*sic*] have no idea of what 'method' means, but have a vague notion about 'techniques' of fieldwork although their minds are so crabbed that I would rely much more on Driberg or Rattray's account of native attitudes.[33]

At this point he claimed to rate the scholarly work of these administrators – government anthropologists – higher than academic professionals, a typical piece of exaggeration that marks his personal correspondence, and not a position that he would 'normally' have maintained.

In presumed contrast to Malinowski, it was Evans-Pritchard who at all times stressed the empirical. In an early letter to Fortes, he sent a copy of his paper on the theory of magic, adding: 'it is eclectic and ideas are borrowed right and left. However, the chief points were a direct response to observation in the field.' In fact the paper represents a careful bringing together of theory and observation, not greatly influenced by functionalism, but certainly much more than a factual statement.[34] But Evans-Pritchard was full of such contradictions which would have led to a conflict with any dominant figure, Malinowski at this phase, but later on with Radcliffe-Brown himself, whom he had initially adopted as a counterweight, intellectually as well as politically, and as the potential focus of a rival school at Oxford.

CHAPTER 6

The Oxford Group

Evans-Pritchard and Fortes believed in an anthropology that was purer, more scholarly, more scientific than Malinowski's, at once more theoretical and more empirically validated. They saw themselves as the spear-point of an opposition to the dominant trend and as closer to the work of Radcliffe-Brown, although the divergences were not as great as they imagined.[1] However the opposition needed to create its own programme, of research, of publications and of teaching, and that required a focus outside the London School of Economics.

Oxford seemed a possibility for both of them when Radcliffe-Brown arrived as Professor of Social Anthropology in 1937. Evans-Pritchard had already been giving lectures there for three years as Research Lecturer in African Sociology, the first post devoted to African studies in the country. However, he now wrote to Fortes saying that he felt something further could be done: 'if I can keep afloat at Oxford you shall float as well.'[2] At the same time he suggests that Fortes come to Oxford from London to write up his notes and asks whether he can do this without too great a row. 'With R-B, you, and me, we would have quite a decent nucleus for a school.' This was the period of their most active collaboration. Plans for *African Political Systems* were put to the International African Institute and accepted in October of that year.[3] Fortes sent the draft of the introduction to Evans-Pritchard which the latter rewrote 'rather drastically', omitted sections on the responsibilities and economic advantages of a chief, but in fact did not add many new points.[4]

African Political Systems, the fruit of collaboration between Fortes, Evans-Pritchard and their colleagues, was also the first of a series of such theoretically orientated volumes, namely, *African Systems of Kinship and Marriage* (1958) and *African Worlds* (1963), which came under the wing of Daryll Forde when he became Director of the International African Institute, the publishers. That was appropriate, since the

Institute had sponsored much of the research and later on arranged a
series of seminars and the resulting publications that continued while
Forde was Director. The first two volumes especially changed the
nature of the understanding of 'traditional' African societies by
presenting a series of excellent case studies preceded by an analytic
introduction of considerable scope.

Oxford did not work out entirely as they had hoped. A permanent
post for Fortes was not immediately forthcoming, partly they felt
because of Radcliffe-Brown's 'inaction', so that Fortes had to take on
temporary jobs. They had only been together in Oxford for two years
when war broke out. Evans-Pritchard and Fortes at once worked out
a scheme for them to be sent to Africa to areas they knew, partly to
carry out research and partly to get involved in the war effort. Evans-
Pritchard was to be financed by the university (and by the Leverhulme
Foundation), Fortes by All Souls. The scheme did not come off, but,
using his private income, Evans-Pritchard went to the Sudan in any
case and joined the administration so that he could carry out the
plan. He considered that the failure of the project was due to
Radcliffe-Brown.[5]

Clearly Radcliffe-Brown's stay in Oxford, interrupted by a wartime
secondment to São Paolo, Brazil, had been a great disappointment to
them. In reply to a request to contribute to his festschrift, which
significantly was edited by Fortes under the title of *Social Structure*,
Evans-Pritchard agreed to do a short piece, saying that he understood
Radcliffe-Brown much better now (in 1944) and could 'sympathize with
his having withdrawn into a shell'.[6] But at the beginning of the war,
when he had gone to the Sudan 'to do research', he declared that he
had had six years of 'disillusionment' at Oxford and welcomed the war
'as a break', wondering if he would ever go back to anthropology; if he
did it would probably be to Yale, where Malinowski had gone at the
beginning of the war, taking the visiting position Evans-Pritchard had
been invited to fill. On the other hand 'The Germans and economic
collapse must do what you and I cannot do – sweep away the dirt
which blocks all real scientific and artistic work in the University – the
R.B.s and Perhams and Coupland, and Adams, etc. etc.'[7] The next
year he again lamented, 'Is it any use trying to get a school going if
R.-B. is going to sit still and dream dreams?' But, despite these
disappointments, he still had some hopes of starting the research
scheme again.[8] The problem with Radcliffe-Brown was nothing
personal. After the end of the war in Europe he wrote to Fortes saying

that he has been to see him. Regretting Fortes' continued absence in West Africa, he remarks that 'There is no one I can talk to now, except, on the rare occasions I see him, R.-B. You know how pleasant those talks are, but also how unsatisfying. One knows that nothing will be done by him so one just talks with him as in a play on a stage.'[9] At this time Radcliffe-Brown was the very opposite of the man of action, which was how Evans-Pritchard, who had become a major in the army, saw himself. Writing of his efforts to get Fortes a Readership at Oxford, he claims that 'The dictatorial military tone I have acquired in the army helped. You know – the "Action must be taken at once" style.'[10]

By the end of the war, things began to change. At the beginning Fortes had filled in for Evans-Pritchard at Oxford when he went off to the Sudan. He remained in Oxford, firewatching, teaching and finishing his books on the Tallensi. Evans-Pritchard wrote to encourage him to complete those works. 'You know I don't flatter. I think it will be the most important advance in theory for the last 15 years.'[11] Nevertheless Fortes did not get a permanent Lectureship at Oxford until 1945, after he had been in West Africa, when the university was also putting in for a Readership for Evans-Pritchard. The latter withdrew his name as in the previous year he had already accepted a Lectureship at Cambridge which was then turned into a Readership. He thought that Fortes might get the Oxford Readership instead (which he did in 1945, but for the following October), and then they would both be in good positions to apply for the Oxford and Cambridge Chairs, the former to become free in 1947 with the retirement of Radcliffe-Brown, the latter in 1950, when vacated by Hutton. That was exactly how things turned out. In this post-war period Firth became Professor at the London School of Economics and Forde at University College.[12] 'In the end', Evans-Pritchard wrote to Fortes, 'we will win our fight and it looks as if the fortunes of war have changed in our favour.'[13]

For a period after the end of the war, Oxford was in the ascendant. Evans-Pritchard and Fortes regarded themselves as working at the cutting-edge of social anthropology. It was their books – on the Azande and the Nuer, *African Political Systems*, the recently published works on the Tallensi – that were making the running. They had taken over intellectually from Malinowski, they were more effective administratively than Radcliffe-Brown. If doubts arose, it was about the work of others. But such doubts also led to self-questioning about the subject itself. On a visit to his wife's parents in Natal in August 1951, Evans-Pritchard wrote to Fortes asking him to let him know 'whether I am going crazy. I have just read Firth's 'Elements of Social Organisation' and just can't make out what he is talking about . . . it just makes me sick and want to give up social anthropology.'[14] Fortes pointed out the strength of the section on economies, to which Evans-Pritchard replied, saying that he had made the same point in the review he was writing for *Nature*. 'I also argue that much of the difficulty lies in the subject, in which a certain hesitation and uncertainty is now apparent – we falter where we firmly trod.'[15] The remark seems strange from the standpoint of their success. The history of anthropological theory does not offer much firm ground to tread upon. On the more general level, it is often characterised by a series of paradigm reversals at the higher level which resemble changes in clothing fashions more than paradigm shifts of a Kuhnian kind. One might have thought that the ethnographic analyses of the two men, which are fine examples of the integration of empirical and theoretical concerns, would have presented as firm a basis as one could expect to find, at least as a first step. But Evans-Pritchard's worries have perhaps more to do with a breach in the certainties of youth faced with the complexities of academic power and scholarly achievement, together with a fear of the resurrection of Malinowskian concerns.

For a few years Oxford was a power-house of academic activity. Students came from far and wide to pursue post-graduate studies, grants for research were plentiful. Since there was no undergraduate course at that time, as there was at London and Cambridge, the staff were able to concentrate on the teaching of graduate students. These students arrived from many other universities. In my Cambridge years virtually all the successful students left for Oxford, attracted by the teaching they had had from Evans-Pritchard. They came too in considerable numbers from the USA as a result of funds made available by the British government: Jim and Paula Bohannan who worked among the Tiv of Nigeria; Grace and Al Harris who studied the Taita of East Africa; Lloyd and Margaret Fallers who went to the Basoga of Uganda; Bob Armstrong who studied and later taught linguistics in Nigeria. Many of the second generation of Africanists spent time at Oxford, except for a few who worked with Forde at University College, London.

The staff also proliferated. Gluckman became a lecturer in 1947, and the Indian scholar, M. N. Srinivas, was awarded a post in Indian sociology. Firth wrote of this period: 'It was a powerful combination – of African expertise from several major quarters, of theoretical skill in social, political and ritual fields, and of common commitment to what then was known broadly as a structuralist position. But it also bore the seeds of dissolution. Given such intellectual strength, and such forceful personalities, it was perhaps fortunate that new opportunities soon opened up.'[16] In 1949 Gluckman moved to the Victoria University of Manchester to start a new department and in 1950 Fortes was elected the William Wyse Professor at Cambridge. In both universities one of their first tasks was to encourage graduate work. At this level Cambridge had been effectively moribund for years. Few promising scholars would have wished to stay there in the 1930s when they could have gone to London, or after the Second World War to Oxford, where the presence of these teachers had attracted a strong bunch of scholars supported by grants from the Colonial Social Science Research Council and wanting to undertake research in Africa. For it was in post-war Africa that most of the money for research was available, stimulated by the reports they had commissioned by leading anthropologists, though deprecated by Evans-Pritchard.

As Firth remarked, it was difficult to see such men sticking together for long, especially with the further opportunities that were opening up, and especially as they each had powerful personalities. Evans-Pritchard agreed with this judgement. In July 1946, new lectureships were established at both Oxford and Cambridge. He proposed Gluckman for the second, writing to Fortes:

I think Max is better away from you and me. We are both very fond of him, but too close an academic association in the same department is, I think, good for neither him nor us. Anyhow, a department wants some variety. Moreover the Oxford post should, I think, be for a younger man who will do research. The Cambridge post is different. It is primarily a teaching post.

The Oxford lectureship became vacant in the following year and Evans-Pritchard suggested it be filled by Godfrey Lienhardt, 'a brilliant man', even if he had done no research; indeed he was still completing his undergraduate degree at Cambridge at the time.[17] Earlier he had been pressing the claims of the Greek Cypriot anthropologist, John Peristiany, who had been trained in Paris at Sciences Po (Political Sciences), for a post at either of these two universities. That all of his predictions came off testifies not only to the quality of the applicants and his power of attracting good people, but to his ability at persuading university authorities, then less subject to committee procedures, to accept his recommendations.

When Gluckman left Oxford for Manchester, and Fortes for Cambridge, they all remained closely in touch, initially at least, regarding the filling of posts. Lienhardt, who worked among the Dinka of the Sudan, neighbours of the Nuer, got a lectureship at Oxford; another student, Emrys Peters, who worked in Libya following Evans-Pritchard's study of the Sanusi of Cyrenaica, went to Cambridge on a temporary position, then took a lectureship at Manchester with Gluckman. Peristiany moved from Cambridge to Oxford. Evans-Pritchard would have liked to help Fortes get rid of Reo Fortune from Cambridge ('an incoherent nuisance in academic life') but found it difficult to write a strong reference to get him a post elsewhere. It is as if all were being planned from GHQ. Perhaps that was so for a short time, the period that saw Evans-Pritchard playing the significant role in founding the Association of Social Anthropologists, very much a professional union. It was not to last long, but in the meantime Oxford played a key role in the development of social anthropology in Africa that had been so stimulated by access to the research funds from the Colonial Development and Welfare sources and from the newly founded Institutes these had established. For those it was the Rhodes–Livingstone Institute that provided the model.

The institute for East Africa was based in Uganda and directed by Audrey Richards; other institutes were established in Nigeria, for West Africa, as well as in the West Indies. They were linked to the newly formed Colonial Social Science Research Council, which was in a real sense the forerunner in Britain of the Social Science Research Council. In all these institutions anthropology was firmly located in the social sciences, along with economics, politics and sociology. During the post-war period many of those engaged in anthropological research were attached to these institutes and it was in this context that interests and techniques were developed and that the subject flourished. It did so too at the universities to which the individuals normally returned after their fieldwork, and where social anthropology was increasingly separated from the fields of human biology, archaeology and museum work, partly under pressure from the Association of Social Anthropologists. The resultant structures were very different from the majority of those in the American scene, where departments cover a much wider spectrum, even within the socio-cultural field. On returning to the States one professor remarked that the members of his department had hardly read a single book in common. That was very different in Britain where the notion of a core curriculum, with roughly comparable reading lists, played a prominent part. That was possible because of the relatively small size of the field and the solidarity encouraged by the Association of Social Anthropologists (the ASA) that included only professional teachers, and partly too because of the common intellectual inheritance from Malinowski and Radcliffe-Brown; and then again it was an intentional strategy for advancing the subject. But it depended upon a structure of scholarly authority. Anthropology and the institutes flourished where there was strong and effective leadership, under Gluckman at the Rhodes–Livingstone and under Richards at Makerere in Uganda. I make this point because British social anthropology developed in a 'highly structured context which is difficult for others to understand (I mean other academic cultures and more recent varieties of our own). Firstly, there was the dominating stature of Malinowski and Radcliffe-Brown (and the undoubted authoritarianism of the former). Subsequently the influential departments in the country were dominated by their students – Evans-Pritchard at Oxford and from there Fortes to Cambridge and Gluckman to Manchester; at the London School of Economics there was Firth and later Schapera and Mair, and at University College, London, Daryll Forde. That layer constituted the professoriate; their lecturing staff consisted largely of members of a different generation.

It was the professoriate that set the tone of discourse not only in the universities but at the conferences which were organised by the ASA, started by Evans-Pritchard as Secretary, with Radcliffe-Brown as the first Life President. Attendance, as football later became for the Manchester department under Gluckman, was virtually obligatory in the fifties. However the general atmosphere was one of camaraderie, of solidarity, of *communitas*, rather than authority; the seminars and the drinking were done together. Socially it was not as objectionable as it may sound. Intellectually it had many advantages. Life was in some ways like an on-going seminar, with continuing discussions of this or that theme, what X thought, what new empirical work had to say on the subject. The closeness of the fraternity was one way in which the highly amorphous subject of anthropology (which can be all things to all men) was given some manageable bounds, and some continuing focus was provided for current investigations.

After the Second World War the situation in Africa had changed in a number of ways. Colonial governments still ruled, but they were more ready to support research in the social sciences. Indeed it was in the twilight of colonial rule that the majority of research has been carried out. Some anthropologists were, of course, producing reports for ORSTOM or other official bodies. But independence was very much in the air, even at an official level. In any case those who felt that not all forms of exploitation or rule are the same, that there are degrees of oppression, considered that to bring the actual situation existing among the people to the attention of the colonial or other authorities, including the newly independent governments, was not universally to be condemned. Otherwise the gathering of any kind of information on social life, here or in contemporary Africa, would be equally subject to attack.

In these post-war enquiries, carried out both from France and from Britain, anthropologists were often the chroniclers of the transition to independence in their particular areas. Indeed many were active supporters of such trends; French Marxists working in Africa – Meillassoux, Terray, Pierre-Phillipe Rey – could hardly be regarded as agents of colonial rule. Nor were their British colleagues in anglophone territories backward in this respect; Ghana led the movement to independence and anthropologists participated. Many of them had chosen that profession because of their interest and concern about what was happening in Africa. Some, like David Tait, the author of *The Konkomba of Northern Ghana* (1961), came from a pacifist Quaker background which was well represented in the University of Ghana, Legon, when it first opened in 1948. Others were sympathetic to the anti-colonial movement for different reasons, because they wanted the post-war world to be different.

The political situation was changing rapidly and the progressive role of anthropology was recognised by a number of African leaders. It is true that after he came to power Nkrumah was somewhat suspicious of the field, but he had earlier taken courses in the subject at University College, London. When he was Prime Minister he encouraged the Africanisation of the university curriculum in which anthropology played a prominent part. Kofi Busia, the leader of the opposition and Nkrumah's eventual successor after the military coup of 1966, had worked with Fortes at Oxford and his thesis was published as *The Position of the Chief in the Modern Political System of Ashanti* (1951). He was in fact the first Ghanaian to become a professor at the university, where he held the Chair in Sociology. The first Prime Minister of Kenya, Jomo Kenyatta, had been a pupil of Malinowski at the London School of Economics, received a grant from the International African Institute, and published an account of his own people, the Kikuyu, under the title *Facing Mount Kenya* (1953). The colonial peoples were never simply subjects of anthropology; it was also an instrument of the colonised in their intellectual struggles.

Like the members of other academic disciplines, anthropologists can be considered as a tribe (Becher 1989). That was especially true of British social anthropology from the 1930s to the 1960s, since the dominant figures had virtually all been students at the same place and of the same man. They were coevals, age mates, who dispersed to take up academic positions throughout the country (and elsewhere) but who kept up their tribal existence by founding the ASA, which deliberately excluded amateurs and those who did not have the same professional training, very much in the early Rockefeller spirit. As subtribes developed at the different universities, they too took on a solidary character themselves, some more than others. In Oxford and Cambridge there was the Friday evening seminar followed by beer at the pub. At Manchester, under Gluckman's more directive leadership, it was Saturday afternoons watching Manchester United (whose obituary Gluckman delivered on the BBC Third Programme after the disastrous accident at Munich airport). Attending one of the early meetings of the ASA at Durham, I can recall that Gluckman took Lienhardt and myself aside when we had gone off to a pub rather than stay in the common room and drink with others. We were considered to be lacking in sociability.

In these subgroups the styles of leadership were very different. Evans-Pritchard, Firth, Forde and Fortes did not dominate their departments and their members in the way Malinowski did at London and Gluckman at Manchester. Perhaps they did not as a consequence establish 'schools' of quite the same kind. Nevertheless they exercised a good deal of influence on the initial choice of research topics of many students, in the manner of approach and certainly in social interaction. Only at Cambridge did Fortes have much competition at this level, having sought an appointment for another of Malinowski's students, E. R. Leach, and having another, A. I. Richards, thrust upon him. Otherwise the professor was the apex of the hierarchy, one who had been trained by Malinowski and Radcliffe-Brown and had had direct access to their wisdom.

There were even rites of passage to attend. I well remember the cremation of Radcliffe-Brown at Golders Green which a number of us

– all research students – attended together with the senior generation, Fortes, Schapera, Lloyd-Warner and others. Anthropologists replaced the family, of which there was but one representative. That phase, cohesive despite the internal factions, did not last long, for anthropology was the victim of its own success; the expansive moment led not only to the segmentation of members but to the diffusion of interests. Yet looking back, as I shall try to do for Africa, its most notable achievements belonged to the early, more tribal, phase. The essential commonality lay not in superficial rituals so much as in common intellectual problems.

CHAPTER 7

Some achievements of anthropology in Africa

The main thrust of the teaching and research in post-war Oxford was on Africa under the aegis of Evans-Pritchard, Fortes (to 1950), Gluckman (to 1949), Bohannan, Lienhardt and others. It was in that context that theoretical interests were largely, though not exclusively, developed and it was to that continent that the bulk of research students went to carry out their work. In the chapters that follow I want to review rather generally some of the achievements of the generation working under the auspices of the International African Institute, then look at post-war developments concentrating on the area I know best, West Africa, and conclude with some remarks on the impact on my own work.

The attraction of Oxford was twofold: firstly, the staff and the students that had come there over the years from 1937 to 1947, but effectively since the war; secondly, the fact that they were largely Africanists and that that was the continent where major socio-political changes were then taking place, where a cluster of independent nations was to emerge within the next decade and a half, where much ethnological work needed to be done, where contributions to knowledge were rapidly building up and where many contacts had been made as a result of the war, the new research institutions and the burgeoning university systems. Kofi Busia, author of *The Position of the Chief in the Modern Political System of the Ashanti* (1951), later Prime Minister of Ghana, and Alex Kyerematen, who also made significant contributions to the ethnography of Ghana, were among the student body. That body found itself working with a series of paradigms developed by the earlier generation, especially by those whose interests were strongly influenced by the work of Emile Durkheim.

LINEAGE STUDIES

I begin with the study of the lineage, since that embodied not simply a technical discussion (though this aspect was important) but embraced much of social anthropology. In the first place, it touched upon religion (especially ancestor worship), politics, law and warfare (especially in societies without rulers), kinship (at all levels) and the economy (the rights in pasture or in agricultural land). The existence of lineages led back to debates not only in sociological theory (to Durkheim and to Spencer) but to the whole problem of order in society discussed by philosophers, lawyers and political scientists. The problem of order touched upon questions of morality and the segmentary structure of norms, the fact that different judgements, personal and legal, were made about delicts depending on whom one was dealing with. In egalitarian societies not everyone was treated equally in relation to ego. At the same time it raised in acute forms the problem of synchronic as against diachronic explanations, shedding new light on the use of genealogies and the problems of historical versus sociological accounts.

I want first to look at some of the contributions that Africanists made to this topic and then touch briefly upon the other major domains. I do not mean to imply for one moment that contributions were not made by scholars working elsewhere; simply that in the period we are considering much of the relevant research took place in Africa, much of the interior of which continent had only been subject to European rule (South Africa was an exception) for some thirty years before these scholars were working there. So it was virtually virgin territory from the standpoint of outside research.

Radcliffe-Brown had been the major channel for the importation of Durkheimian sociology into Britain. He had once described himself as a Spencerian, and Spencer's work was a point of polemical orientation for Durkheim and full of the terms 'structure' and 'function'. But he had also read widely in that field and had been in contact with members of *L'Année sociologique*, as a result of which he encouraged others to take up their ideas. There can be no doubt of the profound influence of the Durkheimian enterprise in defining the problematic, not only of Evans-Pritchard himself, but of so many of those trained at Oxford, as well as those more senior scholars, Fortes, Gluckman, Srinivas who, like Dumont, were on the staff of that university. Among many other ways this influence manifested itself in the attention given to political-jural systems, especially to segmentary ones. That term had been used by Durkheim in his polemic with Herbert Spencer about the nature of solidarity, of social order, the problem attacked in various ways by Hobbes, Rousseau, Locke, Austin and later by sociologists such as Talcott Parsons – the problem of order, or of what in the absence of the state Evans-Pritchard called 'ordered anarchy'. How is order maintained without a centralised authority? The theme had more than a historical or comparative interest; it touched upon the nature of alternative forms of social organisation, a fundamental concern to many in the post-war atmosphere, especially in the context of communes, kibbutzim or other 'socialist' experiments. The classical formulation of the problem was in Evans-Pritchard's study of the Nuer, the results of which had been first published in the thirties, then in book form in 1940. It has been suggested that the colonial authorities were interested in having research done on these peoples with a view to bringing them under control.[1] It is true they were always a puzzle to any central government and remain so to this day. But the attraction for anthropologists was quite different; hence the problems that the Gold Coast official saw with Fortes' conservative (or conservationist) approach. Anthropologists were attracted to them partly because of the theoretical advances in their analysis made since Durkheim and partly because they saw something valuable in 'tribes without rulers'.

Evans-Pritchard's study was important for making sense of the interminable genealogies that we find written down in Biblical, Arabic and Chinese sources; making sense by linking them to the organisation of relationships between individuals and groups. The Twelve Tribes of Israel referred to social groups (clans or lineages) occupying particular areas of Palestine who traced their descent from and organised their relations around their genealogically linked ancestors. These genealogies were not to be read as historical documents (though some historical elements might be present), but as manipulable 'charters' of current relationships. That approach was dictated by the fact that while the genealogy underwent a potential extension every generation, the groups to which they referred did not necessarily expand in this way. Notions such as 'structural amnesia' (Barnes) and 'telescoping' (Evans-Pritchard) came to be seen as significant mechanisms for 'tribal' societies ancient and modern, in the Near East and elsewhere, by which they adjusted depth to span. This notion was one of the important contributions of anthropology to historical studies, since it provided an alternative mode of interpretation.

The politico-jural aspects of the analysis were perhaps the most

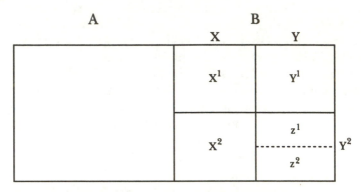

Figure 1 Segmentation model of the Nuer lineage

fruitful and these owed a lot to Sir Henry Maine and his study of a developmental shift from (fixed) status to (negotiable) contract in *Ancient Law*, something akin to Radcliffe-Brown's notion of the lineage as a politico-jural as well as a kinship unit, but above all to Emile Durkheim's idea of a 'segmental' lineage, of mechanical solidarity and of moral density, all derived from *The Division of Labour in Society* (1893). If we look at the earlier versions of what was eventually to appear as *The Nuer*, which were published in *Sudan Notes and Records* during the thirties (1933–5, 1936, 1937–8), the argument is framed largely in terms of Maine's concepts of status and contract. In the later book the influence of Durkheimian theory is much more evident. Evans-Pritchard's contribution to this discussion lay in the notion of differentiated segmentation, that is to say, segments of a corresponding level acted in similar ways but had different interests which brought them into conflict as well as into co-operation. They were structurally and functionally different from segments of another order of segmentation, whether more or less inclusive. The segmentary process meant groups which were opposed at one level of segmentation united at the next higher level in opposition to similar units. The paradigmatic case was that of homicide, feud and warfare, and the principle was summarised in that simple, even simple-minded, diagram in *The Nuer* (1940: 144) (see figure 1) that took on the character of a model, a paradigm, for many other analyses.

The notion of segmentation was closely linked to that of the lineage, the social group based on the genealogical structure to which we have already referred. Fortes reported a discussion with Radcliffe-Brown on the lineage taking place in 1931 as he passed through London on his way from Sydney to take up a professorship at Chicago. The notions that are at times referred to as 'lineage theory' were later elaborated at Oxford where Radcliffe-Brown was appointed to the chair in 1937. In his obituary of Daryll Forde, Fortes records his visit to Oxford and acknowledges the importance of Forde's contribution to the analysis of systems of double descent, of which the Yakö of Nigeria whom he had studied became the paradigmatic case. In such societies each individual belonged to two types of descent groups, one based on patrilineal, the other on matrilineal reckoning. Forde showed such systems to be perfectly 'stable' and not simply to be dismissed as points of transition between one type of system of descent and another. 'What later became known as "lineage theory"', wrote Fortes, 'was being thrashed out at Oxford in the wake of Evans-Pritchard's Nuer studies.'[2]

In that study Evans-Pritchard made few acknowledgements to the influences of Durkheim's work, just as he had done with the writings of Levy-Bruhl in that other important book, *Witchcraft, Oracles and Magic among the Azande* (1937). These lapses, if they can be so called, have been pointed out by Gellner, who notes that although he wrote at great length about his forebears, he said little about Durkheim.[3] Douglas too has observed the contrast between his punctiliousness in gratefully acknowledging evidence from every missionary or district officer and his 'virtual silence as to his intellectual debts', a situation that has also been remarked upon by Barnes in his obituary for the British Academy (1987).[4]

Yet later on he did comment that British anthropologists were still living on the intellectual capital of members of the group known after the name of their journal, the *Année sociologique*, and he went on to say that 'if a personal note be allowed I would, though with serious reservations, identify myself with the *Année* school if a choice had to be made and an intellectual allegiance to be declared'.[5] Certainly he made the debt clear to students at Cambridge and Oxford in the post-war period. Durkheim and his group formed a major part of our reading and several of our contemporaries were engaged in translating their works into English. Ian Cunnison translated Mauss' *Le Don* (1924, 1954), Rodney Needham did the same for Durkheim and Mauss on *Primitive Classification* (1963), while he and his wife translated two essays by R. Hertz under the title of *Death and The Right Hand* (1960). Evans-Pritchard wrote introductions to all these three volumes. I insist on this aspect of his work because one view has stressed his role in a shift from 'function to meaning'.[6] Of course he was always interested in meaning; every fieldworking anthropologist of any merit must be. His polemical orientation to the work of Levy-Bruhl had just that perspective. Levy-Bruhl was associated with the Durkheim group and Evans-Pritchard's work on the notion of 'primitive mentality' among the Azande embodied the comments of a fieldworker on the statements of a philosophically oriented, armchair anthropologist. Later on he occasionally slipped into all-too-easy cultural relativism, asserting for example that Nuer meanings are unique. Such a statement no-one would deny, but is that all there is to say? So too are those of every human being. Even in writing the most detailed ethnography one has to translate concepts into English, French, or some other language of major circulation and hence enter into an enforced if implicit comparison, in other words to draw attention to elements that are not simply unique. Evans-Pritchard of course went much further than his assertion might imply, being interested not only in general principles but in more specific comparisons of the Nuer with their Nilotic neighbours as well as with peoples of the Near East, including Ancient Israel. The most significant aspects of his work remained strongly influenced by the sociological school, especially in the training he gave to others; that defined much of their problematic just as it had done his.

I do not mean that those interests were totally limited by that school. Other currents flowed into the stream of work. But *African Political Systems* (1940), edited by M. Fortes and E. E. Evans-Pritchard, was followed by *Tribes Without Rulers* (1958), edited by J. Middleton and D. Tait, and by the attempts of J. A. Barnes and others, including myself, to define more closely the concepts of segmentation and fission.[7] Other work was summarised by Fortes in an important article on 'The structure of unilineal descent groups' (1953) and later by I. M. Lewis, in 'Problems in the comparative study of unilineal descent' in a volume based on papers given at the 1963 decennial conference of the Association of Social Anthropologists, entitled *The Relevance of Models for Social Anthropology*.[8] There were efforts to examine a variety of acephalous societies, largely in Africa, which did not depend as heavily as the Nuer and the Tallensi on the organisation of the lineage, but emphasised other forms of social grouping such as age sets, locality groups, associations, and so on. These studies served to modify the notion that all acephalous or 'tribal' societies in Africa or elsewhere were based on lineages, or kinship. That is by no means the case.

Hence the notion of 'the lineage mode of production', used by French Marxists, cannot be universally applied, even if the definition of a mode of production with reference to this specific type of social grouping was found to be analytically satisfactory.

There are always problems with any comparison as with any expository or analytic technique. It is impossible to avoid them, even by enclosing oneself in a cultural cocoon. Rather one has to face the difficulties and refine the concepts, as Barnes has tried to do in his article on 'African models in the New Guinea highlands'. At the same time we need constantly to try and improve the rather crude methods we employ, taking into account broad similarities and differences, for example, in modes of communication, in production and in religion, even when we are considering the lineage. For it is important to understand the variety of forms the lineage can take, the lineage of medieval law (from whence came the term itself), the lineage described by Maria Couroucli for the Mediterranean, the lineages of the pastoral Nuer and those of agriculturalists like the Tallensi, lineages in state systems like that of Asante, the lineages of New Guinea, and more importantly the lineages of India and especially those of China with their written genealogies, trust funds and property (what I have called 'corporation lineages' since the term 'corporate' has been used in a much wider sense). Again it is important, as I have pointed out in a critical review entitled 'Under the lineage's shadow' (1984), not to underplay the domestic side of kinship and marriage, that is, the household and other lower level groups and relationships, in favour of the swing to emphasise the politico-jural domain.

Having said all this, we end up a long way from the approaches of M. Verdon (1981) and A. Kuper (1982) who worked in societies in Africa where the lineage had little or no significant development and who argue against its very existence in others. That suggestion seems to neglect the historical changes that have taken place over time (they worked some thirty dramatic years after the anthropologists of the earlier generation on whose work they comment), to misunderstand the use of analytical concepts and to capitulate to terminological quibbles and throw in the sponge before setting about the task of constructive discrimination. In practice the large majority of anthropologists has found the notion of considerable utility in looking at genealogical structures in the societies with which they were dealing. Freedman's application of the notion to Chinese studies, though not without problems, has proved particularly fertile; and that has also been true of the Near East and elsewhere. There is a counterproductive tendency in anthropology, as in other humanistic fields of study, to overplay the idea of the Kuhnian paradigm shift (or the change in 'fashion'). Many practitioners think they have to try to overturn the work of their predecessors at every generation rather than build upon it. One needs to assess and improve their contentions, but aiming towards a cumulative body of knowledge rather than one that starts from scratch with each generation or even each individual. That is the mode of the essay rather than the assay; a respectable genre but not one that should replace the practice of social research.

It was not a slavish adherence to Evans-Pritchard's model that led to the great expansion of lineage studies, and to the utilisation of aspects of his analysis in many other societies and by many other anthropologists. In Africa the greatest development of this type of social group was among pastoral peoples, but other acephalous peoples such as the Tallensi of Ghana studied by Fortes, the Tiv of Nigeria studied by Bohannan and the Lugbara of Uganda studied by Middleton were classic cases where the lineage constituted a core feature of society, along the lines of the original propositions developed by Durkheim, Gifford, Radcliffe-Brown and above all Evans-Pritchard.

KINSHIP AND MARRIAGE

I began by considering the notion of the lineage because it sprang directly from the work of Radcliffe-Brown, Evans-Pritchard and Fortes. Radcliffe-Brown concentrated upon the jural side of kinship studies, as in his influential essay on 'Matrilineal and patrilineal succession' (1935); that element was clearly embodied in his discussion of interpersonal relations which centred on rights and duties rather than 'sentiments'. The latter had played some part in his earlier study of *The Andaman Islanders* (1922), following the social psychological work of Shand, but were now set aside in favour of more 'structural' explanations as in his important contribution 'The mother's brother in South Africa' (1924). The paper became the focus of a considerable discussion as in Homans and Schneider (1955), J. Goody (1959) and in many other attempts to refine, elaborate or reject the hypothesis. These kinship studies tended to stress the jural domain, especially in the sphere of marriage and divorce. For example, Evans-Pritchard adopted the term 'bridewealth' in preference to 'brideprice' in order to characterise the way in which marital prestations were transferred in many African societies where the emphasis was placed on the acquisition of rights and duties over time in both the partners to the marriage (as well as the kin of bride and groom) and the children that were expected to be born. 'Bridewealth is childwealth' became a key concept. Marriage was seen as a process involving a complex set of transfers, partly of material objects but mainly of claims and counter-claims in which sexual access was important but made up only one of the components. One of these other aspects found in a number of patrilineal societies in East Africa was the right of a woman to act as a channel for property to be transmitted to her children rather than to those of a co-wife, what Gluckman called 'the house property complex', which can be seen as a crystallisation of the ties between maternally linked siblings, an important cleavage in polygynous patrilineal societies as well as matrilineal ones.

Social norms as to whom one could or could not marry were also investigated in depth by most anthropologists (especially Evans-Pritchard and Fortes), and the discussion of exogamy and prohibited degrees was linked with that on incest and with the theoretical discussions stemming from Tylor, Freud and others. The interest in cross-cousin marriage generated by Lévi-Strauss' work came in the 1950s but, while some forms of this marriage are widespread, little evidence emerged of the prescriptive systems that occupied so much theoretical attention. That absence followed Lévi-Strauss' prediction since we were not dealing with 'elementary' forms, but rather with 'complex' ones. However the Lovedu of South Africa did present a case of prescriptive mother's brother's daughter marriage which was re-analysed by Edmund Leach in the course of a wide-ranging comparison (1951).

The counterpart of marriage was its dissolution by death or divorce. The study of divorce was considerably advanced by Gluckman's comparative paper on the Lozi and the Zulu in *African Systems of Kinship and Marriage* (1950) where he attempted to correlate patriliny with a strong marriage tie and low divorce rate.[9] The hypothesis was subjected to continual inspection by Schneider (1953), Fallers (1957), Leach (1957), Mitchell (1961), R. Cohen (1961) and Lewis (1962). At the same time Barnes (1948) sought greater statistical clarity in attempting to make such an assessment while E. N. Goody (1962) drew a distinction between divorce and 'terminal separation' in which post-menopausal women return to their kin (and thus re-establish the complete sibling group dispersed at marriage) rather than stay with their husbands. The death of a husband involved similar alternatives, whether a woman returned to her kin or stayed as a wife, notional or actual, under a system either of levirate or of widow inheritance (Evans-Pritchard 1960a).

These were all discussions which the studies on Africa helped to advance and clarify. At the same time, attempts were made, as in Gluckman's case, to relate some of the differences to other variables, in particular to the presence of patrilineal or matrilineal descent groups. The studies by Evans-Pritchard and Fortes became classics on the analysis of patrilineal systems. But in the Trobriands Malinowski had worked in societies with matrilineal descent groups, whose formal and informal workings he had analysed with much subtlety, seeing how they were linked with the norms of interpersonal relations, with notions of conception, with variations on the Oedipus complex and with systems of exchange. It was not surprising that his students, Richards and then Fortes, were attracted to the study of matrilineal societies in Africa, the first working among the Bemba, the second among the Asante. While they wrote much else on those societies, their work is epitomised in their respective articles in *African Systems of Kinship and Marriage* (1950), edited by A. R. Radcliffe-Brown and C. D. Forde. Richards presented a scholarly and insightful comparative analysis of variations in matrilineal systems among the Southern Bantu, stressing the rights established and the variations in timing involved in the bride or groom joining their spouse (that is, by bride-removal and by groom-removal), giving rise to virilocal or uxorilocal marital residence and affecting the location of children and their relationships with parents, with their siblings and with the wider lineage group. It was these domestic relations about which Malinowski was so perspicacious, leaning towards the psychological and 'cultural' rather than the structural and comparative. In this Fortes proved an apt pupil, for his article on matrilineal kinship among the Asante is masterly in being full of insights into their interpersonal relations. These and other less analytical studies laid the foundation for the attempt of Schneider, Gough and their colleagues to produce an omnibus review entitled *Matrilineal Kinship* (1961).

Barnes has remarked of Fortes that his 'work was based on principles that were basically psychological'. He never lost his early interest in that field, however ambivalent he became about introducing those notions into sociological analyses as the result of his understanding of Durkheim, who had insisted on the separation of levels. His essay on

Tallensi education (1938, reprinted 1970) was explicitly entitled 'Social and psychological aspects of education in Taleland'; he subsequently gave a talk on 'Mind' for the BBC (1950) and later he turned back to his earlier interest in psychoanalysis. But 'psychology', at least social psychology, informed his work in two other major spheres, those of domestic relations and of religious activity. The psychologist's interest in the development of the individual led him to go beyond the formal description of the life-cycle and, as he put it in his original research proposal, to look at the 'chronological dimension' of family life, 'i.e. its particular psychological character, as a unit of society which comes into existence, lives, passes away', especially the development through infancy, as the child's horizons expand and he or she acquires 'culture'.

It was out of these ideas that Fortes developed the notion of the development cycle of the domestic group, partly based on the life-cycle of individuals but related to the establishment of reproductive, productive and residential units and the way they were affected over time by the process of fission and occasionally of fusion. Once announced the notion is obvious enough and has become part of the standard analytical framework of social anthropology. Earlier socio-logical investigators would only too often take a household census of a village and then arrive at a modal composition by dividing the total population by the number of households. Such figures of the mean size of households (MSH) were useful for some limited purposes and basic to much historical demography but maladapted for many others. For example, planners would build new housing to such modal specifica-tions. In Europe they would take as the model the cornflake packet family of wife, husband, one girl and one boy, neglecting the fact that households change over the time span of the domestic cycle and have different numbers and needs at different points. The occupants of a house may start as a couple, become a conjugal family (at least a high percentage of them), and possibly later become an extended or expanded 'grand family'. One form is not a deviant version of another, the nuclear is not a variant of the grand or vice versa. It is true that populations differ in the proportion of the varying possibilities, but, if we allow residence in adjacent units to be roughly equal to co-residence, all the various possibilities are found in virtually every society. So one of the practical problems faced by modern architects in the sphere of public housing is to adjust the size of accommodation to the composition of dwelling groups depending on the phase in the developmental cycle. In Africa this adjustment takes place without effort, since unused mud buildings collapse and new ones can be added as the dwelling group expands. With more permanent buildings the problem is of a different order. One possibility is to move the occupants, another to attempt to construct adjustable buildings. It was the second of those alternatives that was pursued by Sir Leslie Martin, Professor of Architecture at Cambridge and advisor to the public-housing authority in London, who discussed the matter at some length with Fortes and myself. But for either solution, planning needs to go beyond the use of aggregate figures and to understand regular changes in the cycle.

The developmental perspective insisted upon by Fortes was part of his attempt to introduce or extend a consideration of the time factor in structural analysis (1949b). It was applied not only to household composition but also to roles and interpersonal relationships. For example, woman's position (even as wife) could not be treated successfully as one unchanging status or even as a sum of her roles over time. There were substantial shifts from her subordinate situation as a new wife under the aegis of her mother-in-law (as well as of her husband), to her position if or when she becomes a mother (especially the mother of a son), and again when she herself becomes a coresident mother-in-law at the marriage of her children. These phases embody important temporal changes which affect individuals psychologically as well as socially. Like the notion of lineage segmentation, the develop-mental cycle has had considerable influence not only on African but on a much wider range of anthropological, sociological and historical studies.

The notion of the development cycle was only one aspect of the study of the family that made great strides in research based in Africa. There were also the broader studies of relationships between close kin in the hands of both Evans-Pritchard and Fortes, but especially the latter. In working among the LoDagaa I was constantly amazed by the perspicacity of Fortes' analysis of the varied facets of interpersonal relations among the Tallensi and I drew back from writing an equivalent study largely because I felt I would be duplicating his account. That study remains the most penetrating account of family life, of kinship and marriage at the domestic level that has appeared in the anthropological literature, either on Africa or, in my own view, on other areas of the world. However, just as the work on matrilineal systems had been greatly stimulated by Malinowski, so this too was built on the brilliant work of his student, Raymond Firth, whose contribution to his own kinship studies Fortes rightly acknowledges. In Fortes' case, the second volume of the Tallensi study is an outstanding example of an individual going to the field not with a definite hypothesis as such but with a defined topic, with adequate training, with a series of ideas and with methods of collecting the data he required to examine them. This achievement in the psychosocial study of the family and the network of domestic groups in a patrilineal society was especially remarkable for the sensitivity to the quality of the relations, the ties and cleavages, between the persons in different roles within the total structure of kinship. Potentially it laid the foundation for a more systematic study of relationships, approached by earlier anthropologists often in the form of studies based on terminologies but in this case of a much more profound kind somewhat along the lines later envisaged by some ethologists (Hinde 1987), and deepened by psychological and sociological knowledge.

Such systemisation is not foreign to anthropology whose major specialism has always been in the study of kinship, marriage and the family, and it is there that the field has developed most of the analytic skills, concepts and techniques that mark it off from others. There is little in other domains of the socio-cultural system to rival the elaboration of the perhaps simple methods they have developed, namely:

the genealogical method
the household survey
the sibling survey
marital histories
personal histories
spatial analysis
the analysis of kin terms (including types of classification, componential analysis and other formalisations)

One aspect of Fortes' work relating to the family lay in the area of demography and census studies. His training in psychology meant that he had none of the only too frequent fear of numbers that strikes at the heart of many anthropologists and he made an early contribution to demographic studies in Africa in his paper in the *Sociological Review* of 1943 entitled 'A note on fertility among the Tallensi of the Gold Coast'. His interest in the topic arose partly out of his contacts in London with Lancelot Hogben and Kuszinski, and it was one he later pursued in Frank Lorrimer's important UNESCO volume, *Culture and Human Fertility* (1954), to which he contributed an essay on 'A demographic field study in Ashanti'. In West Africa that tradition was developed by a number of anthropologists, including Edwin Ardener who carried out a demographic study in the Cameroons. I myself worked with Nelson Addo of Ghana on the constitution of sibling groups, where we attempted to test a negative hypothesis concerning the effects (and causes) of discrimination on the number and sex of children. In his study of the Asante, Fortes compared his data on this topic with the situation in China, remarking that 'no such difference in the care given to children of one sex, be it of males in a patrilineal society or females in matrilineal societies, has been reported for an African people'. That was a most significant observation.[10] He also notes that the sex ratio of live babies seems to differ substantially from Eurasian populations in favour of females, a fact that has been much discussed in recent years. Thirdly he observed that 'in 1945 the Gross-Reproduction rate was 2, so that the population doubles in a generation, mainly because children were highly valued, not only by their parents but also by the elders of the lineage whose influence in local government affairs depends to some extent on their numbers'; he concluded that 'no big change in reproductive habits is likely to occur as long as the corporate organisation of the lineage remains as important in Ashanti social life as it is today'.[11] He went on to suggest that 'education will have little effect if, as seems likely [it] ... postpones marriage or childbearing for a few years and (one might add) reduces the birth interval'. However the pressures from lineage members, from a corporate organisation, from kin, seem less significant than conjugal decisions, continuing high mortality and the general absence of contraception. The first two of Fortes' findings are very much in line with the results of the research carried out by Addo and myself, while the other points have been largely borne out by the extensive work that has been done by specialists in later years.

While there have been some subsequent anthropological contributions to this field in West Africa, especially in the work of Christine Oppong and Wolf Bleek in Ghana, anthropologists have given too little attention to population studies despite their privileged position as students of family, marriage and kinship. For in the absence of registration, and with the difficulties of conducting a census in a population often unable to write, a great premium is placed on small-scale, intensive studies as a check on aggregate data. Moreover the concern of the anthropologists with family structure and domestic production enables them to shed light on the categories used to collect the data as well as on the underlying processes of social reproduction. That vantage point should have encouraged an interest in both theoretical and practical problems. Unfortunately this opportunity has largely lapsed, even though some anthropologists (Wolf and Green- halgh in China, Hammel in Jugoslavia, MacFarlane, Epstein and Moore in India, Segalen and others in France) have continued to develop the field of demographic or population anthropology. While this interest necessarily overlaps with other disciplines, it is one in which the anthropologist has a considerable contribution to make providing he or she is willing to learn about those adjacent subjects. Of course the same applies to any of the increasingly specialised topics which have emerged. It is difficult for social anthropologists to make much significant progress in economic anthropology, psychological anthropology, cognitive anthropology, linguistic anthropology, medical anthropology, without being more expert in these other areas than they have often been in the past. The all-round amateurism of the very early days no longer carries much weight. At the same time a general commitment to some brand-name anthropology (functional, structural, cultural, post-structural, post-modern) is simply not good enough. With such labels anthropology will continue to be the domain of the not-so- gifted amateur, looking at the areas of unspecialised study that other specialists have been unable (often for good reason) to make much of, such as the study of 'symbolic systems'. Earlier it was possible to contribute to the comparative study of human behaviour without much specialist knowledge. However, one noteworthy feature of even this first generation of fieldworkers was that its members were older when they first took up the subject and had already been trained in another field, psychology, economics, history, etc. They were not young students who had studied only a generalised anthropology presented to them as if it alone held the keys to all knowledge. They knew something of what other branches of enquiry had to offer.

In recent years the interest in the cultural factors in human fertility has become of central concern to demographers, economists and to others interested in development. In West Africa Caldwell and his students have carried out much useful work looking for evidence of the demographic transition, that is, the shift from high fertility, high mortality, through lower mortality, to lower fertility. While it is clear that a shift will take place in the long run, many observers are concerned that there is so far little evidence of change over the short term. The problem is a serious one not so much because of the present density of the African population, which has not been high by world standards, but because of the lack of existing resources and the rapidity of the growth, giving rise to high dependency ratios.

The resistance to lowering fertility, to having fewer offspring, has been ascribed by Caldwell and his collaborators to the value of children in providing support in old age for the senior generation, the flows of wealth being from the lower to the upper generation. Whereas in modern societies the flows are seen as proceeding downward, since people do not rely on children to support them but on the other hand support their children, they are held to be more sparing in their procreation. The case is argued between scholars, largely economists working in Western cultures, who perceive children as a burden and those, especially Caldwell and his collaborators, who make the case for children in Africa as an investment (in the literal economic sense), a notion they use to account for 'the survival of the large family'.[12]

Anthropologists have much to contribute to the work on the 'value of children', the assessment of which is often based on too narrow a range of socio-cultural factors, for example, on the measurement of the contribution of children's labour. Wider socio-cultural considerations have been re-introduced with the Caldwells' recent conviction that the continuing high levels of fertility in Africa are related to ancestor worship. In general there is insufficient understanding of differences (and similarities) in economic, religious and kinship systems to allow this heavily financed work to pay maximum dividends. Anthropologists, who study the rich complexity of African society, should certainly be more involved in helping investigators to understand the 'family structures' on which so much welfare in the non-welfare state depends, and will have to depend in Africa for a long time to come since the nature of the productive system allows for no alternative form of expenditure.

I have discussed the importance of lineage studies in acephalous groups, in 'tribes without rulers'. But they were also present in some states in Africa, although there they were inevitably of less significance in the total social system. There were many good studies of states, in southern Africa by the Kriges, H. Kuper, Schapera and Barnes; in East Africa among the interlacustrine Bantu by Maquet on Ruanda, Beattie on the Banyoro, Fallers on the Basoga, and by a variety of writers on the Buganda; in West Africa Lloyd on the Yoruba, Bradbury on Benin. There have also been a number of excellent general studies by historians such as Wilkes on the Asante, which compares with the major anthropological–historical works on francophone areas by Perrot, Tarditz, Terray, Izard and others. Some general concepts were introduced, such as Barnes' notion of the 'snowball state' and Southall's of the 'segmentary state', my own of the 'overkingdom'. However, there is inevitably less by way of comparative theoretical work on complex political systems, except of the abstract kind in the studies of M. G. Smith in northern Nigeria or of the general kind I have carried out in *Technology, Tradition and the State in Africa* (1971) and in *Succession to High Office* (1966a).

However, in the complex states of Northern Nigeria, much influenced by Islam, less emphasis was given to unilineal descent groups, certainly to exogamous groups, the notion of which was violated by the Islamic preference for marriage to the father's brother's daughter (Greenberg 1946). Their social organisation has been studied by a number of authors, especially M. G. Smith and Murray Last, and for the earlier period, S. F. Nadel. Nadel's work on the Nupe was important because it was one of the first, if not *the* first, to examine the operation of a complex African state in sophisticated, comparative terms. Hence the significance of the title, *A Black Byzantium* (1942), which shifted the comparison of African states in Nigeria from feudalism to the more complex patterns of the Near East. The same capacity to deal with complexity emerges in his study of *Nupe Religion* (1954); far removed from the simplicities of tribal rituals and religion, he again produced a pioneering study of the interrelations between local and Muslim practices and beliefs.

Like Fortes, Nadel had been trained as a psychologist and he carried out some explicitly psychological work in West Africa, as well as contributing to the study of witchcraft and interpersonal tensions. But his major contribution, in my view, arose from his capacity for formal 'logical' analysis, acquired or developed when he was a student in Vienna under the logical positivist Maurice Schlich and others, which had led to *The Foundations of Social Anthropology* (1951) and to his work on *The Theory of Social Structure* (1957). These formal treatises did not deal in hypotheses or substantive knowledge, but showed Nadel as the foremost analytic thinker among the British school. On the other hand he was always interested in combining theory and ethnographic research; it was a passing comment from him that set me thinking about the distribution of bridewealth and dowry. But though he taught in England after the war, becoming a reader at Durham University, he left no students of Africa behind since he went to the Australian

National University to become the first Professor of Anthropology. There he was highly successful but he died at the early age of fifty-three, a remarkable and much neglected talent.

LAW

The study of the lineage involved not only kinship and politics but also comparative law and morality. One of the most useful outcomes has been the application of ideas about the segmentary structure of morality, law and sanctions not only to other non-literate cultures, but to early written ones such as Ancient Israel. An outstanding piece of work of this kind was Schapera's analysis of the varied reactions to, and punishments for, homicide in the Old Testament. Legal historians and historians of religion had been puzzled by the fact that the reactions to killing sometimes took the form of a continuing vendetta, sometimes the precise application of the *lex talionis* (an eye for an eye, a tooth for a tooth) while in yet other instances little or nothing appeared to happen; Cain killed his brother and was allowed to wander the world. Schapera showed that these variations were not to be interpreted as random punishments nor yet as relics of different stages of development, as conjectural history only too readily constructed. If one took account of the social (largely genealogical) distance between the actors, then the apparent contradictions in the treatment of homicide could be explained by looking at current social relations; in the Nuer or Bedouin model the counteraction was restricted when the killing took place between close kin, and less so between more distant relatives. Between brothers, exile; between close kin, limited vengeance; and the more distant the relationships the harsher and more violent the reaction. In societies where the central government was weak and did not have the resources to enforce its claim to the monopoly of force, as in Anglo-Saxon England, the recourse to the feud might supplement judgements of the King's court, at least for certain offences and for certain relationships, leading to what Southall called 'the segmentary state'.

The interpretation of the feud in Ancient Israel constituted a paradigmatic case for the analytic priority to be given to the 'synchronic' as distinct from the 'diachronic', at least when the evidence for changes over time was conjectural. Historians often couch their analyses in terms of such changes, while anthropologists only too readily assume continuity. But the analysis of existing societies reveals that in a differentiated structure various types of sanction, burial practice or marriage transaction may exist side by side without any implication of priority, of one being a 'survival' of an earlier stage. In the words Radcliffe-Brown used to describe the studies of his collaborators in the field of African kinship, 'the method adopted here is neither that of history nor pseudo-history but one combining comparison and analysis'.[13] Despite many assumptions to the contrary, the marital assigns of Eurasian societies known in English as bride-price (which is not the same as African bridewealth) exist side by side with those generally known as dotal (dowry); this is not a 'survival', but part of an operating system. That is not to deny the existence of long-term developmental trends; it is only to demand that any such propositions take fully into account the evidence from functioning societies as well as that from the fragmentary reports of earlier communities that appear in written records.

The domain of law in the widest sense of the word (which clearly has links with 'custom', 'tradition' and 'norm') was a major area of achievement in British social anthropology. Law had long played an important part in the development of anthropology because of the interest of the great legal historians of the nineteenth century, and earlier of the Enlightenment, in the precursors of European law, not only in Rome, Greece and Israel but, following the discovery of the relations between Indo-European languages, in India as well. In the post-war period Sir Henry Maine's *Ancient Law* (1861) was included in the reading lists for all degrees in social anthropology in Britain, and formed a critical point of reference for Radcliffe-Brown and his 'school', having had a considerable influence on the work of Evans-Pritchard, Fortes and Gluckman.

The anthropological analysis of law in Africa is primarily associated with the name of Max Gluckman (1911–75). Brought up in South Africa in a Russian-Jewish family of lawyers, Gluckman studied law at the University of Witwatersrand, although he never completed the final stage of the LL B. Meanwhile he had become interested in social anthropology as the result of attending, together with Hilda Beemer (later Kuper), the lectures of Winifred Hoernlé, who had in turn been influenced by Radcliffe-Brown when he was Professor of Social Anthropology at Cape Town in the years between 1920 and 1926. The courses he then gave formed the basis of the development of theoretically inclined social anthropology in South Africa. Rewarded for his sporting as well as his academic attainments, Gluckman left the University of Witwatersrand in 1934 for Exeter College, Oxford, with a

Rhodes scholarship. There he met R. R. Marret and E. E. Evans-Pritchard. His doctoral thesis, based on written material, was entitled 'The realm of the supernatural among the South-eastern Bantu', but he then carried out field research on social change among the contemporary Zulu. His aim was to study the total social situation, so that he deliberately included Whites as part of that totality. In subsequent work he regularly included an analysis of internal conflicts of this and other kinds, in opposition to the more homogenising approach associated with the concept of culture in the hands of Malinowski and others. One reason for this preoccupation was that as a liberal South African his orientation was very different from the metropolitan romanticism of Evans-Pritchard; for him the study of change and conflict was a political necessity, even if others considered it 'applied'. He returned to Oxford from the field in 1938 to join Radcliffe-Brown, Fortes and Evans-Pritchard. But in the following year he left again, being appointed to the Rhodes–Livingstone Institute of Social Studies in British Central Africa and becoming Director in 1942 in succession to Godfrey Wilson. During this time he continued to carry out field research among the Barotse of Zambia, which was the basis of his major monographs on law.

Law, custom and the settlement of disputes was one of the fields that benefited. Gluckman's works on the Lozi of Zambia are not easy to read; few books on law are. At times the extended case-method he employs can become rather tedious, like a collection of fieldnotes. But it was in his analysis of particular cases against a sophisticated knowledge of European law that Gluckman developed his study, showing how similar in certain ways Lozi courts were to our own, but different in others, both similarities and differences needing some kind of explanation. For example, the use of concepts like the 'reasonable man' and equity showed that the Lozi too had multiple sources of law both in the sense of 'judicial decisions' as well as in that of 'rules of right-doing'. Some of the differences were carefully related to aspects of the social structure, as with the nature of the idea of relevance as applied to evidence. Gluckman argued that since relationships in a face-to-face society are multiplex, that is, A is related to B in a large number of ways (as purchaser, as affine, as fellow-villager), any one of these relations may impinge significantly on any other. Hence the judge had to allow people's evidence to roam over a wider range of activities than is the case in societies with a complex division of labour where relations with a shopkeeper, for example, tend to be single-stranded: if I am in a dispute about a purchase I have made, only that limited relation is relevant as far as evidence is concerned.

There are obvious sociological, Durkheimian, aspects of this discussion, as in his treatment of conflict in *Custom and Conflict in Africa* (1955), the theme of which was similar to that of Simmel, although Gluckman claimed he had not read the German sociologist's well-known analysis of conflict when he formulated his thesis. There he stressed the role of conflict as contributing to a more inclusive social integration, 'the peace in the feud', rebellion as reaffirming political values. Thus rituals of rebellion stood opposed to revolution as a way of letting off steam and often involved rituals of reversal of the type in which the choir boy becomes the bishop for the day. Indeed there were some links here with the ritual killing of the king that formed a central theme in Frazer's *The Golden Bough*. To this Evans-Pritchard made a notable contribution in his Frazer lecture, 'The death of the Reth', where he analysed recent research on the Shilluk practice which had formed an important part of the evidence for the original hypothesis.

The work on law relates not only to sociological and anthropological discussions but is also embedded in discussions within the wider field of jurisprudence. His contribution to the comparative study of law was recognised by the fact that his first book on the subject was introduced by Goodhart, Professor of Law at Oxford, and he was subsequently asked to give the distinguished Roscoe Pound lectures at Yale University. Gluckman's work on law gave rise to a series of further studies, especially those by A. L. Epstein, also on Zambia, by Lloyd Fallers on the Busoga of Uganda, by Elizabeth Colson on the Tonga of Zambia, as well as in a broader way the work by Paul Bohannan in *Justice and Judgement among the Tiv* (1957) of Nigeria. These various studies, carried out later in time than Gluckman's, are concerned to a greater extent with the impact of colonial and national law on African societies, and the way legal concepts, legal rationality and moral norms were changing under the impact of political and social conditions. In dealing with topics such as feud, retaliation and negative reciprocity which arose in the examination of dispute cases in acephalous societies, their studies were of much greater scope than earlier 'legal anthropology' as carried out by lawyers interested in comparative law and jurisprudence. For they were undertaken as the result of extensive experience and informed by a deep interest in concepts, in morality, in religion, in the segmental ways by which people relate to others.

Gluckman's influence was considerable well beyond the realm of legal studies; he was a good organiser of research, both in Africa and Israel, a charismatic figure who attracted students and staff to work with him. His abilities as an organiser of research were undoubtedly greater than those of his contemporaries, with the possible exception of Audrey Richards at the East African Institute of Social and Economic Research and of Daryll Forde at the International African Institute. The former arranged for a number of joint surveys, for example, on chiefship, urbanisation and population, while the latter undertook the vast enterprise of the Ethnographic Survey of Africa, as well as editing the journal *Africa*, organising African Abstracts and arranging many conferences and the subsequent publication of the papers. But the Rhodes–Livingstone Institute was a model of co-operative research in which the individuals were also able to follow their own lines of work. In the *Annual Review of Anthropology* (1984), R. P. Werbner begins an article entitled 'The Manchester school in south-central Africa' with the following words:

In the decade after World War II, a major, coordinated project of urban and rural research, perhaps the first of its kind in Africa, was carried out by anthropologists working in what was then British Central Africa ... led by Max Gluckman, the anthropologists broke new ground, empirically and theoretically. Their fresh data were about the observed social practice of specific, recognisable individuals; events were given in detail, with a characteristic richness. The arguments they advanced gave theoretical force to such concepts as ... the social field, situational analysis, perpetual succession, intercalary roles, situational selection, cross-cutting ties, the dominant cleavage, redressive ritual, repetitive and changing social systems, processional form, processual change.[14]

It is certain that Gluckman attracted to him, in Zambia and in Manchester, a body of highly productive scholars who during the 1950s and 1960s published many papers and more than a dozen monographs, in which they made substantial contributions to a number of fields, including the collection of numerical as well as observational material, to the notion of the intercalary role of the village headman, to politics, to kinship as well as to religion and symbolism. Among those who worked with him were John Barnes, Clyde Mitchell, Elizabeth Colson, Victor Turner, Jap Van Velsen, William Watson, Peter Worsley and many others, a remarkable team of productive scholars.

RELIGION

The anthropological study of religion in Africa was heavily indebted to Evans-Pritchard, first, in his book on *Witchcraft, Oracles and Magic among the Azande* (1937) and then in his study of *Nuer Religion* (1956). Evans-Pritchard had written several general essays on the subject of primitive religious thought when he was teaching at Cairo in the early thirties and these had a great influence among his students. His interests were cognitive as well as ethnographic; he was interested in how people understood mystical phenomena, witchcraft, magic, deities. The Azande book was specifically addressed to refuting the notion that such behaviour was 'prelogical' as the philosopher, Levy-Bruhl, had suggested. The later work, *Nuer Religion*, was more theocentric, with lesser agencies being seen as 'refractions of deity'. But the problem of how people understood religious action was always to the fore, as it was in that powerful monograph of his student, Godfrey Lienhardt, entitled *Divinity and Experience: The Religion of the Dinka* (1961).

In the post-war period the analysis of symbolic structure was pursued in Monica Wilson's extensive and thorough accounts of the Nyakyusa of Zambia, which have had less recognition than they deserve. She and her husband, Godfrey Wilson, who wrote on social change, were members of Malinowski's seminars in the 1930s. Much more influential have been Turner's studies of ritual symbolism and the ritual process among the Ndembu, work which has been followed by many anthropologists, particularly in the USA, where he taught after leaving Manchester. In some of the more generalising part of his work, Turner owed a direct debt to van Gennep's classic, *Rites de Passage* (1908) which outlined a progression of such rites through separation, to marginality and finally to aggregation, developing in various contexts the notion of liminality, placing this in a context of societal structure and the idea of *communitas*, and embodied in the in-depth accounts of specific incidents he spoke of as 'social dramas', a narrative form of 'thick description'. But he was also interested in the analysis of the layers of symbolic meaning in a fashion which drew on his earlier studies of literature. Like Turner, Mary Douglas, who had carried out fieldwork among the Lele of Kasai (1963), was also interested in symbolism, especially in implicit meanings and those connected with bodily processes. But her work was more comparative, less ethnographically based than his and she was particularly interested in the analysis of Biblical material. That was a subject of interest to many anthropologists from Frazer onward, including Evans-Pritchard, Fortes, Schapera, Leach and Gluckman. Douglas approached the matter more directly, using the Bible to pose and elucidate theoretical problems to do with classification and taboo, as in her influential study *Purity and Danger: An Analysis of Concepts of Pollution and Taboo* (1966). Subsequently her work took on a European focus, directed at social aspects of the economy, at consumer cultures including the analysis of meals.

Perhaps the most cumulative research in religious anthropology was done in two areas which characteristically were closely tied to the kinship system. The first was ancestor worship, the second witchcraft. Ancestor worship was obviously linked to the presence of genealogies, at least in the more developed examples of this cult. Here the paradigmatic example became that of the Tallensi, the analysis of which drew strength from Fortes' interest not only in large-scale descent groups but in the ties between parent and child. He was especially concerned with the ambivalent nature of the process of succession or replacement in social life, the transmission of conflicts and emotions as well as of 'culture' between the generations. That ambivalence was related to the process of displacement of family bonds and cleavages to the imagined or recreated life of those who were thought to have gone before and beyond, an element that had distinctive psychological and psychoanalytic aspects.

Fortes' interest in the psychology of socialisation had come out in his paper on education among the Tallensi (1938) which was praised for its theory of learning by the American psychologists Miller and Dollard. At the same time he was also concerned with the dual nature of social relationships that ran through the work of Malinowski on the opposed roles of the father and the mother's brother in the matrilineal Trobriands. It will be recalled that Fortes had been introduced to Malinowski by the academic psychoanalyst, J. C. Flügel, and Freud was never far from these discussions, as we see from Malinowski's controversy with Freud's biographer, Ernest Jones, about the nature of the Oedipus complex (1927a) as well as his discussion of *Sex and Repression in Savage Society* (1927b). While other professional social anthropologists flirted with aspects of psychoanalysis at various stages of their career – Evans-Pritchard in the late 1920s, Gluckman in discussing 'catharsis', Leach in his paper on 'Magical hair' (1958) – Fortes' interest went deeper and was more integrated with his work, as we see from lectures he gave later in his career to psychiatric and psychoanalytic audiences, namely, 'Totem and taboo' (to the British Psychoanalytic Society in memory of Ernest Jones, 1973) and 'The first born' (to the Association for Child Psychology and Psychiatry in memory of Emanuel Miller, 1972). In addition there was the work which he carried out with his second wife, Doris Meyer Fortes, herself a psychiatrist, on the evidence of mental disorder among the Tallensi, in particular its emergence among migrant workers as 'migrant madness'. For some years his interest at the theoretical level was subordinated, under the Durkheimian insistence, mediated by Radcliffe-Brown and Evans-Pritchard, on the need to separate social from psychological approaches rather than switching or confounding levels; '*psychological* explanations' of *social* facts were strictly out of order. That was part of Durkheim's effort to establish social facts as *sui generis* and consequently the distinctiveness of sociology, which was not to be reduced to psychology or biology. Indeed even the relevance of such data became questionable. But at the level of practice, Fortes' interest remained; Freud's *Totem und Taboo* (1913) was standard reading for his students, while social psychology was introduced as an option in the Cambridge course (along with linguistics and statistics). Nevertheless there was a tendency for him at this period to interpret ambivalence in terms of structural ties and cleavages; when psychology was involved, it was social psychology.

From some points of view this was understandable. A major problem indicated by the Malinowski–Jones controversy over the Oedipus complex was the need to examine the relation between structural ties and cleavages and interpersonal attitudes. Their discussions pointed the way to the investigation of the linkage between other aspects of intergenerational tension and conflict, apart from those supposedly generated by sexual rivalry, namely, those centring around the transmission of office (for example, what I have called 'the Prince Hal' situation), the transfer of inheritance and the exercise of authority, themes with which my own work was much engaged.

Fortes' work on ancestors looked at their propitiation in the context of the relation between the living and the dead of different generations; but it was also related to the notion of the person, a discussion deriving partly from Marcel Mauss, earlier from Malinowski, and having clear links with both psychology and psychoanalysis. Malinowski had examined aspects of the Trobriand conception of the human being in relation to their ideas of matrilineal descent, to conception in the literal sense and to the question of psycho-physical constitution, blood and semen, flesh and bones. Fortes pursued this line for the Tallensi and the Asante. But his scope was much wider. He became particularly interested in Tallensi notions of destiny (*yin*), which led him to analyse concepts surrounding the make-up of an individual (as distinct from a social person). He was able to approach this subject in a more sophisticated way than others have done partly because of his psychological background but also because of his great command of the language, much greater than that of most anthropologists. That is one of the main problems in anthropological discussion of religious ideas, of symbolism, of cognitive anthropology and complex concepts. Few are sufficiently well grounded in the language of the people they are studying to permit them to analyse such data. As a consequence much of the discussion has to be based upon highly general notions rather than being deeply grounded in cultural activities. But that certainly was not a problem for Fortes.

His work on indigenous 'social psychologies' has been followed up and formalised by one of the most perceptive anthropologists of Africa, a European with some twenty years of residence in West Africa. I refer to Robin Horton's long introduction to the re-issue of Fortes' *Oedipus and Job*. Like Fortes, Horton is deeply versed in West Africa. Like Fortes he has brought to anthropology experience in another field, namely philosophy. His discussions of general issues (always infused with his extensive knowledge of the Kalabari of Nigeria) have had considerable influence, especially his long paper on Western science and African religion. That was a general piece and readily comprehensible. One of the problems of ethno-cognitive anthropology, of understanding how the actors view their own processes of understanding, or of indigenous 'social psychologies', is that the detailed ethnographic description necessary to present the equivalent, say, of the ego and the id, is itself so complex that few investigators or readers have the skills and the persistence to understand what is being said and what is going on.

Fortes contributed to a number of other aspects of the study of religion, stressing early on the political significance of the Great Festivals of the Tallensi in establishing a measure of cohesion and solidarity over the divided groups of Tallis and Namoos, and stressing the role of such celebrations in identity at the group and personal level. His analysis of the role of the cult of the Earth also developed that Durkheimian theme, bringing out the aspects of conflict overcome that was a marked feature of the work of Evans-

Pritchard in *The Nuer* and Gluckman in *Custom and Conflict in Africa* (1955). Gluckman added some Marxist undertones, but the emphasis in all these authors is not on conflict developing out of contradictions that lead to new resolutions, but to tension and conflict as part of continuing social systems, indeed as intrinsic to their unity. A more inclusive view would take into account the contributions of both Georg Simmel and Karl Marx, of revolutionary change as well as of the safety-valve of rebellious threats.

Fortes also turned his attention to themes such as divination, to rituals of succession (close to his kinship interests), and to those well-established anthropological topics, totem and taboo, sacrifice and prayer, to which he added a perspective that was at once psychological and sociological.

The second major topic in the study of religion in the broad sense was that of witchcraft and sorcery, which had been the subject of Evans-Pritchard's volume on the Azande. As I have remarked, he was primarily interested in the cognitive aspects, as well as in presenting the full ethnographic context. However the line of analysis that was developed in the contributions of Wilson (1951), Nadel (1952), Marwick (1965) and many other writers turned around the relationships between witch, victim and accuser. The numerical distribution of accusations were seen as indicating critical tensions in the society. So too in a more explicit way was homicide (Bohannan 1960), for both involved power and gender relations within the family, men mainly being accused of murder, women mainly of witchcraft. Such enquiries raised interesting comparative questions which while rarely capable of a definitive answer did lead to a constructive and cumulative dialogue.

Witchcraft raised the problem of the turnover of cults in Africa. Since these were often directed to specific ills rather than to general well-being, people tended to look for new panaceas when the old did not work. Anti-witchcraft cults, protective shrines of various kinds, spread far and wide, stimulated by the greater mobility of colonial times, although this was by no means a new phenomenon in Africa. The growth and disappearance of cults, some of them of great local importance, meant that African religious practices and beliefs were far from static, providing a window on new cosmological, theological and magical ideas which the advent of Islam and Christianity opened yet further, leading to a proliferation of 'independent' churches throughout the continent.

THE ECONOMY

Contributions to the study of the economy were perhaps less obvious than in other spheres, especially in contrast to the part it has later played in African studies mainly as the result of Marxist studies in France, though much of this was rather schematically formulated in terms of modes of production. Africa even gave birth to a 'lineage mode of production'. Despite the interest in Marxism this approach had little appeal to earlier British scholars of Africa. However, many did pay attention to the economy and their analysis included some acknowledgement of the 'economic base'. That was most explicit in the work of Daryll Forde, who began his academic life as a geographer. Nevertheless, it is significant that Evans-Pritchard, Gluckman and to some extent Fortes, began their accounts of the Nuer, the Lozi and the Tallensi respectively with the economic systems. Evans-Pritchard was studying a pastoral people whose ecology was closely associated with the political and lineage organisation. Among the Lozi, Gluckman attempted to link the intensive floodplain farming with a bilateral kinship organisation that provided individuals with claims to land through the mother as well as through the father. Fortes looked at a version of a more usual type of economy in Africa, that is, hoe farming with shifting cultivation set in a network of local markets, linked to international trade through slavery, cowries and other 'valuables'. The study of pastoral societies was certainly advanced by the work done in Africa but more developments centred around shifting cultivation, beginning with the work of Richards and continued by agricultural specialists, such as Allen and Schlipper. Anthropologists drew attention to the role of the lineage as guardian of the land needed to operate such an economy, as well as refining the associated notions of the tenure of land as a 'hierarchy of rights', to use the phrase of Henry Maine (Gluckman 1945).

On a more detailed specialist level, Audrey Richards, whose background lay in the natural sciences, carried out studies of diet and nutrition in Northern Rhodesia (now Zambia) after having done a comparative survey on *Hunger and Work in a Savage Tribe: A Functional Study of Nutrition among the Southern Bantu* (1932).

In studies of the more complex states of Nigeria, craft specialisation, markets and trade were more to the fore (for example, Nadel 1942). In the post-war period in West Africa M. G. Smith continued this work on the Hausa, Lloyd among the Yoruba, E. N. Goody on Gonja tailors

– as well as editing a more general book on cloth production, *From Craft to Industry* (1982) and on apprenticeship – and above all the economist, Polly Hill, on indigenous economies of the Ghana cocoa industry, of Hausa farming, of butchers and other aspects of the local livelihood. Abner Cohen worked among Hausa kolanut traders in Nigeria (1969), while Hart studied the informal economy of the urban Tallensi in Accra and has produced a challenging general account of the problems of West African development (1982).

Aspects of neo-classical and Marxist economic analysis were employed but since both were based upon European models, there has been a constant problem about applying their terms to indigenous societies and to understanding the process of interaction and articulation – especially the influences from outside, whether capitalist, socialist or mixed – with the local society. Taking the most general level, categories such as the Asiatic or feudal mode of production, modifications such as the tributary mode, like classical models of pre-industrial economies, have proved inadequate, partly because based on inadequate data and working at too high a level of abstraction. Using in part an analysis of Dahomey in West Africa, Polanyi's efforts to draw radical distinctions have proved even less useful, although they have warned us of certain dangers, and were influential for a number of writers on exchange systems in Africa (Bohannan and Dalton 1962). The nature of systems of exchange in non-European society became one of the central themes of anthropological work, as in Douglas' analysis of the Lele economy or in Bohannan's work on the Tiv, partly because it linked up with the exchange of rights and services in a number of other contexts such as marriage and ritual.

Anthropologists have provided intensive data on productive systems, land tenure, markets and other forms of exchange, as well as upon craft activity, modes of tribute and levels of technology. Few of those working in social or economic development realise the immense problems that arise from the virtual absence of the principle of rotary motion or the lever in Africa south of the Sahara, to take but two examples. The earlier absence of the plough and the wheel, the lower levels of water control, of iron technology and of carpentry, the relative lack of 'intensive agriculture' quite apart from the earlier lack of good communications or a system of writing, these are factors that profoundly affect the social and cultural structure of African societies and at the same time place significant brakes on development projects.[15]

There was relatively little work carried out on social change since it was felt that priority should be given to indigenous societies. The main exception was the studies carried out in South Africa where Europeans had been established since the sixteenth century. Enquiries were carried out on the effects of economic changes on African life, especially in Ellen Hellmann's pioneering urban enquiry, *Rooiyard* (1948), about a slum area and in work on migrant communities by Schapera (1947) and Wilson (1964). Migration continued to be a central theme of anthropological research, both in anglophone and franco-phone Africa, but only with independence did serious academic research pay much attention to the changing situation. So the directions laid down by the Rockefeller philanthropies had surprisingly little influence on what research was actually carried out and written up. The foundations were important financially in supporting Malinowski's students but they played little part in determining the outcome of research.

The work of the British school of anthropologists in Africa was presented largely in the form of monographic reports on their intensive field studies which will remain an enduring achievement, especially as it took place in a continent much of which had experienced less than fifty years of colonial rule and just before the major changes that post-war investment and subsequently independence were to bring in the 1960s. As such the ethnographic studies, which were carried out with great dedication (compared with most earlier work), cover a unique period in the history of Africa. But many of these monographs were also sociological analyses of considerable sophistication which raised important issues in the social sciences, some of which were taken up in separate publications and in specific papers. Of general theoretical approaches we have mentioned the work of Nadel, especially *The Foundations of Social Anthropology* (1951), in addition to which there were simpler introductions, such as *Social Anthropology* by Evans-Pritchard (1951), Lienhardt (1964) and Lewis (1976), *Other Cultures* by John Beattie (1964) and the more extensive textbook by Bohannan (1963). Middleton has been energetic in producing collections of papers (with Bohannan and others), a book on Black Africa (1970) and more recently an encyclopaedia of Africa (in preparation).

Specialist fields were initially covered either in the form of essays, or the kind of collection that Daryll Forde edited for the International African Institute, Gluckman from Manchester, or Fortes from Cambridge. But eventually general books emerged such as Evans-Pritchard on 'primitive religion' (1965a) and 'anthropological thought' (1981), on kinship by Fortes (1969) and Barnes (1971), on law by Roberts (1979), on marriage by Mair (1969, 1971), on politics by Schapera (1956) and Mair (1962), on religion by Lewis (1971 and 1986), and on witchcraft by Mair (1969).

I am aware that I have given a selective view of the achievements of British anthropology in Africa. Others would choose different points to bring out. Some would wish to call attention to what was not done; that seems to me of limited interest, given the vast range of possibilities and the advantages gained by a number of research workers concentrating on a limited field of topics. More seriously, I have omitted to mention much of the work of the generation that followed that of Fortes and Evans-Pritchard and which has a claim to be thought of in the same general tradition, the work of Lloyd, Morton-Williams, the Ardeners, of Burnham in Nigeria, of Tait in Ghana, Little and Littlejohn in Sierra Leone, Gibbs in Liberia, of Skinner among the Mossi of Burkina Faso; also, in East Africa of Holy in the Sudan; Beattie, Fallers, G. Harris, James, Mair, Cunnison, Abrahams, Werbner, La Fontaine, Howell, and of many others in Southern Africa. My list of omissions still contains many omissions. But it is sufficient to make the point that we lived at a moment in time when the tradition created by the students of Malinowski (and to a lesser extent Radcliffe-Brown) established certain parameters for research, presented fieldwork in a theoretical frame, trained students in this framework and assisted them in turn to undertake fieldwork and eventually to get teaching positions. It was truly an expansive moment, both qualitatively and quantitatively. Numbers expanded; so did theoretical contributions, which became increasingly wider in scope.

CHAPTER 8

Personal contributions

The previous chapter attempted to spell out some of the achievements of anthropological studies based in Britain and carried out in Africa, especially as they affected neighbouring fields.[1] I focussed in particular on West Africa where I myself had worked and I now present an even more egocentric account of my own work, beginning with field research in West Africa. I do this partly for historical reasons (since I worked closely with those on whom this study is focussed) and partly to bring out the interplay between intensive fieldwork and existing and emergent interests of a wider kind. That interplay between 'theory' and 'practice', the general and the particular, seems to me one of the marks of this tradition of social anthropology, though one that can be pursued in a variety of ways.

I had originally gone up to Cambridge on a scholarship to read for a degree in English literature and became interested, among other things, in aspects of the sociology of literature. After my first year at the university war broke out and for the next six-and-a-half years I was in the army. In the Middle East I was brought face to face not only with a wide variety of humanity, Greeks, Turks, Egyptians, Palestinians, Jews, but with the remnants of ancient civilisations. I already had some interest in archaeology because of a mathematics master at school who had collected flints in East Anglia, partly because I had lived in St Albans and had watched some of the discoveries of the Roman town at Verulamium under Mortimer Wheeler. It was spending time in Cyprus, Egypt and Palestine that widened my interest to the Middle East. In those countries, archaeology had an ethnological side to it. The clay model of a plough from the fourth century BCE in the museum at Nicosia was substantially the same as that used in the fields outside the town. The wells for drawing water went back to Biblical times. The combination of this continuity with the obvious disconti- nuities was intriguing. Directly I had an opportunity I began to read works such as Childe's *What Happened in History?* That opportunity came sooner than I anticipated, since I was captured by the German army at Tobruk in June 1942 and spent the next two-and-a-half years in and out of prison camps in Italy and Germany. Especially in Germany, where the camp had built up an excellent library of gifts from Britain, I was able to read fairly widely, following up various interests. But the situation in which I found myself also turned my attention to the understanding of the variety of human behaviour. While I had an earlier interest in the social sides of literature and history, it was living in the confined space of a barrack-room with a number of persons over a long period when one had to create one's own life within the framework of a prison that so fascinated me and others. A social system was constructed within the camp, under the constraints of our Italian and German captors. While from one point of view they completely controlled the larger structure of our lives, at another we built up our sets of relationships and interactions that were largely independent, or anyhow oblivious, of them. Those included theatre, music, writing, reading, exercise, bridge and just talking. In prison camp one was inevitably thrown together with men of various nationalities, origins and personalities. Outside, on the two occasions when I was able to escape, I lived at close quarters with Italian peasants in the Abruzzi and in Rome with a variety of people of all kinds. These experiences made me think about social relations in a more sociological and psychological frame, and on my release I was particularly attracted to the work being done at the Tavistock Institute of Human Relations in London, which was concerned with returning prisoners of war. Indeed it was reading about the attempt to combine social science with psychoanalysis in an article in *Pilot Papers* by Edward Shils on American sociology that led me to write to him out of the blue and receive a long and valued letter in return, which helped me give up the job in adult education I had taken (like a number of others of my generation such as E. P. Thompson, Raymond Williams, Thomas Hodgkin and many others in Africa) and continue with further study.

When I returned to Cambridge in 1946 I completed a degree in English, then switched to the Faculty of Archaeology and Anthropology. After some years of inactivity in a prison camp I was unwilling to think of spending more time in the rarefied atmosphere of academia, so having completed a diploma, I took a job in adult education of a more basic kind. Even when I decided to return to the social sciences, it was not with the aim of spending my life working on 'other cultures'.

So I went to West Africa not primarily because I wanted to become an Africanist but because I had become interested in the comparative study of human society more generally and intended to return with a perspective that would enable me better to look at European culture, possibly at those Italian peasants who had fascinated me when I was hiding among them, more likely the inhabitants of Britain itself with whose future I was deeply engaged in the aftermath of war. It is difficult to reconstruct the situation that faced many of my generation at that period. If I may put the matter a little more dramatically than an Englishman should, I saw post-war Britain under the Labour government of 1945 as being the natural outcome of many lives like my own. We had grown up between the two wars, with an interval of only twenty-one years from one terrifying destruction to the next, and lived our adolescence under the shadow of continental Fascism with its devastating oppression and annihilation of man by man, in practice and in ideology. This period began with the murderous Japanese attacks on China, the archaic colonial conquests of Italy, the devastating civil war in Spain and the inexorable expansion of Germany, against the background of the widespread suppression and maltreatment that was going on in those countries. That period was followed by some six-and-a-half years of life under arms, during which time all one could look forward to was post-war reconstruction, through the national government and through the United Nations.

That reconstruction obviously involved the dissolution of earlier empires, the whole process of decolonisation that began with India in 1947 and that was envisaged, at least under Labour rule and to some extent by Conservative politicians as well, as gradually extending to the rest of the colonial territories. In a sense the deconstruction of the empire was part and parcel of the reconstruction of Britain. Although we were not fully aware of the consequences, it was a heady prospect, indeed heady in actuality too, for the major part of the process was complete within some ten years, by 1960, the Year of Africa. The Gold Coast where I chose to work led the way and became the independent nation of Ghana already in 1957 under the premiership of Kwame Nkrumah. It was this general background set against five years' residence in West Africa that led me to write about matters that touched on political theory and development.[2] The anthropologists who had taught me often tried to avoid administrators and problems of development. That seemed a churlish way of treating the new Africa that was coming into being so rapidly, which offered so much in prospect and in which our collaborators and ourselves were so closely involved.

That new Africa also demanded an account of its own past and present. Again, earlier anthropologists had often steered away from historical considerations partly because of some of the rash speculations of their predecessors, partly because of an alternative methodological approach associated with fieldwork, and partly for the practical reason that archives and records were officially closed for a fifty-year period. The situation had changed in many respects. Particularly in France where there were fewer inhibitions of this kind (partly because of the *Annales* school, more sympathetic to the social sciences than the Anglo-American tradition of history, partly because of the more explicit influence of Marxist thinking), many anthropologists began to explore the historical dimension. Historians too became interested in anthropological research and approaches. The 'structural–functional' paradigm was ready to be loosened in a number of ways.

My own choice of Ghana was largely personal. At Cambridge I had become friendly with Joe Reindorf, later Ghana's Attorney General, who started a PhD in history, finished a law degree at the same time and then returned to Ghana to work with the firm of a relative, Victor Owusu, closely identified with the Asante opposition to the Convention People's Party, although Joe's own sympathies lay elsewhere.[3] Having a family, I did not want to work too far from Europe; in those days of boat travel, distance mattered. For this reason when I followed my various colleagues to Oxford, after the spell in adult education, I was asked to talk to Meyer Fortes, my first encounter with whom I have described elsewhere.

In his review of social anthropology in West Africa, Keith Hart speaks of the structural–functional Cambridge school of Fortes and Goody.[4] From the standpoint of ethnography and fieldwork, such a characterisation is no doubt correct. But as he goes on to point out the intellectual preoccupations in my research had other roots (as indeed did Fortes'). Few students in the 1930s could avoid having to make some kind of resolution of their interests in two major figures, Marx and Freud. My contact with Marxism had by then been longstanding, but there were other influences. Through social anthropology I encountered Durkheim, through Harvard students of social relations I encountered Weber, as well as Parsons with whom I later worked for a year when he was at Cambridge. But equally important to me in the early phases was Freud, as well as the earlier interests I had developed in studying literature and history.

In literature I was strongly influenced by the 'New Criticism' associated with F. R. Leavis and other contributers to *Scrutiny*, not only regarding the creative arts themselves but also their whole grounding in the moral order of society. One further current that affected many of my generation was the logico-positivism of the Vienna circle and the subsequent transformations that appeared in the Anglo-Saxon world. Of particular importance for me was the work of the contributors to the *International Encyclopaedia of Unified Science* edited by O. Neurath, R. Carnap and C. W. Morris from Chicago (1938–), which included works by E. Nagel, L. Hogben and many others. Two other factors of a different kind played a part in defining my fields of interest. Over six years of war had left their mark: life in a prison camp led to wondering how people got on or came into conflict with one another; life in the army encouraged an interest in the military side of 'other cultures'. As I have elsewhere remarked, Evans-Pritchard's clinical analysis of feud in his lectures in Cambridge in 1947–8 helped to place those years of experience in a wider context, and the threat of nuclear warfare continued to keep 'conflict studies' in the centre of one's vision. So that if Marx drew attention to modes of production, the 'New Criticism' and logical positivism to modes of communication and of thought, so too the army led me to consider modes of destruction and coercion.

Largely at Fortes' prompting I went to work in a community in northern Ghana, not far from the Tallensi. These were the LoDagaa (or Lobi as the British then called them or the Dagari or Dagara as they were known to the French and now generally to themselves), a study of whom had been listed as a priority in Raymond Firth's report to the Colonial Social Science Research Council.[5] The LoDagaa inhabited an area that lay astride the Black Volta which served as the boundary between the anglophone colony of the Gold Coast (later Ghana) and the francophone colony of Haute Volta (later Burkina Faso). As a result I became familiar with the early French writing about the region as well as with French anthropology more generally. That encounter enabled me to indulge my enduring attraction to France and at the same time to modify, in the course of time and in marginal ways, some of my Anglo-Saxon attitudes.

Fortes directed my attention to the LoDagaa partly because he had carried out research among the 'patrilineal' Tallensi and the 'matrilineal' Asante and was interested in those societies of which the Yakö of Nigeria, studied by Daryll Forde, were the paradigmatic case, in which named unilineal descent groups of a patrilineal and a matrilineal kind existed side by side – that is to say, everyone was a member of one of each set. I became involved in the topic of descent of necessity, for it was the subject of lively discussion among graduate students. I also took up other topics on which people were working at the time, such as the developmental cycle of domestic groups (1958), the maintenance of social control in acephalous communities (1957), the role of the mother's brother (1959) and the general theme of incest itself (1956). These topics drew me into comparative analyses which I later pursued with Esther Goody using material on the societies of northern Ghana for the purposes of controlled comparison (J. Goody and E. N. Goody 1966, 1967). Another general question that struck me was the way in which communities and individuals defined themselves not only in opposition to one another, but often in relation to particular activities, so that among the LoDagaa one's identification was with those to the east in one context and with those in the west in another. That is to say, in the Gold Coast at that time there were no 'real' Lobi and Dagari, just a series of communities who defined their similarities and differences by means of these roughly directional terms, Lo (bi, ri) = west, matrilineal, and Dagaa (ri, ra, ti, ba) = east, patrilineal (to simplify a more complex situation).

I was interested both in the subtle differences in the importance of descent groups among and for the LoDagaa as well as in their systems of kinship, family and marriage at the domestic level. Indeed I attempted, in the spirit of the times, to look at the total range of the community's activities and when I came back to Britain after one year, between field trips, I wrote a general account of the first settlement I studied (Birifu) for the B Litt at Oxford which was later published as *The Social Organization of the LoWiili* (1956b). I returned to live in another area of the LoDagaa country where more emphasis was given to the matrilineal clans and both groups were property-holding, and it was in this sense fully 'double descent' along the lines of the Yakö of Nigeria studied by Daryll Forde. That is to say, movable property (cattle, money, grain) was visualised as belonging to the matrilineal clan (or *belo*, species) and was inherited between, first, maternal siblings and then by sister's sons, that is, between uterine kinsfolk, whereas immovables (houses and land) were transmitted within the patrilineal clans, between, first, maternal siblings and then to sons, that is, between agnates. My major interest in this situation lay in the problematic of Malinowski and Fortes relating to the different nature of interpersonal ties in patrilineal and matrilineal societies, depending upon the systems of authority, transmission and organisation, and the way these were related to ritual activities. That is, my interest lay in an attempt to link the social and personality systems in Parsons' terms or the approaches of Marx and Freud in more general ones.

My doctoral thesis, a much revised version of which was published as *Death, Property and the Ancestors* (1962), was initially intended to be an analysis of the religion of the LoDagaa. Having already written a general account of the social organisation, on my second return I completed a historical and ethnographic outline of the region in order to supply a context for my detailed studies.[6] The concentration on religion was partly because Fortes had written two major studies on the political and kinship systems of the Tallensi, which were sufficiently like those of the LoDagaa to make me direct my attention elsewhere. Like Evans-Pritchard he had left the monograph on religion to the end, as was the usual progression in analysing field material at the time, *The Work of the Gods* following on from *We the Tikopia*. I chose to take another direction. My material on the religious life was rich, partly because I had attended so many funerals and sacrifices, partly because of an earlier interest in myth and ritual, partly because I knew people who would discuss these matters and partly because the Bagre ceremony was being performed in the valley below my compound during the first year I was there. Not only could I attend the public aspects of this initiation but I had the good fortune to meet a man who had become marginal to the society itself; he offered to recite his version of the Bagre, a long, secret, recitation reserved for the initiates, so that I could write it down and he then took the trouble to explain many of the details. At the time it was unheard of to recite before someone who was not a member of the association.

In trying to offer a general analysis of LoDagaa religion, I was obviously concerned with those aspects of social organisation linked to relatively permanent roles and groupings (as with ancestors and descent groups, earth shrines and parishes). But I was also interested in the turn-over displayed by cults such as medicine shrines which were adopted from one group to the next over a wide range of territory. The local Kpengkpembie shrine had been very successful around Kumasi, some 400 miles away. Such cults were marked by a rise and fall, by birth and obsolescence, by the recognition of the god who failed as well as by the innovative capacities of those seeking new and different solutions to old and persistent problems. A quest was involved, one that was intellectual, problem-solving as well as emotional and theological. The structure of explicit meaning to the actors had first to be elucidated, including the overt symbolism of ritual acts.

Although the aim of the thesis was to present a study of the whole domain of ritual and religion, I did not get further than the analysis of funerals (and of the ancestors), the topic on which I had begun as representing the point of transition and of transmission between this world and the next. On this one aspect there seemed already too much to say, especially if one tried to take into account what previous writers in a variety of disciplines had contributed. In any case the interest it held for me ranged outside the sphere of religion narrowly conceived.

For, as I have remarked, among the problems with which I was concerned in discussing LoDagaa funerals were those which I saw as relating to the work of both Marx and Freud. There were other influences. The French school including the work of van Gennep and especially Hertz was most relevant and some have seen this trend as dominant. Others have taken the analysis of the role of kin groups based on matrilineal and patrilineal descent to lie at the core. Typical of this first view is the comment of Jacques Lombard: 'De même, J. Goodie [*sic*] reprenant certains thèmes de R.-B., a expliqué la fonction de rites mortuaires en les liant à la structure sociale et plus particulièrement au statut du défunt et de ses proches.'[7] He contrasts the work of Middleton, Turner and myself with that of Douglas, Lienhardt and Beidelman who wanted to 'désociologise le religieux' following the studies of Evans-Pritchard and the book edited by Forde entitled *African Worlds* (1954).

The contrast is too stark. It seemed hardly possible to deal with a rite of passage without building upon van Gennep's pioneering work, nor did it seem useful to discuss 'symbolic' meanings without recourse to the classic but equally simple techniques developed by Radcliffe-Brown and Srinivas, that is, without being concerned with 'action'. While I dealt with the way that social groups, including descent groups, emerged and participated so clearly in the funerals, I was also specifically interested in: (a) differences in funeral practices that were not connected with 'sociological' variables; (b) meaning to the actors of the acts, verbal and gestural, in which they were engaged, as a counterpoise to the interpretations of the anthropologist. Indeed my hesitation to use a variety of hardy anthropological concepts, such as ritual, religion, sacred and profane, except as vague signposts, was precisely because they were not based upon nor did they reflect indigenous categories, which were more complex and more shaded than they allowed.

But, above all, the central thrust lay in another direction, more closely linked to much of my later work. In looking at these aspects of religious action and belief I reviewed earlier studies of ancestor worship, of funerals and in particular patterns of grief and mourning. How was the behaviour of individuals in these situations linked to the wider contexts of their lives? The question raised issues considered by Malinowski and Fortes when they examined matrilineal systems with the aim of specifying the typical patterns of tension and cathexis, of ties and cleavages, in interpersonal relations in these societies; for example, it was a topic pursued by Malinowski when he argued that the 'Oedipus complex' was not universal but was linked to a particular range of social institutions.

The central theme of the enterprise was parallel to one that developed in the study of witchcraft, in particular of witchcraft accusations. Evans-Pritchard's book, *Witchcraft, Oracles and Magic among the Azande* (1937), had attempted to map out the logic of African witchcraft in opposition to the view of Levy-Bruhl that 'the primitive mind' was illogical or alogical, unable to perceive contradiction, a theme which I pursued in connection with a very different line of research. What Evans-Pritchard did not do was look at witchcraft in terms of the relationships of accuser, witch and victim, which, starting with the work of Nadel, came to be an important topic in the first two post-war decades, in Europe as well as Africa, as the work of Favret and others has shown. Gluckman extended the analysis to the realm of gossip and my own work on ancestor worship raised problems of a similar kind.[8] Who were the ancestors seen as most likely to demand sacrifices from the living and were these relationships linked to the control they had exercised in life and to the benefits received by the supplicants? The tensions that arose between those who gave and those who received (the gift relationship) were in turn connected with the incidence of grief, compounded with possible guilt about a deceased parent for whom one may not have done enough or had left on his or her own in old age. That connection was often made at the less explicit levels of the mind in which the general link with the work of Freud is obvious. I tried to elaborate and differentiate the relevant kinds of tension that marked relations between the generations. It was not simply a question of 'splitting the Oedipus complex' (between roles) as Malinowski had argued for the matrilineal Trobriands where mother's brother counterpoised father, but of splitting up the Oedipus complex, the intergenerational relationship of conflict, into its analytic components, some of which were concerned with sexual jealousy, others with conflicts arising in the process of socialisation and others again with those exercising authority more generally. This is where Marx was relevant. For an important element in pre-industrial societies of this kind was the tension arising out of inheritance, the tension between the holder of property and the heirs. My field data came from the two adjacent communities I have mentioned, in one of which all male property was transmitted between fathers and sons, whereas in the other immovables (land and houses) passed in that way and movables between a man and his sister's sons (in both cases after a full sibling – by the same father and mother – in the same farming group). In the second case, which was that of a fully fledged double-descent system, these tensions were particularly evident; they were quite explicit and the splitting was of a formal character. My enquiry aimed at examining differences in the funeral and ancestral ceremonies of the two adjacent communities and at trying to explain some at least of these by reference to the differences in the transmission of property. Not all differences were so explained – I had no monocausal answer. Some I considered to be the result of intellectual exploration, yet others perhaps the result of cultural drift. But certain central differences I did see as related to social relationships and these I discussed in a chapter entitled 'The merry bells: intergenerational transmission and its conflicts', which was the prelude to a general analysis of property and inheritance, before I engaged upon an enquiry into the institutions of the LoDagaa themselves. Those fifty pages are for me among the most critical.[9] Beginning with Freud and Fromm, I went on to refer to Engels' discussion of production and reproduction in *The Origins Of the Family* (1884). I was attempting here, and later in *Production and Reproduction* (1977b), to see kinship and the economy as distinct but related and to do so at a more formal analytical level than those who had treated the topics separately. One key lay in the area of the intergenerational transmission of goods, including the instruments of livelihood, especially in the basic means of production at the domestic level in pre-capitalist (or non-industrial) societies, as well as in the authority relations associated with their management.

By attempting to deconstruct intergenerational relations in this way, tensions based on sexual rights and domestic authority could be given separate consideration from those based on different forms of property rights, and these in turn were linked to the processes of production and reproduction. In addition I needed to distinguish the transmission of office (succession) from property (inheritance) since these situations might well diverge. It was the latter that gave rise to the kinds of tension brought out in the speech of Henry IV to his son, Prince Hal (the future Henry V), when the latter finds the king sleeping in his room and, thinking him dead, picks up the crown. The waking king reprimands his son:

> Thy wish was father, Harry, to that thought.
> I stay too long by thee, I weary thee.
> Dost thou hunger for mine empty chair
> That thou wilt needs invest thee with my honours
> Before thy hour be ripe? . . .
> Thou hast stol'n that which, after some few hours,
> Were thine without offence; . . .
> Thy life did manifest thou lov'dst me not,
> And thou wilt have me die assur'd of it . . .
> Then get thee gone, and dig my grave thyself;
> And bid the merry bells ring to thine ear
> That thou art crowned, not that I am dead.
>
> (*Henry IV, Part 2*, Act 4 Scene 2)

The notion of the 'merry bells' was intrinsic to what I called for short 'the Prince Hal complex', which emerges in anticipatory acts of wish-fulfilment as well as in the mixed reactions to death itself, inducing feelings of guilt and appeasement. Putting together these relationships, which featured conflict as well as co-operation, I presented a schematic table (see table 1).

Problems of succession to high office played a minimal part in LoDagaa life, for there was little or nothing that fell into that category. The last row of the table referred instead to enquiries among the Gonja of northern Ghana where I had been working with Esther Goody and where I was especially interested in one particular aspect of the political system. Instead of direct intergenerational succession, such as we find among contemporary monarchies in the West, each vacancy entailed a lateral shift of power between different segments of the ruling estate. While this rotational movement was sometimes phrased in terms of fraternal succession, the 'brothers' were very distant 'relatives', the kinship term referring to the members of other segments of the ruling group. The important rule was that, in an expression from Mampong in Asante, 'the elephant never sleeps in the same place twice'. No segment should hold office for longer than the reign of one incumbent.[10]

Table 1   *The transfer of rights between roles*

Type of exclusive right	Authorised transfer (prescribed, *propter mortem*)	Role relationships	Unauthorised transfer	Role relationships
Property	Inheritance	Holder-heir	Theft	Holder-thief
Sexual	Levirate, etc.	Husband-levir, etc.	Adultery, incest abduction, etc.	Cuckold-adulterer, etc.
Roles and offices	Succession	Incumbent-successor	Usurpation	Ruler-rebel

Rotational and next-of-kin systems resulted in different lines of tension and alliance. If Prince Hal was not the heir to his father, he had more to gain from keeping him on the throne than from his disappearance. The contrast lay not only in the implications or consequences of rotational as against direct succession, but in the possible predisposing factors ('causal' factors) which pertained to the systems of political power. In rotational systems, power is distributed, for instance, among the members of a mass dynasty each of whom retains an interest in the holding (or holders) of high office. The limiting of the eligibles to high office to close rather than distant kin obviously implies a narrow rather than a mass dynasty. The different ways in which power is distributed may relate, among other things, to the control of the means of destruction (or the means of coercion, as Ernest Gellner has suggested), on which most early states and many modern ones are ultimately based. In West Africa a narrow dynasty tended to arise where the means of coercion were controlled by a professional group, as often occurred when firearms reached the simpler societies, partly because of the technical skills and investment required, since in Africa such weapons had to be imported; whereas a mass dynasty tended to be associated with the equality of status and opportunity associated with a ruling group of armed horsemen. The ruling estate in Gonja constituted such a mass dynasty comprising roughly 20 per cent of the population; power was rotated between the owners of the means of coercion, that is, between the various chiefs with their horses and armed followers.

Interest in the nature of the ownership of the means of destruction ran parallel to that in the nature and the ownership of the means of production and the way that this affected and was affected by the intergenerational distribution of resources. At the political level many anthropologists wrote of feudal and tributary systems in Africa as if they were similar to Europe or Asia.[11] The comparison seemed to me weak not so much because of the distribution of power as such but because of the differences in productive systems (including craft production) within which power was exercised. The major states of Eurasia were characterised by intensive cultivation by means of an 'advanced' agriculture typified by the use of the plough or irrigation, while Africa (and other areas such as New Guinea) was marked by a more extensive hoe cultivation, usually involving shifting, slash-and-burn (swidden) farming. The extensive system of agriculture did not prevent the rise of the state in Africa, but that state had usually to be based on taxes on trade (or exports) and on raiding neighbours for slaves rather than on the internal accumulation of surplus through primary agricultural production, since any such surplus was usually limited in size, in transportability and in exchange potential. The existence of booty production and taxes on trade obviously affected the external relations between peoples, giving rise to the characteristic distribution of states separated by bands of 'acephalous' ('tribal') peoples. Internally too that situation affected the nature of hierarchy, in that under extensive systems the control of land as a factor of production gave no overwhelming advantage to the rulers. All kin groups had to have available a pool of land where members could switch production after a certain number of years, a system that gives great importance to the lineage or comparable unit and severely limits the man–land ratio. For access to land you went to your kinsfolk (or to the 'bush'), not to the rulers.

The differential transmission of resources was also affected. Under a more 'advanced' agriculture land was a scarce good and its control differently distributed within the hierarchy and between particular families. In such a situation different strata would have their own strategies for passing down property and managing the estate, partly in order to preserve their hierarchical position. Indeed different families would have their own strategies of marriage, management and heirship. In *Production and Reproduction* (1977), I tried to sketch out some of the general implications of this difference for kinship relations, for example, in encouraging in-marriage rather than out-marriage. If there are few resources to protect, then the marriage of chiefs to commoners may be a sound political strategy, extending the cross-cutting ties that ensue from marriage between status groups. Such marriages frequently took place in Gonja, where the political benefits were overtly recognised.

It was this interest that led me to ask why, for example, one found formal adoption in Eurasia but not in Africa, although fostering was very common in parts of that continent, as Esther Goody discusses in her work on Gonja and West Africa generally (1973 and 1982a). One function of the widespread adoption that existed earlier in Eurasia was to provide an heir for the heirless, and often an individual to continue the ancestral cult after death. These considerations became relevant when the transmission of property, especially the property in land that differentiated positions in the hierarchy, became of importance. Similar considerations applied to the distribution of monogamy and polygyny as well as of other institutions such as filiacentric unions (the incoming son-in-law), for one aspect of all these practices was their role as mechanisms of heirship and continuity, of transmitting relatively scarce resources between generations, as well as of organising the management of those resources. While none of these features (or indeed any features of human society) are monolithically tied to any other variable, they do constitute a cluster of features which I called the 'women's property complex'. Under such hierarchical systems efforts were made to maintain the position of daughters as well as of sons, especially by means of endowment and/or inheritance. Your daughter could not marry just anyone. She was entitled to property in order to ensure her marriage to someone of the right strata; if she was entitled to property, she had to make a good match, not marry any commoner as in Gonja. Such modes of transmission were significantly linked to advanced forms of agriculture under which dowry as distinct from bridewealth prevailed, for it was then that the maintenance of the position of daughters became an issue.

This distinction was discussed in a volume of Cambridge Papers, *Bridewealth and Dowry* (1973), written with S. J. Tambiah. This work entailed a very broad comparison between Africa and the major societies of Asia and Europe. My interest in European kinship had been partly fuelled by the examination of inheritance systems developed in my thesis. But I was also struck by the fact that in Western Europe, unlike Rome, India and China (but like Islam and Judaism), adoption was not practised after the fifth century CE until the twentieth century, or the mid-nineteenth century in parts of the United States. It was this situation that constituted one of the starting points for *The Development of Family and Marriage in Europe* (1983a). The absence of adoption and of certain other mechanisms of heirship in Europe seemed related to the fact that it was the church that effectively established itself as the heir when family continuity failed (and claimed a substantial share even in other situations). One priestly writer of fifth-century France described the adopted as 'children of perjury'. They cheated God of the goods which He had first given to mankind and which should be returned to Him at death through his church. Some allowance was made for the children of one's own 'blood' but others were improper recipients of the goods rightly belonging to the church and which should be used for God's purposes. So that Christian doctrine and the demands of an ecclesia were consistent with the re-alignment of strategies of heirship at the familial level, and by this and other means the church rapidly became owner of a third of the available farming land of Europe. I argued that this situation radically affected the political economy, since the church became so powerful a landowner that its acquisitions of land had to be limited by the state, but it also affected the kinship system since the church assumed powers over the rites of passage and defined whom one could or could not marry, thus threatening the role of kin groups.

One of my later books, entitled *The Oriental, the Ancient and the Primitive* (1990), pursues this analysis among the major states of Asia, including the ancient and modern Near East. While one can differentiate Christian Europe from the rest of Eurasia on the basis of what the church took and how it did so, certain significant features of the kinship systems in the major states of the Old World are sufficiently similar to one another in a structural sense to cast serious doubt not only upon the way that many anthropologists and sociologists have treated this aspect of 'the uniqueness of the West', but also upon the way that this same theme has been elaborated by numerous European historians of the family (and especially by English ones). This difference with regard to the influence of an established ecclesia with monastic institutions is less clear under Buddhism, which may be why Japan, Tibet and Sri Lanka share certain structural resemblances. It is true that the marriage age for both men and women was later in Europe, that living-in life-cycle servants were more common, but these features of domestic life in the West do not seem sufficient to account in a significant way for any predisposition it had towards the development of capitalism, or modernisation, as has sometimes been suggested or assumed. Indeed as we look at the rapid development of industrial capitalism in East Asia (and elsewhere in Asia) towards the end of the twentieth century, and at the increasing contrast with Africa, the uniqueness of the West seems less significant than the uniqueness of Eurasia. To this 'uniqueness' Asia has contributed a great deal and has never been the stagnant oriental society (though all societies have been this at particular periods) of which European writers have written.

In this book I tried to modify the notion that an unbridgeable gulf exists between the kinship systems of pre-modern Europe and Asia. As I have remarked, this has been a constant theme of European historians. But anthropologists also have been only too ready to compare Chinese and South Indian 'kinship systems' with those of the Australian aborigines, or have singled out features in Ancient Egypt and Arabia to compare with Africa. Such comparisons take a highly restricted view of what constitutes a 'system' of kinship and marriage, selecting a limited number of features to define elementary or complex systems. My thrust has been to look at the entire domestic domain, especially in relation to the domestic economy, and to argue that neither Oriental nor Ancient systems were 'primitive' in this sense but resembled the pre-industrial societies of Europe in significant respects.

This work on kinship inevitably raised matters that touch upon demography and it has often been historical demographers, such as the members of the Cambridge Group, who in recent years have discussed the crucial issues about comparative family structures. Demographic themes have played a consistent part in West African ethnography; intensive census data had to be collected in any examination of the cycle of domestic groups discussed by Fortes (J. Goody 1958) but both he and others such as Oppong made more systematic attempts to integrate their findings with wider demographic concerns. I myself tried to seek a way of assessing the number of individuals that, under different demographic conditions, would be left without male or female heirs, a question that was of direct importance in the resort to certain strategies of heirship. There was also the possibility that the different kinship regimes of Africa and Eurasia might have varying effects on the number and especially the sex of children in a family. N. Addo and I collected a large sample of completed families in Ghana and found no evidence of any discrimination in favour of one sex, but rather a strategy of maximum numbers (Goody and Addo 1977). This evidence was compared with other large samples of sibling groups where these were available but we found less difference than anticipated (Goody, Duly, Beeson and Harrison 1981a and b). However the results were consistent with the fact that in Africa, as distinct from Asia, there was no evidence of any discrimination by sex in, for example, the survival of children. Other enquiries showed that people went as far to hospital for a daughter as they did for a son, and it was generally recognised that in a bridewealth system any domestic group needed equal numbers of both sexes to get the best results from marriage transactions.

I began this account by explaining that I was led to work on the ritual and religion of the LoDagaa partly because of my involvement with the Bagre association during whose rites a long 'myth' is recited. This recitation became a very important strand of my research from that day to this. I had long been interested in myth and other genres, both in oral and written cultures, mainly because of reading medieval literature in English, to which I was directed partly by the interpretative notes to T. S. Eliot's *Waste Land*. In prisoner-of-war camp in Germany I had been fortunate to find a copy of Frazer's *The Golden Bough* in the library as well as E. K. Chambers' study of *The Medieval Stage* and other similar works much influenced by anthropology. One of the first series of lectures I delivered in Cambridge in the early fifties was on the subject of myth, before it had become so fashionable a topic with the publication of Lévi-Strauss' major works. As the result of these interests I was never inclined simply to treat myths and legends in the Malinowskian fashion as 'charters' of social situations, as many of his pupils tended to do.[12] Just as in my ethnological work in the region I saw an element of 'history' in legend and genealogy, so too I saw an intellectual quest in myth, with an important level of meaning located in the actor domain rather than purely in the deep structure posited by those who tended to see the surface meaning as 'absurd' and fantastic. I wanted to understand the explicit as well as the implicit meaning to the actors and hence I was interested in the words as words, in the text as text, or rather in the utterance as utterance.

The advent of the transistorised tape-recorder made this possible to a different extent than ever before. Of course, electronic recording had previously been available and was used in ethnographic research, mainly for recording music and song. That was the case in the important work of Milman Parry and A. B. Lord in Yugoslavia in the 1930s, when Parry set out to study some of the characteristic features of 'oral' epic in order to determine the status of that great interstitial figure, Homer, regarding literary or oral composition. Lord later published a book called *The Singer of Tales* (1960), which has rightly been the source of much subsequent inspiration, research and debate.

But Parry and Lord were working with café singers in Europe, with secular song in a region where electricity was available, and in fact a culture where the use of writing was widespread and where serious religious action had been taken over by the written register. What was left to the oral channel was fragmentary and in any case heavily influenced by the presence of writing. It was a very different story in field situations where the recitals were ritual, often secret, and made only in formal conditions, and where the possibilities for mechanical recording were minimal. The change in technology had important effects on the study of oral discourse in the simpler societies, probably as important as many broad 'theoretical' shifts, especially in the sphere of pragmatics. Its influence has been of a cumulative kind. For the first time this instrument has enabled anthropologists to record long recitations like the Bagre *in situ*, in the actual conditions of performance – in other words, to create a reasonably accurate text from a ritual utterance, one that can be checked back against the tape. It has also enabled them to make repeated recordings over time and so to examine questions of continuity and change in these standard oral forms. In earlier times only one version was usually available, and even that was often a summary of a recitation written down from an 'informant's' recollection of the original performance. Not only did the summary concentrate on the retellable, narrative elements but the impression was left that there existed a single authorised version. So any differences tended to be attributed to the mistakes of observers, or alternatively to structural factors. The new technology made it possible to examine the elements of individual intellectual exploration, or creative innovation, as Barth has done for the Ok of New Guinea (1987) using comparative evidence, or as I have begun to do for the Bagre – more programmatically perhaps than in actuality. Of course such explorations occur within a set of constraints, but which of those will be relevant in any specific case is difficult or impossible to predict.

The first version (published as *The Myth of the Bagre*, 1972) I wrote down from dictation; it took a full ten days. Since then I have worked with my friend, S. W. D. K. Gandah, with whose help we have recorded, transcribed, translated and annotated another four versions of the Black Bagre and ten of the White, a long and arduous programme of work. One of those versions was published as *Une Récitation du Bagre* in 1981 with French and English translations. Having

originally thought the recitation highly standardised, we were surprised
to find the range of variation. Together with Colin Duly, an attempt
was made to analyse this range of variation in the White Bagre (the
most standardised of the two parts because it is tied to the rites) by
means of the computer, the results of which were set out in an
unpublished report for the Social Science Research Council (1981).
Our sample produced a far greater body of data than for any other
long oral recitation to date. It enabled us to compare different speakers
on the same occasion, and the same speaker on different occasions.
The former varied more widely than the latter, indicating that no-one
learnt precisely another's version but always introduced variants of his
own. The result was that surprisingly different recitations were to be
found in nearby communities, though they were all recognised by the
actors to be the same 'Bagre'. Interestingly the dictated version was
longer, richer and more sophisticated linguistically and thematically
than those we recorded electronically, perhaps due to the personal
accomplishments of the speaker, but also to the nature of dictation, the
pauses which enabled him to elaborate to a greater extent than was
possible in the rapid recitativo of the actual ritual performance. It was
also significantly more theocentric, in that greater attention was paid to
the part played by the High God, although he is given much more
prominence in all versions than appears in ordinary social interaction.

I have employed the work of the Bagre in a number of ways, but
chiefly to draw out some features that contrasted with written literary
genres. That contrast has turned on the role of verbatim memorising,
which I find characteristic of societies with writing, the emerging
division between creator and performer (both artists in their own way),
and the tighter structure of written works. As a consequence I would
see both the work of Homer in Greece and the Rig-Veda in India as
the products of early literate societies rather than purely oral cultures.

These studies of the effects of the introduction of writing on oral
genres were published in *The Interface between the Written and the Oral*
(1987). This book was part of a series of studies that began with a
fortunate collaboration with Ian Watt, Professor of English at Stanford
University, on 'the consequences of literacy', which was the title of the
first article we published on the subject in 1963. Watt and I had
attended the same college at Cambridge where we were influenced by
the work of Q. D. Leavis and others on the relationship between
changes in the production of reading material, the nature of the
audience and the content and form of literary works.[13] We had also

been through a period of warfare, and especially of imprisonment, where books were scarce or absent. That led us to pursue an interest in the influence of modes of communication on human societies, especially the introduction of writing. Watt provided much of the initial inspiration, but my later engagement was greater, for it made possible a historical or even 'evolutionary' approach to some of the problems of differentiating 'simple' and 'complex' societies which were the staple of anthropological discussions and certainly of anthropological categories. Differences in cognitive processes could be looked at in a developmental way, which made me less willing to accept the elusive relativism of much anthropological discourse.

In this particular essay we attempted to make a broad assessment of the contribution that writing, and specifically alphabetic writing, had played in the history of human cultures. Acknowledging the work of Havelock and of members of the Toronto School, we looked at the intellectual contributions made by the Greeks against the background of their invention of a fully alphabetic script, especially in regard to ideas of 'myth' and history, concepts of time and space, notions of democracy, categories of intellectual activity, as well as the notions of logic and contradiction which Levy-Bruhl had found absent from 'primitive' societies. While accepting that Evans-Pritchard was correct to refute this proposition, we argued that 'logic', in the limited philosophical sense, as well as the refinement of proof and contradiction were critically dependent upon the use of writing.

Subsequently this research was continued in an edited book, entitled *Literacy in Traditional Society* (1968), which examined instances of the impact of writing on mainly 'tribal' societies. In the course of this later work I came to qualify the weight placed upon alphabetic writing in Greece, partly because the introduction of the alphabet itself was less clear cut than formerly suggested by Indo-European (as distinct from Semitic) scholars and partly because a number of the features which had been seen as consequential on the introduction of that script appeared as embryonic in 'earlier' forms of writing itself. The results of these enquiries into the cognitive effects of early writing systems appeared in *The Domestication of the Savage Mind* (1977a) in which attention was drawn to the role of lists and tables in early written cultures as ways of organising information in non-speechlike ways. That work led to a profitable collaboration in the field of 'literacy' studies with the psychologists Michael Cole and David Olson. The first invited me to co-operate in his research into the uses and cognitive implications of the indigenous Vai script in Liberia, a test case in such investigations since learning took place separately from school education. We were fortunate enough to come across a body of writing by A. Sonie which amply illustrated the powerful role which writing could play in reorganising information for the purposes of recall, 'logical' presentation and accountability.

The research proceeded in two directions. The *Interface* (1987) book gathered together studies on genres and similar topics. Previous to that, in *The Logic of Writing and the Organisation of Society* (1986), I suggested the ways in which the introduction of writing had influenced the domains of religion, economy, politics and law, at the same time as attempting to solve certain anthropological and sociological problems surrounding the broad difference between 'primitive' and 'advanced', simpler and complex societies. One of the major pressures behind the studies on writing had been to get away from the simplistic dichotomies of much social science in order to try and isolate some of the mechanisms behind socio-cultural changes; one such set of mechanisms consisted of the mode of communication. But whereas scholars had paid much attention to the effects of language on social life, the forms and implications of writing had received comparatively little notice. That was a situation I tried to remedy.

The tape-recorder has changed not only the analysis of myth and the procedures of the anthropologist. It has also produced an emphasis on discourse, on letting the actor speak for himself. Before the appearance of sound movies, ethnographic films had to invent a spoken script, a text. Now, as in the Granada series, *Disappearing Worlds*, the natives could speak for themselves. But the result was in some ways disastrous for research. Not only was there an overabundance of material, not only did investigators think less before they turned on the machine, but there was even a tendency, which remains strong, to consider a presentation of the actors' picture as the be-all and end-all of analytic endeavour. That is *verstehen* carried to an illogical extreme. Of course there is a lot to be said for recording as much as we can about 'disappearing worlds' before they finally disappear. But this level of ethnography, of reportage ethnology, does not require any great expertise apart from a journalistic ability to get people to talk into a microphone. It is no substitute for theoretically oriented research or even for the analysis of research materials within the framework of a scholarly tradition. Understanding the meaning to the actor may be the ultimate goal for some literary studies; it hardly exhausts all levels of enquiry.

The remaining sector of my work relates both to the contrasting socio-cultural situations in Africa and Eurasia as well as to the interest in the implications of writing. In reading analyses of cooking, I was struck by the difference from my own experience in Africa, both in terms of the traditional patterns and that which was emerging in interaction with Europe and the rest of the world (*Cooking, Cuisine and Class*, 1982). Quantity apart, I found little evidence of different internal forms of cooking even within the African states where some stratification existed, no development of an *haute cuisine*. But, as we have seen, a different kind of hierarchy was involved, one in which cultural activities and values were by and large held in common. Partly because of frequent intermarriage between the different groups in the hierarchy, there were few tendencies for the emergence of sub-cultures, except in those ethnically distinct and endogamous ruling classes found in some of the interlacustrine kingdoms of East Africa which are even now engaged in a grotesque internecine struggle. Partly because of the nature of the hierarchy, partly because of the productive system, partly because of the absence – except under Islam – of writing, there was little attempt to elaborate a high cuisine such as we find in many of the major societies in Eurasia, with their considerable literatures and institutionalisation of the differentiated production and consumption of food.

My most recent book, *The Culture of Flowers* (1993a), pursues what is on one level a similar theme. Visiting Bali and carrying out some limited fieldwork with Esther Goody in Gujarat, India, I was amazed at the use of cultivated flowers, especially in worship, for which they were deliberately produced and purchased. This 'non-utilitarian' form of agriculture was virtually absent from Africa, where the usual form of offering to a shrine is blood sacrifice. Part of the explanation of the difference is not hard to seek and has to do with the lack of stress on intensive agriculture, although tobacco, onions and rice are cultivated by such methods. When I looked in Africa at forms of ritual, at pictorial representations or at the imagery of poetic forms, I found many references to trees, leaves and roots, but little or nothing on flowers, wild or domesticated, except along the coastal regions of East Africa where for hundreds of years influences from India and the Near East had played an obvious part. My suggested reasons for this state of affairs were several, and partly connected with the nature of agriculture. As a comparison I was led to look in greater depth at the major uses of flowers in Europe and Asia. But initially I concentrated

upon the history of flower use since the Bronze Age: its development in
the Near East, and especially Ancient Egypt, its culmination in Rome,
and then the rapid decline under Christianity – connected with the
earlier role of flowers in 'pagan' worship, as manifestations of luxury,
as well as with a certain conception of God and, as far as representations go, with a Biblical reluctance to represent his creatures. The
effects on the history of Europe were radical. After the collapse of
Rome, that continent saw a dramatic fall away in the use of flowers
which had hitherto so often decorated the altar, the priest and the
sacrificial animal itself, a decline that was paralleled by the virtual
disappearance of three-dimensional statuary. But it also saw the decline
in botanical knowledge which, beyond a certain threshold of folk usage,
was partially dependent upon their representation as separate images
and in manuscripts. In this respect the relative backwardness of
medieval Europe with respect to Asia is a significant comment on the
effects on systems of knowledge, not only of the barbarian invasions but
of Christianity itself.

Europe saw a gradual renaissance in the growth, use and representation of flowers in graphic and literary works from the twelfth century
onwards. The repertoire greatly expanded with the expansion of
Europe, with the demand of the aristocrats and bourgeoisie, with the
supply of new varieties by traders, missionaries, administrators and
later by specialist plant hunters themselves. But their role in cemeteries
and in worship had to overcome deeply established 'puritanical' beliefs
that tended to differentiate Protestant from Catholic regions. The
continuing differences (and similarities) in the use of flowers in Europe
and America, its expansion with the economy and its culmination in a
world market in cut flowers made possible by the aeroplane (and
before that by train and truck) is the subject of several chapters, which
include an analysis of the formal, written 'language of flowers' that
sprang up in Paris in the early part of the nineteenth century and soon
became accepted as the rebirth of a vanished code of eastern origin.

I pursued the themes of specialist production, of the stratifications of
use and of a perpetual ambivalence in the culture of flowers in India,
China and Japan, partly based on observations of the markets and
rituals, of the houses and temples, in those various countries. At the
end I return to the theme of the ambivalence about representation in
Africa itself, this time in respect not of God's creatures but of the High
God himself, and often of other divinities as well. I argue that the
reluctance to portray the Creator God displays a concept of divinity at

odds with the characterisation of African religion as animism and fetishism. The intellectual and cognitive problems appear closer to those of 'western' man than is often supposed but we need also to point to precise reasons for some of the difference. At this level too it is necessary to reconsider assumptions of the uniqueness of the West.

From *The Culture of Flowers* the argument takes two directions. The first is an attempt to summarise and develop the thesis that sees not only the intellectual but the mercantile systems of Europe and Asia as having been on roughly parallel courses, not subject to a great divide. Of course important developments took place in Western Europe after the Renaissance but significant advances had earlier been made in the East. Indeed part of what occurred at the end of the Middle Ages was a process of the West catching up with the East after its earlier backwardness. What some commentators see as inventions of the West are in fact re-inventions of what had existed elsewhere or before. That was the case with mercantile and manufacturing activity which, until the sixteenth century, were more developed in the East, which was less far from producing capitalism, industrialisation and modernisation than either folk wisdom or sociological theory have supposed. In *The East in the West* I try to substantiate this thesis in specific concrete ways, discussing rationality, bookkeeping (*ragioneria*), as well as mercantile (and possibly cultural) activity.

Another thread picked up from *The Culture of Flowers* is the attempt to give an account of the recurrent tendency to reject the use of aesthetic elaborations. Even in some societies that knew about, or had the potentiality to grow, domesticated flowers, they were not always used, or only sparingly. That happened in Judaism, in early Christianity, again under Puritanism, as well as in various revolutionary regimes. The precipitating factors varied and included both theological arguments and objections to luxury and 'waste'.[14] Such aesthetic denial was paralleled in the aversion to icons, especially three-dimensional ones and I discerned implicit forms of this rejection in the reluctance of African societies to make figurative representations of the High God, and in some societies of other gods and even ancestors.[15] As with flowers, I was trying to offer some cognitive explanation of the uneven use of sculptural forms. In this manuscript I attempt to extend the thesis to dramatic representations (mimesis in the Platonic sense), to relics (as representing the person) and in a somewhat different way to fiction, narrative and myth.

I have tried to give some idea of the themes that have been

important in my research in the past and in the present. One constant regret has been the failure of 'socio-cultural' anthropology to become more cumulative. Partly this has to do with the methods that have been favoured over the past half century. Many anthropologists seem imprisoned by their rejection of any method other than fieldwork, being unprepared to see how their enquiries relate in a systematic way to those of others. 'Local knowledge' is essential, but for many purposes it is a beginning rather than an end. We have come full cycle since the nineteenth-century addiction to a version of the comparative method. In my view it is essential to integrate and test our observations and conclusions with material gathered by other scholars in this and related fields using whatever methods we can, imperfect as these will always be. In these resources I include the Human Relations Area Files which I have tried to employ for this purpose. The rejection of techniques other than fieldwork and speculation tends to lead to a withdrawal into deep descriptions of 'my people', combined on the one hand with unsubstantiated global statements and, on the other, with the search for new gods; as with medicine shrines the old ones become obsolescent as they fail to meet impossible demands, so there are shifts, for example, from structuralism to post-modernism, on the basis of a 'global exchange' in computer terms rather than the modification and development of existing programmes.

I have said little about my work on changing social systems and on the history of languages and ethnography of Africa, even though these took up much of my time and energies in the 1960s when I was frequently in Ghana. Especially in the first of these areas, that gap exists partly because I have not completed as much in these areas as I wished. However contributions were made to political culture (1968), to new religious movements and to economic changes (1980). More-over, the bright hopes for the future and the harsher realities of the present have formed a constant theme behind my research. As with other colleagues, that research involved entering some of the no-go areas of earlier scholars and making use of work from other fields.

This breach in disciplinary walls has its dangers, and it could be argued that part of the so-called crisis in social anthropology (though crises exist all the time and in all fields) has resulted from discarding the framework accepted by earlier workers in the field including their tighter paradigms. Anthropology has become very diffuse in a number of ways, which means that there is room for a range of approaches. For me the way ahead is not the way back but consists in supplementing the analysis of socio-cultural 'facts' or situations with a problem-driven approach. That means looking for evidence where it exists rather than confining oneself to arbitrary boundaries, useful as these have proved to be for specific problems or topics. At the same time there are undoubted benefits to be obtained by a group of scholars concentrating on one particular topic for a period of time. While such an approach is adopted in many fields of knowledge, the individualistic approach of anthropologists – each one his 'people', his own problem, his own paradigm, tends to result in a dispersal of effort that is ultimately counter-productive.

I myself have drawn much satisfaction from working with scholars in other fields, with historians (especially those associated with *Past and Present, Annales E.S.C.* and the Cambridge Group), with psychologists and with those in the adjacent fields of literature and oriental studies. An anthropology that does not or cannot communicate with other disciplines stands in danger of placing an excessive value on its own conclusions. It is only too easy to draw back to the safety of the community which one has studied (or even one's individual 'informant' in some American traditions) and about which one may know more than any of one's colleagues. Or perhaps to seek the shelter of a hermeneutic approach to which only the writer holds the key. But knowledge exists in communication, not only within arbitrarily defined fields (for that is essentially what we are dealing with) but also outside them. It sometimes seems to be the case that fields such as cognitive anthropology emerge not to widen knowledge and to provide a link with the work of other students of cognitive processes but to protect and separate off a distinctive anthropological patch. Yes, we anthropologists are also interested, we are saying, but in our own way and on our own terms. That has always seemed to me the way to ruin. There is no 'anthropological' truth, enlightenment or even insight that is not related to the work of scholars in other fields.

CHAPTER 9

Concluding remarks

Before the 1930s social anthropology in Britain was taught in London (at the London School of Economics and University College), and at Oxford and Cambridge. In Scotland teaching only began in Edinburgh in 1946 with the appointment of a student of Malinowski, Ralph Piddington, as Reader. Sir James Frazer held a Chair in this subject at Liverpool in 1907 but remained there for only one term. Earlier Tylor had taught at Oxford and the zoologist Haddon at Cambridge. But serious professional teaching after the First World War began at Cambridge with Rivers (as a Lecturer in Psychology) and Radcliffe-Brown (as a Research Fellow) and at the same time with Malinowski (and Seligman) at the London School of Economics. Both Rivers (as psychologist) and Seligman (as a medical doctor) had been members of Haddon's expeditions to the Torres Straits at the end of the 1890s.

However, a critical mass of research students only emerged at the LSE under Malinowski at the end of the 1920s. That was the true birth of the subject in Britain, and it branched out slowly after the appointment of Radcliffe-Brown to Oxford in 1937. The end of the Second World War, after Malinowski's death, saw the emergence of Oxford as the main centre of research with the appointment of Evans-Pritchard to the Chair, of Fortes to a Readership and of Gluckman to a Lectureship. When Gluckman left for Manchester in 1950 and Fortes for Cambridge in 1951, those departments came to compete with Oxford and London for students and funds.

I myself am far from wedded to the criticism of comparative research and of their predecessors that marked the work of the group of anthropologists that followed Malinowski. On the other hand, by concentrating their efforts they certainly made important contributions and achieved much more than if they had worked in a more diffuse mode. The insistence on fieldwork had its limitations but it also had many advantages. My one programmatic note is to insist that it is an impoverished field that sees itself as having to discard its predecessors at each generation instead of critically building on their achievements, to some of which I have tried to point.

The attempt to dismiss these achievements has taken various forms. Firstly there has been the attack on colonial anthropology, to which I will return. Secondly there has been that on the restriction of topic. It is sometimes said and more often thought that British social anthropology was especially privileged in its access to the 'Empire', and that this has determined some of its significant characteristics. 'British empiricism', writes Boon, 'gaining easy access to a wealth of data throughout the empire and able to find a common ground of common (utilitarian) sense in the most esoteric phenomena ...'[1] British anthropology was hardly alone in being the child of empire. Leaving aside the equally privileged access of other European powers to overseas territories, the immense internal empires of the Americas and Russia (and potentially of India and China) served as parallel sources for their nationals. In fact British social anthropology was more international and opposi- tional than most other traditions, deriving part of its ideological background from a variety of sources, Kropotkin in the case of Radcliffe-Brown, the Austrian logico-empiricists in the case of Nadel, French sociology, Marxism and *Gestalt* theory in the case of others. Utilitarianism hardly seems a dominant theme and the aspects of immediate utility resulted largely from the wishes of its dominant American patron, the Rockefeller Foundation.

Looking back at the development of British social anthropology, one of the key moments in its history was the Anglo-American conference of 1963 in Cambridge, the proceedings of which led to the first publications of the Association of Social Anthropologists. Writing on 'Religion as a cultural system', Geertz argued that the detailed studies of religion in particular societies, which then characterised social anthropology, were in 'a state of general stagnation' suffering from what 'Janowitz ... has called the dead hand of competence', having made no theoretical advances since the Second World War.[2] Geertz summarises the achievements of the anthropological study of religion as:

Yet one more meticulous case in point for such well-established propositions as that ancestor worship supports the jural authority of elders, that initiation rites are means for the establishment of sexual identity and adult status, that ritual groupings reflect political oppositions, or that myths provide charters for social institutions and rationalizations of social privilege, may well finally convince a great many people, both inside the profession and out, that anthropologists are, like theologians, firmly dedicated to proving the indubitable.

At the end he remarks that ' "totemism" and "ancestor worship" [are] insipid categories by means of which ethnographers of religion devitalize their data'. In his final paragraph he begins by pointing out that: 'To discuss the role of ancestor worship in regulating political succession' is in no sense an unimportant endeavour.

But to attempt them with but the most general, commonsense view of what ancestor worship, animal sacrifice ... are as religious patterns seems to me not particularly promising. Only when we have a theoretical analysis of symbolic action comparable in sophistication to that we now have for social and psychological action, will we be able to cope effectively with those aspects of social and psychological life in which religion (or art, or science, or ideology) plays an important role.

The tripartite pattern involved is distinctly Parsonian, assuming a separation of the cultural (effectively symbolic) from the social, a distinction that was either denied in British as in French social science or which played a minor part in discussions.[3] For example, Malinowski tended to identify culture and society and in the end selected the former word.

I recently turned up my notes on this session of the conference, where I was the main discussant. Geertz, Spiro, Turner and Bradbury presented papers, and my handwritten remarks show that comments were offered by Gluckman, Spiro, Goodenough, Leach, Richards, Firth, Fortes, Leach again, Schneider, Stanner, Fortune, Fox, Haimendorf, Homans, Fallers and Spiro again. In my comments, I wrote:

I am not sure after listening to his [Geertz's] paper (i) whether he thinks this analysis of symbolic action has begun, and (ii) what forms he expects it to take. Is it to take the sort of analysis of the actor meaning of symbols, made, for example, by Monica Wilson on the Nyakyusa, by Srinivas, by Radcliffe-Brown etc. etc. in particular societies, with a view to subsequent comparisons, such as Turner has carried out in the paper he presents? Or is it looking for an actor-derived, but observer-imposed 'logic' of concepts, seen perhaps as deriving from social morphology (to use the phrase of Durkheim and Mauss) or perhaps as common derivations from some all-pervading principles of organisation, e.g. in the work of Griaule, Lévi-Strauss and Needham. I have no doubt that both these are profitable enterprises, even though the first sometimes tends to get lost in the particularities of the exegesis (and psychobiology does not get you out of the box), and the latter lost in its generalities since the principles are even more elusive than, for example, some of Radcliffe-Brown's reduction to dualisms.

In any case I see no need to leave aside other lines which are beginning to yield some pay-off merely in order to adopt something 'new' (although this is the title to our symposium). We all wish for greater advances, all desire some panacea for our analytic ills. But this won't simply come about by pursuing some 'new' line, by thinking up some shining 'new' model. Such an attitude resembles the search for New Bearings, New Directions, etc. in English literature, or for new philosophies, new models of automobiles, new medicine shrines. We require data and techniques as well as models for considering data, in order to contribute to theoretical advances.

Today I see little need to modify that view. While there are many ways of manipulating anthropological material, in more or less personal or positivistic ways, a tradition of enquiry should aim at cumulative knowledge of this kind.

Let me first take the point about the 'dead hand of competence'. The very fact that one could be talking of competence in a kind of study that could be considered to have begun only ten to twenty-five years earlier with the publication of the Evans-Pritchard's work on religion, and Fortes' studies of ancestor worship, says something positive about the achievements in that field. However, either the understanding of ancestor worship, animal sacrifice, etc., is superficial – in which case we need greater 'competence' in ethnography; or we possess competent accounts of these features, in which case we can proceed with the proper analysis of, for example, symbolism. But it is difficult to claim both that we are too competent, and not competent enough.

Geertz was of course making a polemical point about what he and others call 'cultural' studies which have been promoted in different ways by a number of American anthropologists in their later work – Schneider in kinship studies, Sahlins in economics. Such accounts are not always clear as to whether or not cultural studies should be limited to the level of *verstehen*, of meaning to the actor. Schneider is much concerned with this problem in the context of kinship. Lévi-Strauss and others have invoked another level of interpretation, implicit meaning, in trying to understand 'what the actor really meant'. However, even getting at the explicit level of cultural meaning is hard enough, especially when that is often stratified and sometimes personalised. In any European or Asian society the level of knowledge of the local language together with the intensity of the fieldwork needed to take the further step of implicit meanings has to be very profound. That is so even when dealing with the literature or religion in one's 'natural' culture, and it is far from clear that in the simpler societies many anthropologists have achieved this level of competence. Do they 'get away with' interpretations that they would be unable to in, say, European studies because of the absence of repeated or perhaps repeatable observations?

For African societies we have in the past often lacked such a body of data derived from a number of observers, although the situation is changing rapidly. For many peoples 'without history', presenting as full as possible an ethnographic record was important. That presentation may involve repeating some of the more general conclusions of others, for example, concerning the relation between initiation and sexual identity. Such statements are not so much a matter of proving the indubitable as of seeing how far one's data confirm existing studies and then of trying to explain any discrepancies. What Geertz seemed to criticise lies partly in the dual nature of ethnographic field studies themselves, which sees a value in offering data on another human group without necessarily adopting a new theoretical stance.

At another level he was criticising the restriction of topic. Any field of enquiry has to engage in such a limitation of the area of enquiry at any one moment in time if it is to be in any way cumulative, if it is to build on earlier knowledge in the way Aristotle desired in the *Posterior Analytics*.[4] If the end rests at 'thick description', one could in principle take any aspect of social action (as with extreme functionalism) to begin the analysis of a culture, just as in extreme structuralism one could take any facet and look behind the scenes for evidence of deeper components that are supposedly homologous with others at the same level. In both cases there could be some advantage in choosing institutions, persons, statements or events that are central to the socio-cultural system, but the question of centrality is not easy to decide either in advance or even in retrospect. Both approaches depend upon holistic assumptions that often take language as the exemplary model. While this holism has its limits, structural-functional analysis does lead one to look at relational sets, for example, at the way the incidence of accusations of witchcraft and sorcery is linked to interpersonal conflicts as between the holder and the heir. Any such focus may restrict the area of study, but it may also lead to a cumulative rather than merely to a repetitive treatment.

An incremental discussion of this kind occurred in studies of witchcraft and of ancestor worship. Both are topics which subsequent investigators took up partly because they saw, or thought they saw, some advance, or the possibility of advance, taking place, some application of the discussion to a wider range of societies. Rather less knowledge of this cumulative kind has emerged from more recent 'cultural studies', the intent of which often seems to lie in reconsidering orientations rather than hypotheses, and of stressing the uniqueness of 'cultures' at the expense of comparable features. With that tradition of enquiry, some recent branches of 'cognitive anthropology' (for example, Boyer 1994) have tried to make a decisive break. The assertion of the uniqueness of groups and their actions is as much a truism as it is of individuals (or of 'things'), but that cannot set aside the need to consider similarities or assessable differences, though this task is rendered more difficult by adopting that particular frame of reference. The subsequent twenty-five years of research may have added relatively less than the previous twenty-five, partly, but not entirely, because of the attempt to establish 'a theoretical analysis of symbolic action', an aim that has proved difficult to define, let alone to attain. For it is not easy to establish what such a 'theoretical analysis' would look like. There are those who have discussed issues at a high level of abstraction without much reference to the results of fieldwork; there are those who have concentrated on descriptive studies of particular peoples. But there seems to have been less of the kind of profitable combination of the general and the particular, of theory (or hypothesis) and practice (or fieldwork), than occurred in the earlier period.

The tradition of fieldwork established by Malinowski involved a relatively long period of 'participant observation' among a particular people. It differed from the antiquarian bent of much earlier American ethnography, against which the Rockefeller Foundation had reacted, as well as from the more superficial surveys carried out by continental ethnologists and even from the interpreter-dependent studies of Griaule and his associates in France. That fieldwork was combined with theoretical interests in a way that was important for the development of social anthropology because it set the stage for the later contributions of scholars trained by these men in terms of both approach and of substantive problem. Subsequently the insistence on bringing together theory and practice has become somewhat diluted both by those who separate highly general 'theory' from highly specific fieldwork, as well as by the kind of ethno-methodological approach which limits its aim to recording the words and action of the people (or a person) themselves. This ultimate empiricism is embodied in the work of some anthropological film-makers who claim to let the 'actors' speak for themselves. In the extreme case, you no longer need an anthropologist, just a tape recorder or a camera. Anthropology, as distinct from this kind of primitive ethnography, is analytic or it is nothing.

The second feature that marked these students of Malinowski was the constructive formalism of the methodology, the use of diagrams, figures, tables and similar techniques, as well as the insistence on systematic note-taking. The formalisation is brought out very clearly in the joint memorandum which Fortes, Nadel and Hofstra prepared for their teacher at the end of their pre-field training (Appendix 1), but schematic tables are equally evident in the practice of Firth, Richards and many others. As for note-taking, Malinowski was insistent on writing up fieldwork each evening, recommending various ways of categorising and recording information. He also wanted his students to send him back regular monthly reports, though few fully met this requirement.

Thirdly, although research was to be directed in terms of theory and topic, it was also holistic, seeing how one facet linked with another, that is, it employed methodological functionalism. Carrying out research meant producing comprehensive and comprehensible accounts of particular societies, or at least of communities, of writing ethnographies that considered the major aspects of social life, the ecology, economy, the kinship system, political organisation and religion. One investigator was supposed to cover all these domains (or sub-systems in Parsonian terminology), partly to elucidate aspects which were functionally interrelated, one affecting the other, like land tenure and mystical notions about the earth.

One obvious way in which scholars like Firth, Fortes, Evans-Pritchard and others differed from many more recent anthropologists was in the comprehensiveness of their ethnographic treatment of a particular society. In this they followed Malinowski rather than Radcliffe-Brown. Malinowski's corpus consisted of a series of books that analysed Trobriand society in the context of theoretical issues. Firth followed with books on the social organisation of Tikopia, covering religion, the economy and kinship. Evans-Pritchard wrote a book on the Nuer political and economic system, one on kinship and marriage and a third on religion. Fortes wrote two major books on the Tallensi political and kinship systems and a number of essays on their religion which have been brought together in a volume called *Morality,*

Religion and the Person (1987), together of course with *Oedipus and Job*. Gluckman wrote on the Lozi economy, and then several important books on the judicial system. All contributed to the consideration of wider theoretical issues.

There is little in subsequent African studies from Britain that can compare with these extensive analytic ethnographies. Take anglophone West Africa. We have had individual books on a number of different people (often resulting from doctoral theses), such as Stenning on the pastoral Fulani of northern Nigeria, Lloyd on the Yoruba, Horton on the Kalabari, Burnham on the Hausa. But there are few bodies of ethnographic analysis of the same kind as issued from the pens of the previous generation. For Nigeria, M. G. Smith's work on the Hausa is extensive but largely on the politics and economy. Esther Goody has produced two books on the Gonja of northern Ghana, mainly devoted to an analysis of the domestic domain. I myself have written two books on the LoDagaa, one general, one on funerals, ancestor worship and property, and then two books on the Bagre. But the same attempt at comprehensive analytic coverage does not emerge, except perhaps in the Bohannans' work on the Tiv of central Nigeria, which includes books on social organisation, law, the economy, together with a series of publications that present their fieldnotes. That presentation seems to presage, firstly, the information revolution, and secondly, the extreme ethno-methodological approach which leaves the field in the hands of the speakers saying their own thing, and goes no further along the analytical road.

The situation does not greatly differ in francophone Africa which was earlier characterised by the series of studies on the Dogon. Now we have a number of long *thèses d'état*, often more historical than sociological, but, apart from the work of Marguerite Dupire on the Fulani, few analyses of the comprehensive ethnographic kind.

On the face of it this situation is curious, since owing to the changes in the mode of transport continuing ethnographic research has become increasingly possible. Like every other part of the globe, West Africa is more accessible; individuals have the chance to return frequently to the field, Africans come to Europe in great numbers, and under late colonial rule and the early years of independence many Europeans spent time teaching or carrying out other work on the spot. Opportunities for grants were greater than before, while the last quarter of a century has seen the advent in strength of African anthropologists who have continuous access to the 'field'. Nevertheless, there is a dearth of large-scale ethnographic studies.

Part of the answer to this problem lies no doubt in the quality, maturity and formation of those who went before, partly in the wider range of interests of those who followed. The rapidly changing scene now leads some to study urbanisation, others politics, social change, the new states, aspects of development, often reflecting the local call for research useful to a new country. In this way energies and efforts are dispersed. But in Britain more relevant perhaps is the fission of the group of scholars that came with increasing size, the widening of interests, the consequent loss of focus, and the impact of a much more diffuse American anthropology. The loss of homogeneity, of research-group status, meant that comparative or cumulative work was less likely to develop.

At the same time, increasing productivity has meant that studies have become more and more specialised within the field of social anthropology. In the *Newsletter* issued by the *American Anthropologist* one sees advertisements for political anthropologists, for development, for feminist and Marxist anthropologists, with academics defining them-selves in very different ways, as Indianists or as Africanists. While Fortes and Nadel did fieldwork exclusively in Africa, they would never have defined themselves as Africanists but as anthropologists. Indeed they were not very interested in the establishment of institutes or associations based on regional ties. While they were critical of the comparative method as practised by Tylor and Frazer, and committed to intensive fieldwork, to understanding the actors' point of view, they mainly regarded themselves as comparative sociologists in the sense that their understanding was not, in their view, limited to one culture alone. It was rather human culture itself.

The desire to complete the ethnographic record was in part a continuation of older approaches to presenting anthropological data that were used by those writing about the Amerindian population, in the work, for example, of Lowie on the Crow. Accounts by colonial administrators such as Rattray on the Asante and Labouret on the Lobi lie down the same path. In the period after the Second World War this trend, which attempted to combine the study of documentary work with fieldwork, was embodied in the extensive series of volumes published in the *Ethnographic Survey of Africa*, which was edited by Daryll Forde and owed its being and its range to the energy he put into that scheme, and into the organisation of the International African Institute.

The insistence on intensive fieldwork carried out over an extended period by living in close association with the people themselves (known as participant observation) was an obvious but essential way whereby oral cultures (and those working with the unwritten traditions of literate cultures) could be given the scholarly attention, and even the human dignity in the world at large, that had hitherto been accorded only to the members of literate civilisations. Those who spent long periods in oral cultures had previously done so with other purposes in mind, as missionaries to convert them, as traders to sell them goods, as administrators to rule them. What little professional anthropology was done consisted largely of survey work or of brief visits. The results may have filled gaps in the written record but they were not impressive from the scholarly point of view. What would be thought of a Chinese scholar who tried to write a serious academic study about rural France based on a visit of short duration, possibly without any opportunity to learn the language beforehand? But such procedures were standard in, for example, Rivers' work in Melanesia, Seligman's in the Sudan, Lévi-Strauss' in South America, and in numerous other cases. While Evans-Pritchard respected the work of John Peristiany, the Greek scholar who came to join him at Oxford, he was critical of his field procedures. He had lived in town and driven out to work among the Kipsigis, publishing a photograph of his tent that, it was suggested, he probably never slept in. When I received a grant from the Colonial Social Science Research Council to work in northern Ghana, the offer of motor transport was vetoed by my mentors at Oxford on the grounds I would have less contact with the people with whom I was working and would be unable properly to appreciate their concepts of space and time. As far as intensive understanding was concerned, I undoubtedly benefited from this restriction on my mobility since I was forced to get down to fieldwork in one place. As in archaeology or any other field, where little else is known survey work has a value of its own. But its role is limited when it comes to studying any more complex features of social life or to seeing how particular activities take place in the context of the wider community. It can too easily be forgotten what a different approach intensive fieldwork represented to earlier traditions in anthropology and even to much current practice, especially that carried out in and from the better-endowed environments.

In this account I have directed attention to two general discussions about the influence of the providers of funds, permits and intellectual credentials on social research. The specific case of social anthropology in Africa has been subject to some controversy since there are those writers for whom research undertaken in colonial times is seen as strongly influenced by the demands of the administration and by the spirit of the times.

Despite the apparent power that foundations and governments wielded, their influence on anthropological research appears to me to be much less than in more recent times. Whatever bows had to be made to the interests of Rockefeller benefactions, the International African Institute (IAI) and the colonial authorities, by and large people were allowed to pursue their own academic purposes (as Rockefeller and the Institute intended). An interest in lineages, for example, had little or nothing to do with colonial policy, though of course the general problem of social control is of interest to all governments everywhere. The point is that control of the policy-making process at the providers' level was not always the central question. Fisher argues that control came increasingly into the hands of trustees and of certain foundation officers. But in a field like anthropology, consisting of individual researchers working on their own, the direction of the research was largely under their own control. That is what mattered. In the work of the Fellows of the IAI the results of their research in terms of 'culture contact' were minimal.

It is possible to see attempts at comprehensive accounts of a functional kind as an emergent characteristic typical of English empiricism and even of British imperialism. If by empiricism we mean a non-theoretical approach, or at least working without hypotheses, the contention is invalid. About the relation with colonialism the argument is more complicated. It is true, in general terms, that any social science research (indeed research of most kinds) can be seen as supporting the *status quo*, in this case as helping the colonial powers to govern. But as we have seen very little funding came from the authorities until the dying days of imperialism; they tended to regard professional social enquiry with understandable suspicion. The bulk of the resources came from a Foundation with reformist tendencies, an American Foundation that was hardly concerned to support the continuation of European empires.

It is true that the Rockefeller Foundation offered its support to a London-based institution and that one of the reasons was so that the Fellows could gain access to the colonies for their research. But the acquisition of an entry visa did not involve submission to the colonial authorities, although the Fellows tried to avoid antagonising them. Not too much should be made of this, certainly in contrast to the present day. For wherever people work and whatever they do, they have to establish some kind of relationship with the political authorities, albeit the local ones. This is as true of working in contemporary India, China and Ghana (not to speak of Eastern Europe and Central America) as it was in Africa before independence. The nature of the regime, the personality of its agents and the position one takes towards them, as well as the kind of conditions that obtain in the country, differ. The simpler or the more disturbed these conditions, the more one has to depend upon the government, unless of course one chooses to work through that other highly effective network, the church.

But perhaps the most important fact that leads one drastically to modify the account of British empiricism and imperialism lies in the type of scholar who was recruited, and the climate of opinion in which they worked. In the first place most of them were not from Britain and were often marginal to that society in other ways. In the second, they were mainly recruited in the period after the Great Crash of 1929 and following the rise of Hitler. Opinion among anthropologists at the London School of Economics and in the other intellectual circles in which they moved was predominantly left wing and intellectually influenced by those dominant figures, Marx and Freud.[5] It is true that neither of these plays an obvious role in their anthropological writings, but both strands were there in the background. In the years to come a number of them contributed to radical journals such as the Fabian bulletin on colonial affairs. For those who came from abroad were attracted to anthropology partly because of their concern for native peoples, and that in itself was seen as a threat by some colonial authorities.

It has been suggested that British social anthropology was too ethnographic, and at the same time too theoretically simple (too 'empirical'). There can be no adequate understanding of particular cultures, of other societies, without a deep immersion in their experiences. That cannot, in my view, be attained by the examination of a single 'informant', much less of a unique 'text', but only in the fullness and totality of people's interactions. That means fieldwork, ethnography and 'empiricism'. Without the 'ethnographic present', analytic anthropology is gravely hampered. We need that level if we are to study the meaning of events to the actor. With that level every field worker must necessarily be concerned and it is hard to achieve the same understanding by decontextualising techniques like questionnaires. Not that such meaning is the be-all and end-all of everyone's enquiry; there is also the meaning to the observers, perhaps of a structural or functional kind. Then there is the comparative dimension, intrinsic to the very notion of an outside observer but capable of a wider extension to neighbouring groups, to regions, to continents and to humanity as a whole. Of course such investigations are possible without engaging in fieldwork. But observational, participatory enquiry is an important dimension for understanding the way different individuals and groups interact and different aspects intermesh, as well as for gaining a sense of the problems that are realistic to examine, and pretesting, in however limited a fashion, the profitability of lines of investigation.

As for theoretical simplicity, of which Malinowski was accused by Lévi-Strauss, there is little virtue in complexity for its own sake; quite the reverse, we need only as much theory as is necessary. Its complexity or simplicity is determined by the problem and material under discussion, not by academic fiat. What is significant is not the 'general theory', which only too often becomes a subject either of dead-end philosophical enquiry, such as the nature of truth, or of broad conceptual clarification (or confusion), such as the relation between culture and history. These are matters influenced by 'opinion' to a greater extent than types of discourse closer to the empirical (and such questions of degree count for much). Where attention should be focussed is on the 'hypothetical' rather than the 'theoretical' level, the middle rather than the long range.

At a programmatic level, the comparative and developmental perspectives, the systematic investigation of the perspectives of space and time outside the 'ethnographic present', were largely set aside by the anthropologists working in this ethnographic tradition. That meant setting aside not only the methods but also the content of much earlier anthropological work in the nineteenth century. And yet the total rejection of neither was feasible in the longer term. Malinowski confessed he was attracted to anthropology by *The Golden Bough* of Frazer; Radcliffe-Brown and his students gave much attention to work in historical jurisprudence, such as that of Maine, or of Robertson Smith in comparative religion; E. B. Tylor and Lewis Morgan were constant points of reference. Those authors combined the comparative and the developmental, constructing long-term 'evolutionary' sequences. For the purist, comparison neglected the particular, the contextual, while the proposed long-term sequences were often considered to be 'pseudo-history', in Radcliffe-Brown's phrase. Nor was even history relevant in a strictly synchronic, structural-functional, framework that looked for explanations (or relationships) in the present rather than in the past.

That formal framework owed much to Durkheim and his associates in France. Their writings were often mediated by Radcliffe-Brown, who had early been attracted by their work and who was interested in systematic frameworks and in general theory, his training having been in the moral sciences (philosophy). Radcliffe-Brown's book, *The Andaman Islanders* (1922), had made great use of ideas and approaches derived from scholars writing for the journal *Année sociologique*; Evans-Pritchard continued to seek inspiration from the same source, not only in his writings but in encouraging students to translate works of that school.

British social anthropology of the period was marked by building upon the level of hypothesis, for example, around the developmental cycle, the lineage, the 'social' dimensions of witchcraft or of 'segmentary' systems. That means more than simply having a point of polemical orientation but engaging in a relatively constructive consideration of earlier discussions. Methodological rather than theoretical considerations tended to lead to these ideas being developed on a one-to-one basis (the Tiv against the Tallensi), an approach arising from the focus on fieldwork, and working best among a small group of scholars who continually discussed their own intensive studies (as did Evans-Pritchard and Fortes). But the method embodied some basic contradictions which have been faced by few ethnographers. Comparisons were made, but over a limited range of material. Meanwhile one future tendency of the concentration on fieldwork was solipsistic withdrawal into culture-specific studies and personalised accounts. From the standpoint of cumulative social science such accounts are yet more problematic than the earlier set, whatever they contribute to other fields of the humanities (and those are not contributions to be neglected, peripheral as they may remain from that standpoint).

The whole endeavour was facilitated by the fact that the strength of social anthropology in Britain lay in research and graduate training rather than in undergraduate teaching. As in France, general courses had been offered to those being trained for the Colonial Service from early in the century. But Malinowski was primarily interested in research, as were those he trained. It was his energy, his engineering, his charisma, that helped attract both funds and students at a time when many were looking towards change and reform. These students Malinowski acquired were not new graduates in search of a career. They were often scholars who had already done substantial work in other areas such as psychology, economics or sociology. Malinowski himself was also aware of much that was going on in these fields, whether in Europe, America, or the Pacific.

Some too were drawn by his control of funds. But whatever the motivation, Malinowski encouraged them to work in constructive, co-operative ways, partly through his seminars, partly through the IAI. One result of their work was a series of important symposia, namely, *African Political Systems* (1940), *African Systems of Kinship and Marriage* (1950) and on a lesser plane, *African Worlds* (1954), which were not simply collections of papers or conference reports, but examples of partially linked research drawn together by wide-ranging theoretical introductions.

One aspect, perhaps condition, of this activity was that under-graduates were relatively few. A great deal of emphasis was placed on seminars and training when other faculties outside the hard sciences directed virtually the whole of their attention to undergraduates. That created an attractive ambience for research students from other parts of the world, which in turn reinforced the international aspect of the work.

But it also meant that paradigms were tight, initiatives controlled. Absent was the amorphous quality of much 'anthropology' in the USA, where the term embraced fields from linguistics, archaeology, through to human biology. In restricting anthropology to the social, Malinowski placed himself in opposition to Seligman and to much of the academic establishment. In effect he excluded from the field not only the kind of psychological anthropology then associated with Ruth Benedict but also much work of the longer-term development kind, making co-operation with historians and others more difficult than, say, in France.

In the longer term such restrictions were impossible to maintain. Marxists, Weberians, sociologists and the public at large insisted on comparison; the temporal dimension had always been a problem, increasingly so as archives became more available. Later the field could profitably have divided up into interest groups in order to prevent the tendency to diffuseness. But earlier the advantages of such concentra-tion by a tight group of scholars are equally apparent. Without that episode, without that expansive moment, social anthropology would have much less of a enduring kind to show.[6]

Changing research schemes

The kind of research that anthropologists do sometimes seems to amount to parachuting themselves into another group of human beings and finding out as much as they can about their way of life. Undoubtedly, as with bird-watching, there is a lot of underrated ethnographic work of that kind, which has its uses in getting a general picture of a particular people. But needless to say, every observer goes to the field with some framework for his observations. In the case of Malinowski's students this was especially marked, partly because as experienced scholars they came in with their own foci of interest (Fortes, the family; Nadel, music; Hofstra, individuality). So I thought it would be of interest to present the research projects they submitted before going to the field, which increasingly bear the strong marks of Malinowski's influence on them. In Fortes' case he presented three versions of his project at different times and I have included all three in order to give some idea of the way he shaped his project under Malinowski's influence so that it moved from a general psychological enquiry to a more specific anthropological one. But it still retained a psychological component which when he later presented the results of his research under the influence of Evans-Pritchard, Radcliffe-Brown and Durkheim had largely disappeared. Only in his account of Tallensi education did he retain an explicit orientation in that direction, although later in life he returned strongly to the theme of the interpretation of sociological and psychological (even psychoanalytic) frames.[1]

There are three versions of Meyer Fortes' plans for research of a psychological nature in an anthropological setting. The first is attached to a letter to Malinowski, dated 2 July 1931, which must have been written soon after they met in the same year at the house of the psychoanalyst, J. Flügel. The second is a proposal dated 26 March of the following year entitled: 'A psychological approach to the study of African society: the social development of the African child', which was submitted to the International African Institute as part of an application for a Fellowship. The third is the plan formulated at the end of the year's study of anthropology at the London School of Economics in association with S. Hofstra and S. F. Nadel; it forms part of the joint submission to the Secretary of the International African Institute on 23 October and is headed, 'Sketch of a plan for the study of the African family'.

PLAN NUMBER I

This proposal was enclosed with a letter to Malinowski, dated 2 July 1931.

My object is to study the primitive child, in the setting of his family and community, by the observational methods which have hitherto been used only with civilised children. After nearly four years of work with children, I was driven to the conclusion that my main problem – the acquisition and growth of social behaviour – could never be solved by the usual psychological methods of tests and interrogation. I concluded that it was necessary to observe the child living and acting in the context of his family and group life. For this reason I have, during the past six months, been trying to collect some empirical data on the sociological functioning of the family in that part of London from which the children I have to deal with come. It has long been my ambition to carry out similar observations on the primitive child. One might thus obtain a check on the data already available from the study of the civilised child. But, above all, one should thus be able to discover facts and viewpoints which are marked by the complexity of the social factors in civilised life. At the moment, for example, a controversy is being waged about the nature of children's thinking. Some investigators say that the thought of children is animistic, syncretistic, and prelogical, hence quite different from that of adults. Others maintain just the opposite. But both sides have neglected to observe that they are dealing with children drawn from entirely different social milieus.

The only fruitful method of dealing with these problems is, I believe, one which would commence with a sociological analysis of the child's domestic, cultural, and community setting, and then proceed to study the child's behaviour in this setting. It seems to me, in other words, to demand the application of the methods of functional anthropology to the solution of problems which have for the most part been regarded as purely psychological.

Before proceeding to the field, I should want

(a) to survey all the material available from the study of the civilised child

(b) to find out as much as possible about the culture of the people selected for the work

(c) to prepare a plan for the inquiry.

This preliminary plan obviously proceeds from a conversation with Malinowski and arose out of his interest in Fortes' declared desire to pursue an enquiry into the 'primitive child' using observational materials to test a psychological assumption against a background of sociological and anthropological enquiries.

PLAN NUMBER 2

The second plan, dated 26 March 1932, is headed 'Confidential' and comes from the minutes of the Executive Committee of the International African Institute.

A psychological approach to the study of African society: the social development of the African child

Somewhere in his well-known article on Anthropology in the new *Encyclopaedia Britannica*, Professor Malinowski remarks that 'psychology is indispensable for an understanding of culture'. He means, I think, that we shall never completely understand any primitive society until we turn our attention to the individual human beings who constitute that society, and cease to regard them as mere ciphers, significant only as repositories of curious customs. This lays down the cardinal principle for any psychological approach in anthropology.

To the psychologist, a society is primarily a group of inter-acting individuals. Its social organisation presents itself to him as a system of habits, attitudes, sentiments, and values, rather than as a system of social institutions transcending the human beings 'carrying' them. Some of these habits, attitudes, etc., are directed to frequently recurring situations in the life of the group, others to rare events. Some are peculiar to individuals, others are met within practically all the members of a given society. Every society offers its members a variety of values: goals towards which to strive, rewards for some kinds of conduct, and penalties for other kinds of conduct. Such, in brief, are the conceptions by means of which a psychological analysis of a primitive society would proceed.

Hitherto, most anthropologists have been content to study primitive societies along one co-ordinate as it were. They have confined their attention to a cross-section through the society under consideration at a given moment of time. They have consequently been interested almost solely in the adult members of the community. This incidentally, has no doubt contributed greatly to the prevalent view that primitive societies are as a rule very homogeneous, and stable over long periods.

Recent psychology has however shown that the habits, attitudes, motives, etc., which control individual conduct, within our own society, have their roots in the experiences of early childhood. The adult man or woman can be understood only as the end-product of a long process of growth and development in infancy, childhood, and youth. Social conformity, whether in belief, conduct, feeling, or perhaps even thought, is gradually *learnt*. Indeed, learning, and its correlate teaching, are the concepts which in the psychologist's view give the clue to most of what the sociologist calls custom, convention, ritual, etc., both in our society and in primitive society. When, therefore, we envisage primitive society in terms of psychology – that is, in terms of individual conduct and interaction – we are led to shift the emphasis from the anthropologist's cross-section to a genetic line of inquiry. We are led to investigate the gradual acquisition of the modes of behaviour current in a given society, by the members of that society. The machinery and processes of culture transmission become the centre of interest.

This genetic approach is of particular value, in my opinion, in connection with the less tangible aspects of culture, which are usually treated perfunctorily by orthodox anthropologists, but are of central significance for educationists and students of culture contact: I mean what we describe as moral conduct, standards of value, and even the ways of everyday social intercourse. Any attempt to understand these aspects of a society's life leads the psychologist back directly to the study of the child. It is in childhood, as we learn from psychology, that the foundations are laid for these phases of social behaviour. Indeed, this principle has already proved of service in unravelling certain problems of primitive social organisation. It has, for example, been found to illuminate the problem of the function of the classificatory kinship system, from a new angle.

It is possible to pose the problems involved here even more

specifically. It is generally agreed that the royal road to the re-organisation of African culture in conformity with Western civilisation lies through the education of the African child and adolescent. Psychologically, this may be formulated as the task of inculcating new habits, motives, and attitudes in the African child, and setting before it new goals towards which to strive. There is, however, the further necessity of avoiding a disruption of African society in the course of this new teaching. In other words, there must be some relationship between the new habits, etc., taught to the child, and the modes of behaviour of the older members of its group. The psychologist would maintain that a merely formal relationship between what the missionary or government school teaches, and what the given society practises is not sufficient. The new teaching must be related to the growth and social development of the child within the framework of his own society. We need to know how much the African child has learnt at each stage of his growth, what sort of conduct is expected of it and how well it fulfils expectation, how it is integrated with the life of the group as a whole, at every stage of its development. If we were in the possession of such information, we should, at a moderate estimate, at any rate be in the position to relate the process of purposive education more vitally to the actual mental condition of the African child. To take a hypothetical example, we should be able to tell whether the group life imposed upon the African child in school is consistent with the habits and attitudes expressed in his group life in his own community.

I have brought up the instance of group life for the following reason. It has been shown that the acquisition of social conformity among European children, is largely dependent on the types of contact they have with other children and with adults. This is no doubt true of the African child, the kind and range of its contacts with others will have to receive special attention. In our own society, education by primary contact is practically limited to the transmission of manners and morals. In a preliterate society, the scope of education by primary contact is far wider. Since the most decisive educative contacts in the child's life are known to be those it has with members of its family, and in savage communities, no doubt, its kindred group, it follows that our investigation would have to include a consideration of the family and clan in relation to the child.

Experiment has shown that European children are socialised, especially in regard to moral conduct, not by forms and formulas of instruction, but through their concrete experiences in particular situations. Assuming this to be true of African children, we have to inquire what are the situations in the African child's life which practise him, as it were, in the conduct and the sense of values requisite for good citizenship in his community? Can these situations be reproduced by the white educator, at least in respect to those character traits which are valuable? Professor Malinowski's observations on Trobriand children indicate that it is quite possible to make an inventory of the educative situations recurring in the life of a savage child. With such an inventory as a standard, we should be better able to grasp the significance of the new situations introduced into the African's life through contact with the West.

A final problem: It has been maintained that the African child's mental development ceases at puberty. Psychologists have made us familiar with the fact that a crisis frequently occurs in the life of a European child at puberty, and that these crises are bound up with the experiences of early childhood. The question arises whether the African child's apparent cessation of intellectual development at puberty is not due to a puberty crisis, and what the relation of childhood experiences is to this crisis.

Having thus outlined some of the psychological problems which present themselves in regard to the African child, I should perhaps say something about a possible technique of investigation. *In the last resort this will depend upon the conditions met with in the field.* Certain general standpoints may however be indicated.

(1) A working knowledge of the language of the people to be studied would seem to be indispensable, if the intimate contact required by the sort of investigation proposed is to be possible.

(2) Before undertaking the actual psychological inquiries, it would seem essential to obtain a working ethnological basis. The psychological investigation must of necessity proceed within a framework of ethnological data. Hence it would be advantageous to select an area for which some ethnological information is available.

(3) The actual technique of investigation would be based on the observational methods being perfected in recent child psychology, coupled with 'case history' data about particular individuals or families, obtained by the methods of interrogation and observation employed in functional anthropology. The dominant principle here, is that the data be obtained as far as possible through direct contact with the children. By comparing the behaviour of children

at different stages of growth, it should be possible to set up a sort of scale of development.

(4) Finally, simple experiments should not be beyond trial, although it is difficult to predict which kinds will prove feasible.

Just as the practical educator or administrator often finds it difficult to frame the sort of questions which guide the scientific investigator, so does the latter find it difficult to indicate the practical utility of his work. It seems evident, however, that an inquiry of the kind sketched above, cannot be without bearing on the concrete problems of African education and administration.

As regards the area to be chosen for the work, the officers of the Institute will probably be able to judge best where such a research could most profitably be undertaken. I have suggested the Northern Territories of the Gold Coast, for the following reasons: Captain Rattray's recent ethnological survey of this territory will greatly facilitate the preliminary work of establishing the sociological frame of reference for the inquiry. European contact has apparently not yet destroyed the tribal life of the peoples in these territories, but this process will presumably not be delayed much longer. There may therefore be an opportunity of actually testing the value of inquiries such as the one proposed for directing, or at least understanding cultural change in Africa. Then also, the languages and cultures of the different tribal groups inhabiting these territories appear to be sufficiently allied to enable comparable studies to be undertaken, in different parts of the area, having different degrees of culture contact, both with European and other native culture. Finally, as has been pointed out, it would seem necessary to study the child against the background of its family environment. A people showing a distinctive form of family organisation might thus lend itself more readily to the sort of investigation proposed. This condition seems to be met with in the tribes of the Northern Territories.

M. Fortes, 26 March 1932

This second proposal places more emphasis on ethnological enquiry, learning the language and culture of the people, which was the remit of the International African Institute. It also emphasises 'culture contact' and practical implications, which lay at the core of the Rockefeller grant, even though the Northern Territories were chosen partly because Rattray's recent survey, published that same year, had shown a region where 'the tribal life of the peoples' had not yet been destroyed. This notion of the rapid *destruction* of traditional ways is based upon a rather static view of pre-colonial social life in the area, combined with experience in 'colonies of settlement' (the USA and the Americas more generally, Asiatic USSR, Australia and South Africa), where the advent of massive numbers of largely European immigrants changed earlier modes of life and quickly turned anthropology into a kind of social archaeology.

The second member of this group of fellows was the Austrian, S. F. Nadel, whose report dated 12 December 1932 I present for comparison with that of Fortes, together with his later plan for fieldwork presented in the joint memorandum submitted by the two in conjunction with Hofstra. It was not the first proposal he submitted to the Institute.

PLAN OF RESEARCH, DR SIEGFRIED F. NADEL

As area of my prospective anthropological field-work I want to propose the Territory of Northern Nigeria and within two areas which I may suggest as alternatives:- (1) Nupe-Country and (2) the Bauchi-Hill-Tribes.

General considerations

There were several reasons which induced me to choose the Territory of Northern Nigeria. First of all, the amount of scientific investigation done in the country, both from the general anthropological and the linguistic point of view, was up to now very small. Nearly all parts have been investigated but very superficially owing to the rather short time which the official-anthropologist could afford to spend, in coherent anthropological research work, among different tribes. Other parts may be called still scientifically uninvestigated.

Besides this, the particular tribal distribution in Northern Nigeria, i.e. the interpenetration of different cultures, races and languages, which is so highly characteristic for the Western Sudan, points out a great number of most essential problems. Not only in a vague concept of 'cultural contact', but according to well defined, strong and effective influences, which are working at present among the tribes of Northern Nigeria and which offer to the anthropologist the opportunity to look, so-to-say, into the machinery of cultural action and reaction, into the psychological background of cultural interrelation and to approach the problem of the ability of special cultural facts to survive or to disappear, to be taken over or to be refused, etc. I may enumerate in a preliminary way these various interrelated cultural influences working in Northern

Nigeria: paganism and Islam, Hamitic influence and Sudanic Negro-element, herdsmen and agriculturists, the powerful political organisation of the Negro-kingdoms and, on the other hand, loose village-cultures, or finally, in the special case of the Fulani, the division of one ethnical unit into the two different culture-forms of nomad and settled tribes.

It is obvious that all these questions are also highly important from the political and colonial point of view. Not only because those influences are actually forming the cultural life of Nigeria today, but because colonisation itself, the inevitable influence of western civilisation, represents in a special way that process of 'permeation', the inner mechanism of which must be completely known in order to calculate or to control its consequences.

Moreover, the modern anthropological school of Functionalism we are trained in, here in London, has to pay special attention to these problems of cultural change and disintegration (as Professor Malinowski calls it). Here the 'functions' of cultural or sociological elements can really be tested, by pointing out the varying contextual relations and interpretations that the same cultural element might gain in this or that cultural unit; here the inner mechanism of a living culture can be observed in action by following up the lines along which cultural elements are transformed, taken over or refused, developed or dropped, – apparently according to some inner tendencies of the respective cultures.[2]

These general considerations formed the basis for the two concrete propositions which I am submitting to the African Institute. But I also tried to join in these suggestions the scientific ideas with the standpoint of practical field work and, moreover, with the colonial-political point of view, as far as I could learn it from the literature and from personal information which I was glad to receive from some authorities on Northern Nigeria, as Mr G. J. Lethem of the Colonial Service, Major H. Vischer and Mr G. P. Bargery of the School of Oriental Studies.

Nupe-Country

The rich culture of the Nupe, full of interesting and far-reaching problems, has always attracted the attention of anthropologists (e.g. Frobenius, Meek, etc.), but nevertheless has been studied but very superficially, and nearly no investigation was made on Nupe-language. Nupe is certainly to be ranged among the most important and most interesting of the West African cultures; there are the highly developed handicrafts, the famous goldsmith work and the manufacturing of glass, which made the Nupe widely renowned from the ancient times; on the other hand the highly developed social organisation, the complicated religious system but superficially islamised, etc.

(a) From the historical point of view the Nupe have obvious relations to the Jukun-culture and probably to the Nuba-people of Southern Kordofan, but, on the other hand, also to the Western and Southern cultures of Ashanti, Dahomey, Yoruba and Benin. Here we touch one of the most important problems of African historical anthropology; the racial and cultural relation between the Western Sudan and the East.

(b) More interesting in an actual sense is the fact that the Nupe preserved themselves practically untouched from the surrounding cultures. They represent one of the few if not the only culture in Northern Nigeria, upon which Hausa and Fulani influence had no effect at all. So the culture organisation of the Nupe can be studied under most favourable circumstances and especially one particular problem can be approached: the problem of the 'state-building power' (*staatenbildende Kraft*) of the Negroes, which has been overcome and reduced in the other parts of the Northern Provinces by the Fulani rulers.

(c) Yet one point complicates the situation. Though the Nupe culture proves this effective strength and vitality, the population is subject to permanent diminution. These two facts, going side by side in Nupe country, raise the very important problem of the interrelation between POPULATION (number, in accordance to its density and economic situation, physical status, etc.) and CULTURAL ABILITY.

(d) As far as the Fulani living among the Nupe are concerned, I want to add some remarks. When I first worked out a scheme for prospective field work in Africa, I liked to lay most stress on the problems of the Fulani, – which again was very little investigated and which seems to be urgent in a way, e.g. concerning the actual change among the Fulani from nomadic herdsmen into settled agriculturists. The study of the Fulani, however, especially of the shy and wide-spread Nomad-Fulani, would appear a much too large and complicated task for a first field-work, moreover limited in time. Yet, in Nupe-country, owing to the mutually uninfluenced living-together of the different tribes, the conditions would be given to start with the study of the Fulani; first perhaps as a side line, but working out the basis for future research in the large area of the Northern Provinces.

(e) Nupe-country itself, from the practical point of view, is a well defined and, in a way, limited cultural unit. It presents an excellent opportunity of being studied monographically, i.e. above all of being thoroughly and satisfactorily investigated in the TWO-YEARS-TIME, we can dispose of.

Bauchi-Hill-Tribes

The Bauchi-Hill-Tribes or, with the new official name, the Jos-Plateau-Tribes, represent probably the most primitive stage of culture among the tribes of Northern Nigeria. They represent the characteristic type of primitive pagan village culture and they again have not yet been really investigated.

(a) First of all they seem to have preserved entirely their old pagan customs, tribal institutions, etc., which are everywhere still alive and have not been influenced but very little – and only on the boundaries of the area – by the surrounding cultures of the Hausa and Fulani.[3]

(b) the special environment of the mountains has certainly contributed in forming the culture of the Plateau-tribes. The mountains served for centuries as 'the refuge of communities fleeing from Hausa, Fulani and Kanuri pressure' (Morel, 1912: 184), they preserved most ancient culture forms but they also split up and separated tribes and languages into numerous small units. New questions arise here. How far did independent cultural peculiarities develop in these small and someway isolated communities? Or, on the other hand, how far did the same environment work upon these cultural peculiarities?

(c) There is one special point which makes these questions important, and perhaps urgent too, from the political and sociological point of view. The Plateau-tribes have got an old knowledge of iron-melting and manufacturing of tin. Tin-production is now carried through in Bauchi Province on a large scale and with the most modern means of industrial exploitation. The work in the mines brings together people of all parts of the country. The new roads and railway lines enable the primitive hill-men to come around the country, to walk down to the towns and to come in touch with other tribes, much more than ever before. So most primitive cultural stage and most modern industrial development are facing each other in the Bauchi-Plateau-territory. A

wide range of new possibilities, new aspects, new economic situations
suddenly opened for the people. All this must become of extreme
importance; not only for the people themselves and not only for the
student, who finds here an exceptional material for studying cultural
permeation and the conflicts and processes of adaptation rising here;
but also for the Government, which has to reckon with these results,
brought up inevitably by the new state of things. So here again, as far
as I see, the scientific point of view meets with the political and colonial
interest.

Supplementary remarks on music

I want to add still one personal point – according to what I have
explained in my former Memorandum for the African Institute –
concerning my interest for the investigation of native Music and
Dance. The scientific investigation of native art can certainly not be
done fruitfully without the basis of the general anthropological
research. By no other means can one learn to understand the important
part which music plays in the native life and, above all, learn to
approach the fundamental and almost virginal problem of understanding and explaining the musical culture of a people out of the
general structure of its cultural life. The music investigation will
become by this way, so to speak, a last chapter in the general
anthropological monography.

But besides these theoretical questions, music plays a very important
part and has specific scientific significance in both areas, which I was
describing. Nupe music and Bauchi-Hill music are scientifically almost
unknown. The Nupe culture encloses a great number of problems of
musical ethnography; highly characteristic instruments, which cover
the whole Bantu area and reach as far West as Senegambia (Marimba,
Panpipes, some drum-forms), make a sort of detour, in their distribution, around the Niger-Benue-territory; on the other hand other music
instruments are found here in interesting isolation or in peculiar
relation to other parts of Africa (square bells, bells with tongue, special
types of horns and signal flutes). Also the question of the strength of the
Hausa-Islamic influence in Nigeria can be approached through the
medium of music and dance, – e.g. Arabic influence in melody and
style of singing, influence of the dances of the Islamic religious orders in
the tribal dances, etc. The Bauchi-Hill tribes again present the
opportunity to study music bound up with the most primitive forms of

culture and, perhaps, the adaptation of native music, songs and dance to the new circumstances of the life in the industrial districts.

The third member of this particular group of fellows was the Dutchman, S. Hofstra whose report, also of December 1932, presents an account of what research he intended to carry out in Sierra Leone, complementing Fortes' work in the Gold Coast and Nadel's in Nigeria.

PLAN OF RESEARCH, DR S. HOFSTRA

Before setting forth the problems I should like to investigate it may be advisable to state at the outset that my approach to these problems will be that of the functional method. This method, as presented by Professor Malinowski, seems to me to be the most fertile one for field-work. It will therefore be my aim to study in the most concrete way possible the functional relationship between the different social phenomena connected with the subject.

I should like to submit *three* problems in which I am especially interested. The *first* is that of *the influence of Mohammedanism on primitive communities*, especially in West Africa. Under this head I propose to deal with: the effect of Mohammedanism on family life, economics, law, religion, morals and knowledge.

A few questions arising from this problem may be indicated here, namely: the conditions under which primitive peoples become Mohammedan, and the motives, religious, material or other, which lead them to do so. The methods of conversion that Mohammedanism employs. The genetic relationship between Mohammedan brotherhoods and secret societies. The means of propaganda. The way in which Mohammedanism maintains itself in primitive communities. The religious leaders (an important question in relation to the problem of individuality in primitive society and to that of the genesis of leadership). The relationship between Mohammedanism and the means of existence (many Mohammedans in West Africa are traders). The spread of Mohammedanism (according to Brevié Mohammedanism in the French Soudan is losing ground, while in other parts of West Africa as in Guinea and Ivory Coast it is, according to Marty, making headway). And the extent to which assimilation is taking place between primitive religion and Islam.

These are, of course, only a few aspects of the subject, which, since it is very extensive, has to be limited according to the conditions prevailing in the field.

It seems to me that this problem is of great importance, both from the theoretical and from the practical point of view. From the theoretical, because we have here a most interesting opportunity of studying the functional relationship of the religious factor to the other factors of life, and of studying the effects of the intermingling of two different culture elements. And from the practical, because Mohammedanism has a considerable influence in West Africa. It seems to me to be of the greatest possible importance to know as exactly as sociological and psychological methods of investigation permit, how far this influence goes and in which direction.

I may add that my concern is predominantly with this problem, since I am especially interested in the sociological and psychological analysis of religions; also my former training and descriptive sociological work lay in this field of research. The technique of my enquiries would be based on the *observational* methods employed in functional anthropology. I am already acquainted with a great deal of the general literature dealing with the social side of Mohammedanism and with the ethnography of the area I should like to investigate. In regard to the area to be chosen for making a study of this subject, I should like to suggest French West Africa: firstly because the conditions for studying the problem are very favourable in that region; secondly because I have studied two languages spoken in this area, Dyoula and Bambara. It would also be possible, of course, to study the problem in Nigeria, Sierra Leone, the Ivory Coast or the Gold Coast. The officers of the Institute, however, will be able to judge best where such a piece of research could most profitably be undertaken.

The *second* problem I should like to suggest for investigation is that of the *social conditions prevalent amongst the Sierra Leonese*. Sierra Leone has a special interest because we have no good descriptions of this country. It seems to me that a study of one or more of these tribes and the different levels of civilisation found among them would be well worth undertaking. I should like to compare certain social conditions among various groups, taking first Freetown and the Coast population; second, the primitive tribes in the Central and Southern Provinces (Mendis, Veis and so on) and third, the Mandingo in the Northern Province. A study of the land tenure and or vital statistics, for instance, should be of great importance.

The *third* problem in which I am interested is that of *Individuality among*

primitive peoples. The place of Individuality in their society, the relationship of the individual to group life has not so far received due attention,
and we know very little about the social function of individual differences
among primitive peoples. This subject is of importance, both for genetic
psychology and from a practical point of view.

It is for instance important to know the opportunities of leadership
open to outstanding individuals and to discover the real power of
initiative given by a position of leadership. And there is the further
problem of the extent to which successful adaptation to new conditions
is related to differences in individual character. This problem I should
like to study in one of the Mandingo speaking tribes in West Africa.

To sum up, these are three problems which would especially interest
me:

1. The influence of Mohammedanism in West Africa.
2. A study of some vital problems in Sierra Leone.
3. The place of individuality in primitive community (to be investi-
    gated among one of the Mandingo speaking peoples).

12 December 1932

In the following October, after nine months' work and joint discussion, the
three fellows sent the following joint memorandum to Oldham at Malinowski's
request.

REPORT TO THE INTERNATIONAL AFRICAN INSTITUTE

To Dr Oldham   London, 23 October 1933

In response to your request for an account of our collaboration during
the past year, we have drawn up the following statement. It is
necessarily brief, but we hope that it will be sufficient to convey a
general idea of what we have been aiming at. Unfortunately a great
deal of what emerged from our joint discussions cannot easily be
summarised on paper, as it was concerned with clarifying issues raised
in the Seminars of Professor Malinowski and Professor Seligman, and
with threshing out some of the more difficult problems we discovered
to be common to our respective areas of future field work.

These common problems, the scientific interests which we shared,
the stimulus which we received from seminars and private talks with
Professor Malinowski and Professor Seligman, and the Institute's
programme formed the basis of our collaboration. The areas which we

have chosen for our field work have many sociological features in common. They have, for example, linguistic affinities; the forms and functions of the family are similar in the three areas; the type of political organisation is in many ways uniform; and the history of contact with foreign cultures, both in the past and at present, is alike in its general features for the three areas.

Our main efforts were thus from the outset directed towards working out a methodological approach which would enable us eventually to compare the results of our field work. Three problems of method have particularly engaged our attention. Although we shall have to formulate them rather abstractly here, they actually emerged from frequent discussions of concrete field-work tasks, which we shall illustrate later.

1. The problem of classifying social facts in a way sufficiently systematic to permit of comparing those we shall bring away with us from the field, and yet flexible enough to meet empirical requirements. We are still far from a practical solution of this problem, and hope to gain much new insight into it this term, when it will form one of the main subjects of Professor Malinowski's seminar.

2. The problem of establishing the functions of the social institutions of our respective communities, the interrelations of these institutions, and their 'powers of resistance' to foreign influences.

3. The problem of investigating the psychological and biological factors in social institutions and social relations.

Although our main concern has been to develop a practicable plan for dealing with these broad problems of method in connection with our field work, we found that it was essential to regard them as parts of far more general problems pertaining to Occidental as well as African societies. Thus we hope to be able to bring our field work into relation with the work of students of European society.

To give one or two illustrations of the specific questions round which our discussions have revolved:

Firstly, The Family. The family is the pivot of social organisation in West Africa. We have been discussing ways and means of studying it, in our respective areas, as a concrete social grouping made up of a number of closely linked individuals, rather than as an abstract appendage of the kinship system. In this connection we were brought up against such questions as the economic, legal, educational, religious, etc., functions of the family, and the probable consequences for its stability of a changing economic and political context. We have found, also, that special problems arise, in our selected areas, from the relations of the family as a distinct social unit to other social groupings of a religious, educational (secret societies), political (a 'ruling class'), and professional (craftsmen), nature.

Secondly, the problem of social control. One of our main interests has been to arrive at useful concepts and methods for investigating the processes – legal, economic, religious, traditional, and educational – by which conduct is regulated in the interest of social cohesion. We have thus been led to pay special attention to the question of social differentiation and individuation, and its relations with institutions like chieftainship, religious leadership, magic and witchcraft, economic enterprise; and with new phenomena like conversion to Christianity or Islam, and response to the demands for labour on mines, etc. We believe that the problems arising from culture contact can be approached from this angle with fruitful results.

These two instances will, we hope, suffice to indicate the direction of our joint work, as well as its bearing upon the practical issues with which the Institute is concerned.

M. Fortes,
S. Hofstra,
S. F. Nadel.

INTERNATIONAL INSTITUTE OF AFRICAN LANGUAGES AND CULTURES

SCHEMES OF RESEARCH

JOINT MEMORANDUM BY DR FORTES, DR NADEL AND DR HOFSTRA WITH APPENDICES ON PARTICULAR SCHEMES

(*Note.* The three Fellows of the Institute who have recently gone to West Africa have acceded to a request of the Directors that they should submit an outline of the plan on which they propose to work. The following joint memorandum with attached schemes is circulated for the information of the Council. The Fellows desire that what they have written should be regarded as entirely tentative, since it is based necessarily on secondhand material and may be considerably modified by experience in the field. – J. H. OLDHAM, Administrative Director.)

The work of the field-anthropologist consists of two main parts: firstly the *descriptive* part, and secondly the *interpretation* of the descriptive data. These two parts, or more accurately phases of investigation, naturally merge into each other. Our schemes will try to bring out the significance of each phase and the point of transition.

To facilitate the descriptive work of the anthropologist and sociologist it is necessary to have a working classification of social facts. We have adopted the following:-

I *Classification of Social Facts*

(a) *Institutions.* They represent organised bodies of activities, relatively permanent, subserving a more or less discernible social purpose; e.g. a typical economic institution is the market; a typical political institution is chieftainship; a typical religious institution is the ancestor cult; a typical legal institution is a court of law, - etc.

(b) *Social Groupings.* E.g. family, clan, local community, tribe, religious associations, professional groupings, castes, recreational associations, economic associations, etc.; to the same category would belong also the looser types of grouping, such as friendship, comradeship, accidental associations, etc.

(c) *Aspects of Social Life.* E.g. economics, law, education, religion, political system, science, art.

The system of relations which constitutes a particular grouping may comprise a variety of institutions and *vice versa*; e.g. the family comprises economic, religious, legal institutions; a typical economic institution, e.g. market is the centre of activities of family, tribe, local groupings. In the field we are in touch primarily with concrete social behaviour, i.e. with *Groupings plus Institutions*. This means, in effect, that every concrete constellation of social behaviour can be viewed under the aspect of its 'Institutionalisation' or its 'Grouping'. The *Aspects* do not enter until the final interpretation and synthesis. This synthetic correlation of groupings and institutions with one another and with the Aspects of Social Life will yield the significant general characteristics of a particular culture. For the Aspects are not of the same order in all types of culture; they have different powers of resistance against the influences which induce culture change; and they are of varying importance within the culture; their hierarchical order thus characterizes the particular culture for comparative work. We thus arrive at problems such as whether or not it is true that Religion and Magic completely dominate the life of the African to the exclusion of other interests?

II *Function and Relation of Institutions*

The consideration of this problem arises out of the fact previously mentioned that in Groupings, Institutions and Aspects we are not dealing with discrete social phenomena, but that all three are integrated in one unitary system. We classify Institutions according to the *purposes* they subserve, i.e. the *needs* they satisfy. It is important to note that every single institution may be correlated to a variety of needs; these needs appear in a certain structure, some being primary, fundamental, and generally the more permanent, others secondary and variable. One of the main problems of fieldwork is to determine the structure of needs characteristic of particular institutions. Since this structure can not be predicted *a priori*, it is essential to obtain as complete a description as possible of the activities which constitute an institution.

The relations between Institutions are revealed in so far as (a) they can be allocated to specific Aspects of culture (e.g. hunting, agriculture and market are related with each other as economic institutions, i.e. as belonging to the same Aspect: Economics); (b) in so far as they exist in the context of common groups. This type of correlation of Institutions can only be established in the process of fieldwork. Examples, based on second-hand material, will be given in the special schemes appended (e.g. chieftainship, as an element of political organization, and courts of law, as a legal institution, are interdependent in virtue of the common 'personnel' factor).

III *Problem of Psychological Factors*

Here the factor of the organised grouping which is essential for every institution is envisaged from the point of view of what makes cohesion and cooperation in the group possible.

Psychological Factors, however, are not deducible from sociological observations unless these have been undertaken with the specific object of revealing the former. The Psychological Factors seem to be most accessible in two contexts:-

(1) Life History of the Individual.
(2) Life History of the Group.

The investigation of these two contexts will lead to the recognition of the inner dynamics of institutions which express the strength and quality of the Psychological Factors. The two dimensions manifest themselves in the following way sociologically:-

(1) The Life History of the Individual is correlated to the sociological problem of continuity and transmission of cultural norms and patterns.

(2) The Life History of the Group is correlated to the sociological problem of size, distribution and constitution of groups.

(3) The correlation of both dimensions with each other leads to the sociological problem of the elasticity of 'norms'.

In connection with (1) arise questions for investigation such as: the psychological factors maintaining authority, e.g. in the family; the system of social sentiments which governs the conduct of the individual, e.g. his consciousness of being [a] member of a community and of all that this entails. This has special reference to problems of culture contact, e.g. to the problem of disintegration of family solidarity.

(2) Psychologically this factor is significant in virtue of the types of relationship which individuals can enter into, either *inter se*, or with groupings. Here again culture contact problems emerge, e.g. redistribution of population due to industrialisation leads to types of social relations which did not exist before; or, as a result of concentrated missionary effort, the constitution of a group may change considerably, and thus affect the whole system of social relations and individual conduct.

(3) In the widest sense this is the problem of Social Control. It is reflected in the existing system of values towards which the life of individuals and groupings within the society is organised. Specific instances are Ancestor worship and Magic. From this point of view we are faced with the problem why, under certain circumstances of contact Ancestor worship may become transformed or assimilated to Christian or Mohammedan belief, whereas Magic persists in distorted forms, but in full strength.

The best practical means of presenting the concrete application of the points of view elaborated above are diagrammatic schemes as suggested by Professor Malinowski in his seminar. We have so far been able to test the value of this scientific device on secondhand material only. We append as illustrations three schemes covering respectively a typical *social grouping* (Family), a typical *institution* (Religious Cult), and one phenomenon which shows a typical *overlapping* of the two categories (Secret Societies).

SKETCH OF A PLAN FOR THE STUDY OF THE AFRICAN FAMILY

M. Fortes

The family in Africa is the pivot of social life. It is defined spatially, genetically, in terms of social organisation, of economic relationships, of religious cult, of legal ordinance, and of political structure. The first problem of family research is to establish the complete sociological definition of the family for a particular culture, as a more or less permanent grouping, subsuming a series of institutions. We thus plot the family in that culture along the co-ordinate of its place in the whole social scheme, as a functional unit, bound to other groupings – other families, clans, various associations, etc., as indicated in the preceding general scheme – by specific ties and sanctions, and playing a defined role in societal life.

I. The most methodical procedure would be to describe the institutions by means of which the family satisfies the basic needs of its members. To give an instance:- the economic needs of the individual in many West African societies are satisfied by a complex organization of institutions, in some of which (e.g. those concerned with land tenure, agricultural technique, knowledge of plants and animals) the economic need is paramount, while in others (e.g. the religious practices associated with agriculture) it is secondary; a full inventory of the series of institutions grouped round the basic need for food might be represented as follows:

Need	Institutions clustered about						
Food	Locality	Ownership	Production	Exchange	Consumption	Legal rules	Religious practices

A similar enquiry undertaken for the other basic needs, such as that for security, shelter, etc., would lead to the sociological definition of the family for the particular area.

II. This is the first stage of research. At the next stage, it is necessary to treat these institutions as the regular, recurrent activities of an organized and permanent social grouping, with a distinctive life history. We focus attention upon the family as a permanent microcosm which comes into being by well-defined social processes, maintains itself, counteracts or succumbs to subversive forces, passes away.

We are thus concerned with the twin questions of what keeps the family together as an integral unity, and how does this inner cohesion react upon the institutions of the society and upon the society as a whole. A study of the literature suggests several lines of attack upon these fundamental questions of family research:-

(a) It is clear that the very nature of the institutions correlated to the basic needs of the society, both as individuals and as a group, constrains family cohesion. Thus the division of labour is a strong force in favour of family solidarity, in an agricultural community. The political structure of many West African societies is only workable as long as the family remains a corporate unity, under a strong patriarchal head, and thus reacts in favour of family cohesion. When, as a result of culture contact, new means of satisfying the basic needs arise, or the political structure atrophies, an early symptom may be family disintegration.

(b) There may be other factors of conduct or belief, only indirectly connected with the basic needs, but institutionalised as distinctively familial, and hence conducive to family integrity. The ancestor cult in West Africa is a specially good instance. The belief in descent from a common ancestor not only unites the group sharing it, but differentiates that group from other groups. What may seem a superfluous superstition thus appears to be an important principle of social cohesion. To appreciate the value of the ancestor cult as such a principle, it is necessary to investigate how it gains validity from its acceptance as a norm of belief by the whole community. This is what characterises it as a religious belief and not merely as a family tradition. In short, the unity of the family in this connection is derivative from its place in the religious scheme of things.

(c) The prevailing principles of social organisation. In West Africa the family pattern pervades all social organisation. Thus the village community and even larger tribal units are constituted on the family pattern. As a consequence no individual can enter into wider social relationships except as a member of a family – this applies even to slaves – and family integrity is greatly emphasised.

(d) The specific psychological results of the fact that the family is a continuous grouping – that the child grows up in the family environment. Sentiments of respect for authority in the family, emotional bonds with the family home and family members, a system of values in which the family occupies pride of place, are inculcated. Unquestionably these serve as the basis of family cohesion. But they do not by themselves ensure family cohesion. Unless emphasised and sustained by the whole structure of the society they may remain at the level of feelings which do not reach expression in conduct. It is necessary to find out what are the social processes which actualise these sentiments and feelings. Here the 'ritual of family life', which often has the combined sanctions of the religious, the legal, and the economic systems, operates as a determining factor. Funeral customs are such 'rituals' in West Africa. While they undoubtedly evoke the psychological bonds which link the family members together, matters of inheritance and succession, and public opinion also motivate the collaboration of all branches of the family on such occasions.

III. We thus arrive at the final and most significant stage of research in family problems, the enquiry as to how the family functions as the matrix of conduct, in the widest sense of that term. To explore this, it is necessary to study the family along the 'time co-ordinate', biographically. We have to investigate how, from earliest infancy, knowledge, skills, norms of behaviour, religious and magical beliefs, kinship attitudes, loyalties and hostilities are inculcated by parents and other kinsmen. We have to investigate, too, if possible, how the subtler features of personality which give the clues to individual variations within the group, are generated in the family environment.

The method most adaptable for this problem is the study of individual life histories, not in abstraction from but against the background of the changing family and community milieu. This may be represented graphically as follows:-

Individual's life-line in terms of the major phases of social development

— →

/   /   /   /   /   /   /

Birth Infancy Puberty Marriage Parenthood Elder-ship Death

Each phase must be established specifically for every culture, and studied in its context of (a) the personnel involved (grouping), (b) the institutions concerned. Thus the birth of a child among the Ashanti involves the ritual participation both before and after its birth, of various members of its family and kin. The rites which take place are institutionalised religious and magical acts.

As we trace the child's development through infancy and puberty, we find its life-horizon gradually expanding. It acquires the skills and knowledge incumbent upon it for each stage of growth, and learns to canalize its emotional drives along institutionalised lines (e.g. in kinship relationships). An (institutionalised) stage such as marriage involves a re-crystallisation of its relationships with a large section of the social milieu.

The purpose of such a plan of investigation is to cover, as exhaustively as possible, the two chief dimensions of family life: the 'spatial dimension', i.e. the place of the family in the social scheme, as part and parcel of a wider whole, at a given time; and the 'chronological dimension', i.e. its peculiar psychological character, as a unit of society which comes into existence, lives, passes away.

SCHEME FOR THE INVESTIGATION OF RELIGIOUS INSTITUTIONS

S. F. Nadel

The idea of this scheme is to trace the empirical investigation of *Religious Institutions* in its gradual deepening into more and more general problems. It starts off by concrete, observable constellations of human behaviour, and leads into the functional correlation of general aspects of social life.

According to the structure of social institutions, implied in its sociological definition, three initial categories are chosen. They correspond (1) to the centre of every institution, namely *organised activity*, (2) to the necessary factor of *grouping*, and (3) to the existence of a certain *theoretical charter* which is essential for every institution: for it accounts for its purposive contents, its regularity, or, translated into terms of subjective principles determining the behaviour of the grouping, the essential conviction that the Institution is permanent and continuous. These three factors may be formulated for the religious institution proper as follows:- Dogma, Ritual (being the central organised 'activity') and Personnel.

The first layer gives the full descriptive account of concrete happenings, organised in these three categories. It gives a first, more or less coherent, evidence of the material from which the deeper insight into the essence of the religious institution will emerge. The transition to the second layer is marked by placing each category in the wider connection of the implications which lie within the first statements, and are now expanded. The 'key' of transition is the question after the correlation of Dogma with the other dogmatic (or, more general, theoretical) factors in Society, or Ritual to the whole realm of organised activities in Society, or Personnel to the other existing forms of organised grouping in this Society. Evidently this must lead beyond

Religion proper to the neighbouring fields of Science and Social Organisation, which is indicated in the scheme by widening the basis of our diagram [figure 2].

Yet the connections worked out on this layer stand only in *lateral* relation to each other. They do not yet show inner, i.e. functional correlation; e.g. in the case of the West African 'Bori' we find that the 'material substratum', which is characteristic for the ritual, is of an aesthetic nature (musical instrument), the 'formulated aim' is quasi-scientific (cure of mental diseases) and there is no fixed place in the 'Life Cycle'. On the other hand a ritual might use a significant agricultural object as 'material', might formulate its aim as bearing upon agriculture, and take place only at times characteristic for agricultural enterprise (e.g. this is the case in the ordinary fertility rites). On the second layer we are directed to *find* and *see* these connections; what they *mean* in the life of the society cannot be answered yet. This will be part of the deeper 'functional' study, which, for this special question will turn into the problem of the psychological background of these 'lateral' correspondence and correlations.

It is necessary to note that empirical investigation can begin from every datum corresponding to any category of the first or second layer. If this datum which might form the empirical starting point belongs really to Religion, then it must be possible to work it into the whole scheme and to complete the material accordingly; if this is impossible, then it was not part of Religion (e.g. the observation of a ceremonial dance whose religious nature might be doubtful at first).

The transition to the third layer is marked by the logical transition from 'lateral' to 'functional' correlation. The problem of the place of religious beliefs amongst other organised beliefs becomes here the problem of *Transmission*: how does Religion work as transmission of ideas and beliefs, keep them alive, and maintain them as specific religious ideas and beliefs. The problem of the Grouping and the characteristic observances and activities which distinguish and, at the same time, unite 'Actors' and 'Congregation', lead to the problem of the *Norms of Conduct*, which are necessarily involved, and which enable and control these specific activities and observances. The central Column of *Ritual* finally leads, as we have seen, to the problem of the *psychological background* behind the ritualised activity.

Again, new larger categories have to be added to the right and left in our diagram: Education and Social Control (Legal and Political).

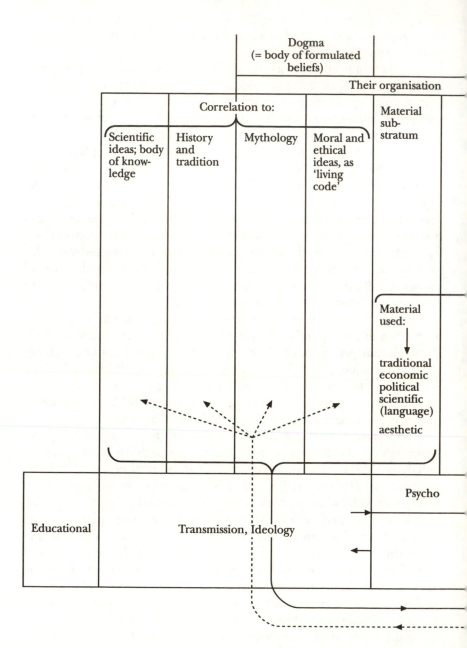

Figure 2 Nadel's diagram for the investigation of religious institutions

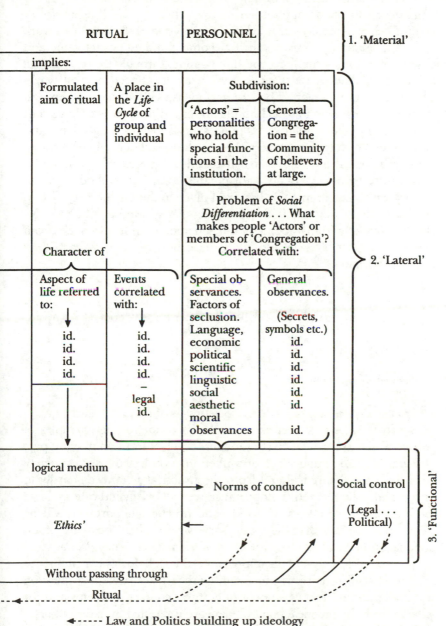

RITUAL   PERSONNEL   1. 'Material'

implies:

Formulated aim of ritual	A place in the *Life-Cycle* of group and individual	Subdivision:	
		'Actors' = personalities who hold special functions in the institution.	General Congregation = the Community of believers at large.

Problem of *Social Differentiation* . . . What makes people 'Actors' or members of 'Congregation'? Correlated with:

Character of

2. 'Lateral'

Aspect of life referred to:	Events correlated with:	Special observances. Factors of seclusion. Language, economic political scientific linguistic social aesthetic moral observances	General observances. (Secrets, symbols etc.)
↓	↓		
id.	id.		id.
id.	id.		id.
id.	id.		id.
id.	id.		id.
	–		id.
	legal		id.
↓	id.		id.
			id.

logical medium

Norms of conduct →   Social control

'Ethics' ←   (Legal . . . Political)

3. 'Functional'

Without passing through

Ritual

◀----- Law and Politics building up ideology

◀——— Education working as factor of social control

And here the inner meaning of Religion discloses itself as the ultimate result of the application of this scheme. The *Transmission* of certain beliefs, not necessarily religious (e.g. general ideology) can work upon the *Norms of Conduct*, which become manifest in activities and observances of a grouping, without passing through the *psychological medium* embodied in the Ritual. And, *vice versa*, Social control works back upon Transmission of beliefs, and ideas, without passing through Ritual and its psychological implications. But then we have not Religion, but the regulative influences of Education, and Law and politics respectively. Only where this regulative influence goes through the psychological medium, which is based upon a significant material substratum, revolving round a formulated aim, and embodied in an activity which has its more or less fixed place in the Life cycle of Group and Individual, *only then* is this influence really *religious* influence. Its effective working from one side of our scheme upon the other, i.e. from one large aspect of social life upon the other, represents the '*Ethical Power*' of Religion.

SCHEME FOR A STUDY OF SECRET SOCIETIES

S. Hofstra

Explanation of the scheme

1 *Importance of the subject.*   Secret societies as they exist nearly everywhere in West Africa offer some of the most interesting examples of groups which are strongly institutionalized. They form an integral part of tribal life. The importance of a phenomenon like the secret society both from the theoretical and from the practical side needs hardly to be stressed. The theoretical importance we will briefly indicate as far as the data available allows us to do. The practical importance will be clear from the fact that the secret society very often forms the main political and educational organisation of the natives. They do not seem to have considerably lost in importance through European influence and in what direction this process of change takes place is a question equally important for the student of cultural contact problems and for all who from the practical point of view are interested in native affairs.

The adjective 'secret' may be somewhat misleading. Certainly the activities of the societies are to a great extent secret, but not in the sense that they are against public opinion. Secret here does not necessarily mean anti-social.

Migeod (cf. *The Mende language*, p. vii) asserts that things of which nearly every boy and girl knows cannot be very secret. Professor Westermann (cf. *Die Kpelle*, p. 233) rightly criticises this opinion. He remarks that in the first place the boys who go through the secret societies (Porro) are not familiar with all the secrets of that society; in the second place men and women have their own societies and are not allowed to know of the affairs of each others' societies. Moreover, it is not only *within* the society that there are degrees of secrecy. The extent of secrecy depends also upon the *type* of the society. It is obvious that, for instance, the Human Leopard Society was much more secret in character than the Porro.

2 *The aim of the scheme.* The appended scheme [figure 3] aims at giving in a diagrammatic form a survey of the main elements of our subject. The value of such a scheme lies mainly in providing the fieldworker with an apparatus for his work. The scheme is not intended to give a brief final formulation of results of investigation, but will be a summary of the most relevant facts which the fieldworker ought not to neglect.

3 *Its content.* The several sections of the scheme as outlined give an indication of the main subject matter of the society we want to study, viz.:-

Locality (comprising headquarters of the society, houses for the initiates, extent of influence).

Mythology and beliefs (beliefs about origin of society, relation to ancestors and spirits).

Organisation (membership, grades, fees, symbols, meetings).

Initiation (age of boys and girls when they enter, ceremonies connected with the initiation, teachings, special purpose of training).

Personnel (head of society, council, minor officials).

Language (secret language, songs).

Activities and special purpose of the society (political, legal, educational, religious, magical and medical, recreational activities; special purpose according to whether the society has a general character as the Porro or a special character as the Kufong. A few remarks may be added as to the *activities* of the secret societies. With this point may be included *their functional importance*.)

Locality	Mythology and beliefs	Organisation	Initiation	Personnel	Language	Activities
Headquarters	Mythological origin	Memberships	Age of boys and girls	Head Council	Secret language	Political
Houses of the initiates	Relation to ancestors	Grades	Ceremonies	Minor officials	Songs	Legal
Extent of influence		Fees	Teachings			Educational
		Symbols	Special training			Religious
		Meetings				Magical
						Medical
						Recreational

Main subject matter

Further analysis

Functional relationship of secret societies to other institutions and groupings as chieftainship and family.

Human relations within the societies (leadership, relation teacher–pupils, authority, degrees of secrecy) and *place of the individual* in the societies.

Figure 3 Scheme for the investigation of West African secret societies

Political aspect. Although our knowledge of the West African secret societies is still very limited and lacking precision, yet their political importance will be clear to everyone who is acquainted with them either from experience or from the literature available on the subject. Where, for instance, the Porro exists it may be called the main political body in native culture. A thorough investigation, however, would have to make clear how far this political influence goes. Another interesting point about which more information is needed is the relation between chieftainship and leadership of the secret society, the division of power between them.

The legal aspect is shown is the following points:- (a) in some cases a legislative function exercised by a special group of chiefs and elders within the society; (b) teaching of the laws during the initiation period and the general guardianship of native customs; (c) the degree of legality which the different societies enjoy; the Human Leopard Society, for instance, was only in the opinion of the Europeans but also of a great many of the natives of criminal character.

The educational aspect is in the first place of a general nature: every boy or girl has to enter a society (Porro and Bundu in Sierra Leone, for instance) in order to undergo a training in their later duties as members of the tribe and family. A transmission of social values thus takes place. In the second place the societies train for special vocations; those of magicians, artisans, etc.

The relation to *magic* and *medicine* consists in the fact that some of the societies function as the guardians of the magical and medical store of knowledge of the tribe. The societies of magicians play a considerable and mysterious part. They act very probably as transmittors of the magical knowledge.

The relationship of the different secret societies to one another and of them to *other institutions* (as chieftainship), and *groupings* (as the family), will be part of our subject. Further, the relation of the professional groupings to the societies has to be considered. Also the influence of rank and wealth on their activities (great influence of chiefs and magicians; wealth enables to pay fees for higher grades).

Finally, the subject of secret societies is of considerable interest in relation to the *position of women*. Where the women have their own society (as in the case of the Bundu in Sierra Leone), the social status of the women can only be fully understood in connection with these societies. Through the facts mentioned above runs a system of *human relations*, which are of great interest to the student of social psychology. We mean relations as between leader and members, between teachers and pupils, between the members of a same age-group.

A problem as to how *authority* is secured and exercised, what are the *binding forces* amongst the members and between them and their leaders demands a closer investigation.

Closely related to these questions is the problem of *the place of the individual* in a group like a secret society. For an understanding of the processes of individuation and differentiation (and at the same time of association) the secret society will probably prove to be of no less importance than the family (for a more detailed analysis of similar problems I may refer to my *Differenzierungserscheinungen in einigen Afrikanischen Gruppen*, Amsterdam, 1933). The secret society acts on the one hand as a binding force by its obligatory character; on the other hand it provides an opportunity for differentiation through leadership and through training for special professions. For instance in the case of the magical and medical professions the selection according to individual ability seems to play a considerable role.

Towards the study of the history of social anthropology

Writing about the recent history of social anthropology in Britain has made me think more tightly about the writing of history, especially when I compare my own approach with that of individuals who were neither anthropologists nor participants. Participants do not make the best historians, nor do practitioners make the best historians of science. But historians too are at a disadvantage. In the first place they are dependent on the written record or, with contemporary or oral historians, on recollections about the past. As we have seen in the case of the letters of Evans-Pritchard and Malinowski, the written record is very partial in a number of ways. Not simply because much is left out, much destroyed, but because the presentation of the self in writing is often a caricature of what occurs in the intercourse of everyday life. Obviously the written record of an incident covers a greater span than the understanding of any one of the participants, perhaps of all of them. But in so far as it does so it may well override subjective meaning, meaning to the actors. Of course, the presentation of such a meaning can rarely constitute the be-all and end-all of scholarship. Equally it can never be disregarded.

Of nowhere is this more apparent than in intellectual history. Historians of this domain are intent on placing people in schools, to which various characteristics are allotted. This is done partly for their own understanding of a complex situation, partly to make comprehension easier for the reader, who likes to have his phenomena tied together in neat packages. There are of course some explicit 'schools' of this kind that have a common programme. There are also general trends that characterise certain periods. But 'general' trends are not universal ones and their elucidation tends to underplay the contradictions, the disagreements, the multiplicity, that mark any human endeavour of this kind. The effort to aggregate may well lead to a measure of distortion of the evidence.

It is sometimes suggested that, under colonial regimes, research in the social sciences was limited by the constraints of the metropolitan powers and by the nature of its funding. It is true that wherever and whenever one carries out fieldwork, constraints of these kinds exist. But regarding finance, we have seen that the research carried out from Britain in the 1930s was largely financed by an American foundation interested in social reform, not by the colonial authorities. After the war, the Colonial Social Science Research Council offered grants to scholars, including a number of Americans and citizens of other countries (including a Chinese anthropologist who worked in Sarawak, returned to China, and was later accused of being a British spy). But the administration of these grants was enlightened and largely controlled by university teachers themselves.

In her account of British social anthropology, Kuklick remarks of anthropologists of the interwar period that 'their research was conducted largely in Africa, because their patrons expected their findings to prove useful to colonial officials then developing administrative structures there'.[1] The patrons however were largely an American foundation interested in 'cultural change' who did not have as a primary aim the provision of administrative help to British officials. In fact, as she later remarks, 'their work proved of little use to colonial rulers', and that aim was certainly not a prime mover. To claim that 'Functionalist anthropologists reassured colonial officials that indigenous politics maintained order even in the absence of political institutions recognizable to European eyes and that indigenous peoples were capable of adjusting to change', seems a strange attribution to 'functionalists'. Was there any serious doubt in the minds of administrators that change was impossible or that even the 'tribes without rulers' maintained a modicum of order? If anthropology provided 'reassurance', it did not come from one particular brand. But that is just one example of a tendency to attribute some general characteristic to a specific school or specific profession. At one point the author claims that 'anthropologists were concerned to justify the emergence of the middle classes, to which they belonged'.[2] They were 'the ideologues of meritocracy'.[3] It is difficult to see why anthropologists are selected for this particular role when there are so many other possible candidates: historians, sociologists, even philosophers.

Having made this suggestion, Kuklick reverses the position. She acknowledges that 'anthropologists' understanding of political order was in some measure a function of their field experience'. But there is a sting in the tail. Because they lived among them and came to identify with them, they imputed to them 'the values they themselves held dear. Thus, their idealization of stateless societies is better interpreted as an appreciation of the virtues of egalitarian democracy than as an apology for colonial power.' The concern with stateless societies had other roots, including a concern with lineage, kinship and the varieties of social sanctions. Some were undoubtedly attracted by the notion of 'ordered anarchy' but the 'egalitarian individualism' of the Nuer cannot reasonably be equated with democracy, nor do I think Evans-Pritchard always had much time for egalitarianism, if that meant the abolition of rank and authority in a complex society. Certainly there was, following the analysis of Evans-Pritchard, much interest in the workings of 'tribes without rulers', and some ideological elements were certainly present. But that interest also arose from an (international) tradition of discussion in political anthropology, from the work of Montesquieu, of Maine, of Spencer, Durkheim, and Lowie, as well as from the analysis of the mechanism by which order could be sustained in 'acephalous' or 'segmentary' communities. The source of order was not difficult to perceive in state systems but the elucidation of these mechanisms among the Nuer followed up an important line of political and philosophical enquiry that was not confined to the western tradition, let alone the British.

In her concluding chapter on 'The Politics of Perception', the author admits to treating the subjects of ethnographies as 'nearly inert – little capable of modifying Westerners' propensities to cast exotic cultures in familiar forms'. She goes on to state that 'anthropologists themselves, recognising that they take their own cultures' obsessions into the field, have identified the solipsistic element in their work'. Indeed 'ethno-graphic evidence can be appreciated *only* if it is translated into local terms ... In the context of local use, it makes no difference if anthropological accounts are complete fabrications.'[4] Kuklick recog-nises that accounts of the Nuer all have some points in common but these are phrased at such a general level as to be meaningless. For the most part she is prepared to emphasise the solipsistic element in anthropological work; 'ethnographic evidence can be appreciated *only* if it is translated into local terms', as with the appropriation from abroad of a technological innovation or of an idea. Appreciated perhaps by the subjects largely in those terms, but there are also general problems in the innovation of technology which cannot be discussed in this way and which go further than local knowledge alone.

Once again, the possibility of distortion in making observations applies not only to anthropologists in the field but to historians with their documents and indeed to any form of scholarship, one of whose main aims is precisely to reduce such 'interference'.

Following Malinowski, these anthropologists had been concerned to describe and analyse the local situation in great detail, a process that has been seen by some as a failure of their work. In an introduction to a volume of essays entitled *Reading Cultural Anthropology* (1992), George Marcus writes of the 'agenda' of anthropology (as distinct from that of cultural anthropology) as being identified 'with the finely-grained, merely descriptive study of primitive, exotic peoples'. Leaving aside the question of the primitive nature of Japan, China, India and the Middle East, on which earlier scholars such as Embree, Fei, Srinivas and Abu Zaid carried out studies (in the latter three cases of their own societies), it is the phrase 'merely descriptive' to which attention needs to be drawn. Some students of cultural anthropology would deny the possibility of 'merely descriptive' enquiry. However the authors we are dealing with certainly saw themselves as carrying out analytical as well as descriptive work, and when one compares their studies to earlier ethnographers it is difficult to disagree. They aimed to combine the two in the classic manner of Evans-Pritchard's study of the Nuer and did indeed create a new genre of analytic studies. The alternative course, deriving from the assumption that we can never know the other, is to sit back and contemplate our own navels instead of those of other peoples. For me that is a less satisfactory mode of understanding the other, more in the line of *belles-lettres* than with anthropology in the literal sense of that word.

That observations, any observations, may be influenced by one's own preconceptions is no special attribute of anthropology; it is as easy to foist one's interpretation on other groups in one's own society (such as on the lower and upper classes, or on gypsies and anthropologists) as it is on exotic societies. History (including the history of science) is subject to similar distortions, anthropology is in no sense peculiar. Especially when we take into account that in the later period, the period when intensive field work became the norm, a number of anthropologists were themselves of 'exotic' origin, working on their own peoples. I am referring here to Jomo Kenyatta's work on the Kikuyu, to M. N. Srinivas' studies of south India as well as to Kofi Busia's enquiry on the Asante.

Regarding both funding and relations with the authorities, the situation changed after the Second World War. Anthropologists who then received grants from the Colonial Development and Welfare Funds are described as 'skilled practitioners of an established technique of grantmanship, promising utilitarian research while pursuing strictly academic concerns'. The only evidence produced is a letter from Evans-Pritchard about the research of his student, I. M. Lewis, in Somalia. Neither he nor Evans-Pritchard made any promises of utilitarian research, which would have strongly contradicted the main positions they both held. No-one I know made such promises, nor were they asked to. Under the thoughtful secretaryship of Sally Chilver, later Principal of Bedford College, London (1967–71) and of Lady Margaret Hall, Oxford (1971–9), that would have been inconceivable. The anthropologists concerned were men and women recently released from the services, including an American contingent (the Fallers, Bohannans, Harrises, etc.). Most held strong views about the coming independence of African territories and were more interested in the end rather than the perpetuation of colonial rule. At this stage they were hardly skilled in obtaining grants and were certainly not in the business of making promises to carry out work with practical implications for the colonial government, except in so far as post-war Britain was making preparations for handing over the reins of government. To help the independence movement was more important for Fallers in East Africa, for R. T. Smith in British Guiana, for many in West Africa, than to assist the colonial regime.

The relationship between research workers and the relevant committee was far from onerous; in general individuals carried out what research they wanted. That is also broadly the case with the earlier anthropologists of the twenties. Much of the criticism is based on conjecture rather than history, as the work of Brown on Northern Rhodesia (Zambia) has shown regarding the supposed co-operation or coherence between anthropology and colonialism. In his discussion of the work of Godfrey Wilson and Max Gluckman at the Rhodes–Livingstone Institute in Northern Rhodesia between 1937 and 1947, he brings out the conflicts that the anthropologists working there had with colonial governments and with settler interests, as well as their own problems in deciding whether to work independently of such authorities (carrying out 'pure anthropology') or whether to try and influence the course of events (by means of 'applied anthropology', but not of course as government employees). In each endeavour they were colonial only in the same sense that somebody who wishes to work in any society (America, Britain, France) can be described as 'capitalist' or 'hegemonic'. I make this point because Brown, like others, tries to see changes that take place in the anthropological landscape as closely reflecting wider social processes, the movement from colonialism to imperialism. To regard intellectual traditions as tightly isomorphous with socio-political processes is to underrate the contradictions within those traditions, the often critical nature of intellectual production and the degree of structural autonomy which the written mode promotes.

Kuklick compares the authoritarian relationships of earlier 'colonial' anthropologists to the supplicatory position of contemporary ones, whose attributes are lauded. As an example of the first she quotes the comments of Margaret Mead about her ex-husband's manner of conducting research. Some anthropologists may have received benefits as representatives of the colonial regime and its hierarchical attitudes. Others certainly suffered from this association and tried to keep clear of contamination, especially as the authorities were not always co-operative. But the same problem exists today because the important point is most anthropologists come as Westerners or outsiders (which carries a cachet), even as men of the book. Amita Ghosh's experience as an Indian anthropologist in post-Nasser Egypt, of being addressed as 'Ya, doktor' is very revealing in this respect, and not all that different from my own. In talking to them I have found it quite possible to compare my fieldwork experiences with that of insiders, like Srinivas or Beteille in India or of Busia or Arhin in Ghana, though their command of the language was obviously better than mine. Shaded differences between earlier and later, between inside and outside observers exist but they are not of the order of deference versus supplication.[5]

Of course there are many different kinds of relationships between academics and the authorities, as well as between their disciplines and the life that goes on around them. To characterise these in any simple way is profoundly unsatisfactory, empirically and theoretically. In the first place the observer tends to present both the groups and the ideas in an over-homogenised form. Conflicts within groups and differences of ideas are underplayed, while both are given names which the actors themselves would not always recognise. The works of the evolutionists and functionalists are dismissed in ways that suggest the notions of evolution, diffusion and function are themselves of little or no use in examining human society. That is evident nonsense. Some of the applications, some of the hypotheses, were certainly mistaken; that does not warrant a refusal to entertain the general notions, either in anthropology or in any related fields.

It is in the nature of the history of ideas and the sociology of knowledge that its practitioners group together a number of scholars under rubrics that the actors would not have recognised ('colonial') and that stress resemblances (sometimes superficial) rather than differences. That is a necessary part of the endeavour but it does mean that the currency of such discourse is often a simplified constellation of ideas. Take for example, Kuklick's conclusions in 'Tribal exemplars: images of political authority' (1984). She tries to show that anthropologists' responses to national developments were not random; the 'anthropologists' she cites include the practitioners of a wide variety of fields, medicine, ancient history, folklore, human biology and so forth. At the beginning and end of the period in which she is interested (1885–1945) their work was critical, in the celebrations during the period before the First World War of established order and national glory. In both cases their observations were 'refracted through cultural lenses'; the history of British anthropological thought is held to demonstrate the extraordinary persistence of the folk tradition of British political theory. This 'folk tradition', equated with the 'British political debate' especially as it centered on the Norman conquest, is specified in such a way that its central opposition would be found in most other societies. That is just as well since leading social anthropologists such as Malinowski and Nadel could hardly be described as reared in that tradition and were certainly not 'proselytizing secularists of provincial dissenting origins'.[6]

As part of this attempt to force anthropological discussions into a simplified framework of 'British folk political theory', Kuklick draws attention (as others have done) to the difference between the central Nuer areas and those newly acquired from the Dinka. But she links that comparison with the British folk tradition. The Dinka she sees as fitting the pattern not of the democratic ('Anglo-Saxon') pole of this theory but of the aristocratic ('Norman') end, 'incorporating the elements that have been seen as essential features of aristocratic government, military pacification, inherited leadership', and 'exaggerated divisions among social classes'.[7] So that 'Evans-Pritchard's rendition of the relations between dominant Nuer and subordinate Dinka ... constitutes an apology for British colonial power, cast in the standard formula of Whig liberalism.' There is no evidence that 'Evans-Pritchard and other anthropologists ... by denying that a conquered people could be forcibly compelled to follow an unwanted way of life ... denied the reality of colonial domination'. Neither parts of this statement are true; what anthropologist could possibly deny the colonial domination of America or Australia over subject peoples who were forced to change their ways of life? It may be the case that some aspects of Evans-Pritchard's picture of Nuer-Dinka relationships need to be modified, that he may have exaggerated the 'democratic' tendencies of the former. But he also studied the Azande and was well aware of colonial domination in Ethiopia and elsewhere. If the deliberations of British anthropologists were 'reflections of the national mood', how is it that their discussions were so readily taken up in other countries (for example, in the States) or that they borrowed so freely from French and German writers? Of course there are some local, time- and place-specific links with academic activity, but the use of the word 'reflection' betrays a mechanistic view of the relationship.

The problem for historians and their readers lies partly in the concern with general labels rather than particular hypotheses, or other lower-level contributions to the subject, such as work on the developmental cycle. Historians and philosophers of science tend to look at individuals and their contributions in terms of evolutionary versus historical, functionalist versus structuralist, labels that easily take on pejorative significance, as when, in an admirable article on the contribution of the Rockefeller Foundation to anthropology, Stocking writes of 'an ideological milieu befogged by evolutionary racist assumptions',[8] or stigmatises C. B. Davenport 'as another Galton Society racialist',[9] as if neither 'evolutionary' (long-term developmental) nor physical factors were relevant in the analysis of human affairs. Of course one can make wrong assumptions about development or about genetics, but one can just as easily do so about socio-cultural or social factors.

In her account of British anthropology, Kuklick claims that 'functionalists were ... able to strike a responsive chord in official hearts because they echoed ideological refrains long dear to colonial rulers'.[10] The theme is a persistent one in other recent comments on British anthropology of the period,[11] especially those emanating from some American and left-wing sources. For Americans, the word 'colonial' refers to the period of British rule of what became the United States. It tends to exclude the devastating conquest of the indigenes by the settlers (or colonialists) within the country that gave rise to considerable anthropological scholarship under the American Bureau of Ethnology in the nineteenth century. In the present context the use of the term overlooks the different attitudes to colonisation as well as to anthropologists held by individual administrators, by the Colonial Office at home and colonial governments overseas, and by different political parties, not to speak of the very different attitudes taken by anthropologists, many of whom were certainly left-wing in their thinking. To speak of 'functionalists as striking a responsive chord in official hearts' seems to carry classification to a point at which it ceases to be able to explain the actual course of events and the thoughts of the participants. Why functionalists rather than all those American anthropologists working with the Department of Indian Affairs? It is of course true that any political regime lays down some rules of 'proper behaviour'. For a number of years it was impossible to get into the United States as an alien unless one concealed one's left-wing past. More radical compromises were sometimes made by those seeking funds to carry out social research in colonial territories just as they are today, often to a much greater extent, in many newly independent nations. Or in 'socialist' countries. To see this relationship as striking a chord between the two is to oversimplify and even seriously to distort the situation.

Her notions of the operation of functionalism make the views of anthropologists (and others) often seem more like a caricature than the considered opinions of intelligent men and women. Kuklick writes that 'Denial of the special character of Western society was basic to functionalist anthropology, which was premised on the assumption that all societies were essentially alike.'[12] The material trappings of civilisation were 'superficial' and progress was an illusion. Treating every society as an organism she regards as making nonsense of directional social change. But since functionalism does not create such a problem for biology, why should it do so in sociology? There is no necessary connection. In any case the view attributed to the actors is hardly representative. Even extreme relativists did not go that far.

Functionalists, declares Kuklick, restricted their scholarly attention to simple societies, so that their analyses evoke 'the lost Anglo-Saxon village community beloved of centuries of British radicals'. Her definition of simple emerges on the following page. 'Anthropologists of the 1920s and 1930s turned for preference to the study of simple, "acephalous" (i.e., stateless) societies. A number of factors *conspired* to direct anthropologists' attention to such societies'.[13] This interest distinguished these scholars from amateur investigators; it was a new topic and it provided new employment opportunities.

The facts are very different. The Trobriands studied by Malinowski were hardly acephalous; chiefship was critical. Evans-Pritchard's first study was of the Azande state, Fortes' second of the Asante, while Schapera and Gluckman worked in African kingdoms.

Once again the strains in the tight network of relations she tries to discern are seen in the claim that 'colonial anthropologists' such as Cardinall looked not only to evolutionist but to diffusionist work 'for guidance'. This approach was betrayed 'by a propensity to compare African societies with those of ancient Egypt' rather than with classical societies.[14] That was a characteristic of the 'Children of the Sun' school of diffusionism centred at University College, London, but in fact other comparisons took place, with classical Greece and with feudal systems. In any case, the propensity to think in terms of diffusion was never confined to 'diffusionist anthropologists', who were attached to a very special set of doctrines. Nor did 'the consolidation of peoples into larger units' require either a diffusionist or an evolutionist legitimation; it followed from the nature of colonial conquest. If '[c]olonial officials were able to use evolutionist arguments to resist innovations they saw as threatening to their authority', it was not Frazer that provided them.[15] They themselves introduced many changes that were 'incongruous with the cultural patterns characteristic of each stage of development', of which public transport was only one. Was not the introduction of schools among these modernising innovations which according to Kuklick would have 'had to be resisted' in favour of gradual change?[16] Once again, the author tries to impose her own consistencies on situations that contained inevitable contradictions and in which views were often dependent upon specific situations. The political objections to disruptive change, either in the Gold Coast or the USA, do not rest upon anthropological analyses.

The grouping together in 'schools' can take extreme forms. Kuklick understands that 'the evolutionary school had a lower level of consensus than its successors' (because it did not have 'the social cohesion of an established profession') and that one is 'bound to err' in giving any account of its development and ideas. But despite the fact that Rattray declared his indifference to theoretical abstractions, she perceives the evolutionary influences of Tylor and Frazer when he draws analogies between classical and feudal societies. 'Because he regarded cultural development as a uniform, linear process, he ignored cultural differences between the peoples of the Gold Coast ...'[17] There are three *non-sequiturs* hidden in these statements. Any educated man of his generation would employ such analogies, which continue to be made by many without any connections with these 'schools'. Secondly, there is no adequate evidence that he regarded 'cultural development as uniform', and finally, while it is always possible to overlook differences, he certainly did not 'ignore' them; his works such as *Tribes of the Ashanti Hinterland* are full of the recognition of differences of all kinds.

One aspect of the problem comes from lumping the views attributed to individuals into labelled groups (evolutionist, diffusionist, functionalist) that they would be reluctant to recognise, and would in many cases reject. At the same time these labels are extended to include a range of views possibly held by one or more members of these groups rather than the totality, and finally these views are attributed an influence that over-rates the significance of anthropology and indeed of all academic life on practical policy.

It is possible to discern some small groups that called themselves functionalist or diffusionist at a certain moment in time, and it is possible to recognise the influence of the doctrines they espoused on others. But to speak of the psychology of Rivers as diffusionist because he was at one time interested in the migration of peoples and associated with the work of Elliot Smith and Perry, seems an error. The ingenuity expended by Kuklick in positing connections of this highly general kind results in attributing to anthropology a force it never had. Rivers was after all a medical psychologist before he was an anthropologist and his psychological work was more influenced by developments in those fields (for example, by Charcot and Freud) than by ones in anthropology. Kuklick recognises this manner of proceeding as a possible criticism when she writes that 'unlike virtually every other chronicler of Rivers's career, I see intellectual continuity in the various aspects of Rivers's scholarship and political activity' and she concludes that the more fragmented approach arises out of the desire to dismiss as aberrations 'those aspects of his work that have fallen out of scholarly regard'.[18] One can grant a measure of truth in her approach, in the desire to establish the existence of a degree of intellectual continuity and the desire to account for both the less enduring and the more enduring views (as in the case of Newton). But it is the way this intellectual continuity is constructed that poses the problem. For example, 'the reality of functional disorders' that distinguished wartime psychology and industrial psychology after the First World War is seen as 'an insight that derived from the Torres Straits Expedition as the result of the work of 'the diffusionist anthropologist-psychologists'.[19] The model of battle-induced mental disorder was 'anthropologically informed'.[20] The common premisses that informed 'both ancient migrations and contemporary social disorder' seem so general as not to require any such specific attribution.[21] That seems equally true of the remark that the 'diffusionists' ascription of the relationship of social factors to the expression of instinctive tendencies was derived from their understanding of the evolution of the brain and the nervous system', a remark which would appear true of any selected set of individuals.[22]

The 'evolutionists' include not only a specific set of anthropologists but members of the colonial administrative service who 'could not afford to abandon evolutionist views during the 1930s', because policies based on, for example, the 'evolutionist maxim' that 'progress was associated with the development of hereditary kingship' made 'negotiations with their subjects more efficient'.[23] I would suggest that evolutionist arguments also saw progress in the abandoning of hereditary succession. But those arguments do not depend upon a specific school of anthropologist; in the academic community, they are hardly seen as the property of 'evolutionist anthropology', and had been in the air of the Enlightenment (or of Ancient Greece) long before Darwin. In the second place, is there any need for any specific derivation at all? It seemed 'natural' among the District Commissioners I studied to list the potential successors (or methods of selection) in order to avoid disputes without recognising any need to rationalise the course of action by reference to 'evolutionist anthropology', as Kuklick suggests.[24] But then as a historian she is inclined to look for derivations at times when others might see structural-functional arguments of a sociological kind as more relevant, especially those with a knowledge of the human agents who were interacting with the social environment.

In his fascinating account of notions of human ascendancy in the early modern period, Keith Thomas examines the maintenance of boundaries between man and animals, pointing out the 'inferior humans', outsiders, foreigners, the Irish, infants, women and the poor were often seen as brutes, near the animal state.[25] These are the same categories whose debasement Kuklick uses as evidence of evolutionist views. 'Analogies among primitives, children, the underclass, women were accurate because physical and cultural evolution were interdependent', analogies which are linked to 'racial characteristics'.[26] But these analogies clearly could not have arisen from the views of nineteenth-century anthropologists since they were found among their sixteenth-century predecessors, and are indeed found much more widely. While we do not necessarily see the view as pan-human (not all societies have an underclass), they are nevertheless very widespread, as are (at this broad level) notions of 'evolution'; Frazer even found them in many non-literate societies.

The aggregation takes other forms. One person is held to represent the whole. 'The permanent staff of the Colonial Office claimed ...; the reference is to an individual.[27] We know that, especially after 1940, opinions were heavily divided. A similar aggregation takes place with ideas; talk of progress, development or administrative action is viewed as realising 'evolutionary ideas'. No doubt all social engineering, whether by the United Nations, the US Congress or by some Commune in France, is guided by some general notion of amelioration; that has no more to do with evolutionary ideas in British social anthropology than had the installation of sanitation in Pompeii or the administrative reorganisation of medieval China.

The same tendency emerges from the comparison of different colonies. After an examination of the Gold Coast (now Ghana), Tanganyika (now Tanzania) is taken as 'the counter example that proves the rule'.[28] It is the 'rule' of one against one. In that country the investigations of 'anthropologists were essential to develop strategies for ruling acephalous societies, and not to make acephalous societies into centralized ones'. The implication that this latter policy was general and deliberate in, for example, the Northern Territories of the Gold Coast, is wrong. The work of Rattray described in *The Tribes of the Ashanti Hinterland* went in quite another direction, as did that of Fortes and Tait. All examined those societies without any suggestion that chiefship should be imposed on non-centralised peoples. It is true that some states were made more centralised than they had become following invasions of one kind and another (for example, the Gonja), while others (for example, the Asante) were made less so by the fact of colonial rule itself. It is also true that any central government has to have intermediaries for its rule, hence the interstitial role of the village headman, even where none had previously existed. It is also true that the politics of acephalous societies could be better understood after the work of Evans-Pritchard. But many anthropologists and anthropologically minded administrators (Cardinall, Eyre-Smith, Duncan-Johnstone and others in the Gold Coast) called attention to the way this situation was changing the leadership roles in acephalous societies and they paid considerable attention to the 'priestly' role and fate of the Master of the Earth, the *tendaana*, in their works.

The author's globalising approach, this swallowing up of the concrete situation, is well illustrated in the final comment which tries to draw a connection between ethnographic observation and the use made of it. If the writer and reader lead lives in a different 'social milieu', there need be no such connection. Nevertheless she interprets T. S. Eliot's use of Rivers' comments on the failure of Melanesian society to reproduce itself in a different light, since he sees the whole world as possibly going the same way. Kuklick comments: 'both the breakdown of Melanesian social order and the changing character of British society reflected a reconfiguration of international relations'.[29] But Eliot is talking of worldwide events, not those confined to Britain or its anthropologists. If Kuklick is claiming that the same worldwide matrix of events influenced all mankind (for example, the rapid growth of industrial capitalism), there can be little disagreement. Eliot did not need to read Rivers; Ezra Pound saw things clearly without such an aid. It was a common enough notion.

The image of 'evolutionism' and 'evolutionists' the author pursues is based on collapsing the thought of many into one mould. For example, it is claimed that the 'central idea of evolutionism ... is that of "recapitulation"; the growth of each individual summarized all previous development along a linear evolutionary sequence, patterned after the geological model of developmental stages'.[30] But the animal model was just as prevalent an element as the geological in the thought of the period, while 'social evolution' certainly did not automatically assume the equivalence of the child, the savage and the lower class (though this was one possible variant). To suggest otherwise represents a vulgarisation of the thought of thoughtful men and women who were influenced not only by Darwin and geology but by earlier ideas about the general lines of societal change.

Kuklick's analysis is phrased in terms of class as well as nation. For her, anthropologists' analyses celebrated 'the middle-class virtue of individual achievement'.[31] Later on the situation changed and 'the careers of members of the anthropological community ... exemplify a general social trend: the increasingly standardized pattern of middle-class lives'.[32] This development was related to 'the hardening of class lines' which seemed 'to substantiate their hereditarianism'. For functionalists concerned with 'stable social orders ... an individual's character was formed by general cultural patterns'.[33]

Class is sometimes intellectual class. Anthropologists were 'specimen members of a developing intellectual class, whose positions on national issues reflected their social status'.[34] Alternatively their views reflected the loss of the self-confidence Britain once enjoyed as the first industrial nation. However, as we have seen, social anthropology in Britain was dominated by *émigré* scholars during this period, often with left-wing views. Kuklick argues that 'the *émigré* scholars' schemes were welcomed in Britain because they could be reconciled with indigenous ones', and partly too because they took pains to adapt them to their new surrounds.[35] That mechanical determinism seems to grossly under-estimate the part played by *émigré* scholarship as a whole in London at this time, as well as to discount the measure of structural autonomy which intellectuals sometimes display towards the dominant values of society. Can the support given to Kirchhoff or more generally to decolonisation movements, can the conflicts of interest between the International African Institute and colonial governments be explained by notions of reflection and adaptation?

Some comments on individual anthropologists seem quite inappropriate. To declare that Rattray, the author of the two-volume monograph on *The Tribes of the Ashanti Hinterland*, 'ignored cultural differences among the peoples of the Gold Coast' is very wide of the mark. Of course any observer, however meticulous, is bound to overlook some cultural differences and to overstress others, whether in Africa or the USA. Rattray made mistakes.[36] But his observations certainly made an important contribution to knowledge at the time and have been recognised as having done so by later anthropologists of Asante extraction such as Busia, Kyeremateng, Sarkpong and Arhin. To declare that he based 'a good deal' of his analysis on responses to questionnaires issued to political officers is to misunderstand his relationships with the Asante and his extensive travels and interviews in the Northern Territories. Of course he used other approaches and information as well and could hardly be said to have carried out a 'community study'. But that does not justify the comparison with armchair anthropologists of the nineteenth century.

Not only is anthropology found to be influenced by a long-established cultural tradition, but its connections with the colonial authorities are seen as less contradictory, less oppositional, than was in practice the case. For example, Malinowski can hardly be said to have established himself as an 'adviser to the Colonial Office ... by virtue of his connection with the International African Institute',[37] although he had associations with that department in his attempt to place students in research situations. Kuklick appreciates the necessary role a supervisor has to take in the case of Evans-Pritchard but not for Malinowski (though Stocking does).[38] In this same vein the journal of the International African Institute, *Africa,* is described as 'almost a house organ for the Colonial Office personnel'.[39] Over many years I encountered only one (from, say, a total of fifty colonial officers) who even glanced at it; it was essentially an academic journal, while the administrators had their own (*Corona*).

Anthropology is seen by Kuklick to have been applied by colonial regimes to encourage 'the shift of individuals' loyalties from small-scale societies to large ethnic groups'. As a consequence this process 'left a destructive legacy for new nations'.[40] At first social scientists emphasised the 'quasi-natural forces' such as migrations that brought people together; then stressed the positive contributions ethnic groups made to nationalist agitations. 'But it is now clear that ethnic partisanship has impeded the creation of political order in new nations and, moreover, that the divisive loyalties experienced as primordial are in fact in good measure of imperial design.'[41] It is an old accusation, not only of colonial regimes, that governments (and individuals) 'divide and rule'. But there seems something curious firstly in attributing so powerful a role to anthropology and social scientists, and secondly in seeing this process as necessarily linked to a shift from small-scale societies to large ethnic groups. Were the small-scale societies not also ethnic groups? What is involved in conceptualising the shift as one of 'society' to 'ethnic group'? From *gemeinschaft* to *gesellschaft?* It is true that new nations (like older ones, such as Yugoslavia and the USSR) are plagued with ethnic tensions. That was bound to be the case in Africa where some 4,000 linguistic groups were forcibly brought together by conquest into some fifty colonies which then became nation states. Any efforts made by anthropologists, colonial administrators and politicians could only have a minimal effect on this basic problem. Ethnicity was no invention of the invaders. While 'tribal' or 'ethnic' conflicts have taken many different shapes in Africa, often manipulated by local politicians much more effectively than they were by expatriates, the violent conflicts that I have witnessed in Ghana in recent years have tended to break up rather than consolidate the political units established under colonial rule, mainly because previously subordinate groups have struggled to free themselves from their pre-colonial masters (as with the Vagala, the Nchumuru and the Konkomba of northern Ghana). To say that 'colonial policies exaggerated cleavages within populations' is to suggest that they broke up some previous unity. A knowledge of local wars and conflicts in the period before colonial rule casts serious doubts upon the correctness of the verb 'exaggerate'.

Kuklick's desire to promote the importance of the subject she has chosen leads her to speak of anthropologists 'dictating policy' to the administration and their wish that authority be ceded to them.[42] The second point refers to Fortes' comments on the reorganisation of local government among the Tallensi. Far from attempting to dictate, he made these remarks at the request of a local administrator, Kerr, who had become a friend and who later incorporated some of the points in a semi-official memo. As we have seen, Fortes was initially held in low regard by the local administration and he gained a reputation for non-interference rather than for interference. It certainly was not 'Fortes' determination that the Gold Coast Tallensi had no traditional secular offices whatsoever' that 'led to the deliberate transformation of their religious leaders into Native Authorities'.[43] The administration was well aware of the general problem of 'acephalous' peoples long before Evans-Pritchard and Fortes came on the scene; that was evident at the time of first contact and indeed had been evident to local states before that. Like any ruling power coming into such an area, they had to appoint local leaders, though 'local religious leaders' in the shape of Masters of the Earth usually avoided such an ambiguous promotion, as Rattray, Cardinall and others have pointed out.

While overestimating the role of anthropology both with regard to colonial rule and to British society as a whole, Kuklick changes her mind (or is undecided) about the role of anthropologists. At one point she admits that Evans-Pritchard, like other anthropologists, was 'determined to prevent colonial rulers from subverting indigenous institutions to service their own ends'.[44] At another she claims that 'systematic misunderstanding of indigenous cultures was often promulgated by anthropological investigators'.[45] Or suggests, in passing, that Evans-Pritchard's analysis 'constitutes an apology for British colonial power'.

Although Kuklick gives passing recognition to the differences in the perspective of traders, at others times she ignores those of other participants. Thus on the Nuer, the work of the missionary Hoffman, the administrator Howell and the anthropologist Evans-Pritchard are treated as equivalent. All are outstanding reports of their kind, but sneering at 'participant observation' cannot hide the differences of approach which must give different weight to their reports on the indigenous society.

This lumping together of anthropologists and ideas in single categories makes it difficult to understand their work. That is as true of those called 'evolutionists' as it is of the 'structural-functionalists', since it tends to homogenise for no apparent reason, except simplification itself. While it is right to point to Evans-Pritchard's analysis of the acephalous Nuer to which he was undoubtedly attracted, not only theoretically, it is wrong to overlook his study of the centralised Azande (not mentioned in Kuklick's bibliography), and quite wrong, in my view, to conclude that 'by denying that a conquered people could be compelled to follow an unwanted way of life through the use of force, they [these anthropologists] in effect denied the reality of colonial domination'.[46] Both parts of this proposition seem equally untenable. Neither Evans-Pritchard nor Fortes denied the role of force, either internally or externally, much less the reality of colonial rule, though this is not always as prominent in the studies of the majority of anthropologists as their claims to synchronic analysis might suggest.

Writing the history of a recent intellectual movement involves achieving a balance between the actor's and the observer's points of view. There is no formula for achieving such a balance. But as with Weber's *verstehen*, as with most anthropological enquiry, it first involves understanding the actor's position at the historic moment, which is often shaded, ambivalent and differentiated from that of his or her colleagues. This understanding has been the aim of this essay.

Notes

INTRODUCTION

1 For example, Kuklick (1991) on the relations with colonialism, Fisher (1983) on the relations with capitalism as embodied in the Foundations.
2 Fisher 1983: 212.
3 See especially the work of H. Kuklick on which I have commented in some detail in Appendix 2. I do so as historian of the 1930s and participant in the post-war period.
4 R. Firth kindly commented on a draft of the first chapter, and M. Bulmer has supplied many references. I am also indebted to anonymous reviewers as well as to G. Hawthorn and J. A. Barnes.

I. THE ECONOMIC AND ORGANISATIONAL BASIS OF BRITISH SOCIAL
ANTHROPOLOGY IN ITS FORMATIVE PERIOD, 1930–1939: SOCIAL REFORM
IN THE COLONIES

1 Fisher 1983: 206, 224; Bulmer 1984: 575.
2 J. Goody 1973: 186.
3 J. Goody 1973: 190.
4 Fisher 1983: 209.
5 Bulmer 1984: 573.
6 Bulmer 1980, 1982; M. and J. Bulmer 1981: Stocking 1985 (and the substantial bibliography).
7 Fisher 1978.
8 Coben 1976: 231
9 The decision was accepted by the academic council of that body in order to protect their funds.
10 Fisher 1983: 210.
11 Bulmer 1982.
12 Cambridge acquired a Professorship of Political Science as a result of Ruml's suggestion but showed little interest in a Chair in Sociology (Bulmer 1981). Malinowski must have been disappointed because later on he claimed he had intended to back Reo Fortune for the post (Malinowski to Keppel, 27 March 1934, LSE library file Malinowski 494; hereafter

these files will be cited by the writer's name and the relevant number only).

13 Malinowski to Foundation, 2 October 1930. Rockefeller had also given support to research in the Pacific, under the auspices of the Bishop Museum and the University of Hawaii, as well as to Australia. When Radcliffe-Brown was appointed the Rockefeller people invited him to tour anthropological institutions in America on his way there (Stocking 1985: 120).

14 Firth 1963: 3.

15 Firth 1963: 5.

16 Fortes 1949c: xi. Up to 1936 Rockefeller gave almost 250,000 dollars for research in social anthropology in Australia and the Southwestern Pacific (Stocking 1985: 121).

17 A major exception was N. W. Thomas who served in Nigeria and Sierra Leone (Kuklick 1978: 102), though M. J. Field began her work in the Gold Coast in that capacity, having come from teaching in a local secondary school. Subsequently a number of people were trained as anthropologists who had earlier been school teachers, members of Voluntary Service Overseas or Peace Corps personnel.

18 There was more support for ethnographic work in French and German territories in Africa, but again largely channelled to governmental personnel.

19 See Brown 1973.

20 Berman 1980: 185. See also Bennett 1960, King 1969.

21 Berman 1980: 187.

22 23 September 1930, Malinowski 493.

23 17 September 1930, Malinowski 493.

24 Vischer to Malinowski, 1 June 1931.

25 Malinowski to Kitteridge (Rockefeller), 1 February 1933.

26 30 January 1933. Firth, he remarks, remained neutral.

27 Oldham to Malinowski, 19 December 1927, Malinowski 495, British Library of Political and Economic Sciences (hereafter BLPES).

28 Malinowski to Oldham, 22 March 1930, also referring to a memorandum to Beveridge.

29 The key article here is Malinowski's piece in *Africa*, January 1929, together with the printed memo to the IAI of March 1930.

30 Bulmer 1980: 80.

31 Oldham to Malinowski, 26 March 1930, referring to a conversation with Bott, Vice-Chancellor of Toronto University.

32 Oldham to Malinowski, 6 September 1931, Malinowski 533.

33 Malinowski to Oldham, 13 September 1931, Malinowski 533.

34 Malinowski to Oldham, 20 December 1931, Malinowski 533.

35 Radcliffe-Brown to Oldham, Paris, 5 September 1931, Malinowski 533.

36 Radcliffe-Brown to Oldham, Paris, 5 September 1931.

37 12 September 1931.

38 Richards to Malinowski, no date ('Thursday'), Malinowski 533.
39 See Evans-Pritchard to Fortes, undated, 1937(?). 'Best of luck in your contact with the Faithful [I got +o from it].'
40 Malinowski to N. Hall, 26 April 1932.
41 Malinowski to Firth, 16 March 1931, Malinowski 520.
42 See also Malinowski to Brackett, 27 December 1931, reporting that Evans-Pritchard was going to take up a post in Cairo.
43 Richards to Malinowski, 21 September 1931.
44 Radcliffe-Brown to Malinowski, 24 March 1931.
45 Malinowski to Foundation, 2 October 1930.
46 I am indebted to Raymond Firth's comments to me in a letter, dated 26 September 1983.

2. TRAINING FOR THE FIELD: THE SORCERER'S APPRENTICE

1 Malinowski to Oldham, 13 September 1931.
2 Kitteridge to Malinowski, 21 July 1932.
3 Malinowski to Van Sickle (Rockefeller), 21 March 1934.
4 30 May 1933, Malinowski 494.
5 These others included Lola Gisaricius, C. F. Meyer (from Oxford), M. Kramer, Miss Kemp and Bocassino.
6 Fisher 1983: 211.
7 Fisher 1983: 216.
8 Fisher 1983: 212.
9 30 May 1933, Malinowski 494.
10 Fortes to Middleton, 7 November 1973.
11 Fortes to Malinowski, 2 July 1931; Malinowski to Hall, 17 August 1931, Malinowski 582.
12 The dates here are uncertain since in March 1932 Malinowski wrote to Oldham that 'he has known Fortes for the last 3 or 4 years off and on' (7 March 1932, from Toulon).
13 22 March 1932.
14 4 March 1932.
15 Malinowski to Rockefeller Foundation, 14 August 1932.
16 Fortes to Malinowski, 12 March 1932; Malinowski to Fortes, 7 March 1932, Toulon.
17 Malinowski to Oldham, 13 June 1932, Malinowski 494.
18 7 March 1932.
19 Malinowski to Rockefeller Foundation, 24 June 1932, Malinowski 582.
20 3 July 1932, Malinowski 582. But did he send it? The original is unsigned.
21 15 March 1932, Malinowski 582.
22 Malinowski to Oldham, 26 October 1935.
23 In London on 1–2 March 1934.
24 Fortes 1930; 1932.
25 Malinowski to Oldham, London, 26 February 1934.

26 Fortes to Malinowski, 14 June 1934.
27 Oldham to Malinowski, 16 November 1934; Malinowski, 21 October 1935.
28 The seminar began on 17 October.
29 Malinowski 613. Seminar notes, 1935–36.
30 Seminar of 12 December.
31 Malinowski to Fortes, 11 March 1936.
32 Srinivas too was told by Meyer Fortes that Malinowski had asked him to sign a document stating that he had got all his ideas from him. He refused to do so, but the result was unlikely to endear him to the teacher.
33 Fortes 1978: 4.
34 To T. S. Van Sickle, 27 June 1933, Malinowski 582.
35 Malinowski to Keppel, 27 April 1934, Malinowski 494. Presumably a revised proposal, as the original one connected with Ruml was in 1924.
36 Kuklick 1978: 105.

3. MAKING IT TO THE FIELD AS A JEW AND A RED

1 To Lugard, 4 November 1937, concerning the future of Rockefeller grants.
2 Barnes 1987.
3 Malinowski to Oldham, 13 June 1932, Malinowski 494.
4 Memo 4, Malinowski 582.
5 Oldham to Malinowski, 16 February 1932.
6 Oldham to Malinowski, 18 February 1932.
7 Brackett to Malinowski, 7 March 1932.
8 Brackett to Malinowski, 21 April 1932.
9 Malinowski to Oldham, 5 February 1932.
10 18 March, 1932, Malinowski 582.
11 26 March 1932.
12 Seligman to Malinowski, 19 April 1932, Malinowski 582.
13 9 September 1932, from Toulon.
14 Malinowski to Kitteridge, 21 September 1932; Firth, personal communication.
15 Letter, 12 August 1932, Malinowski 582.
16 Memo 4, Malinowski 582.
17 Malinowski to Kirchhoff, 15 April 1932.
18 Malinowski to Oldham, 3 November 1932.
19 Malinowski to Kirchhoff, 17 June 1932, Malinowski 582.
20 Malinowski to Van Sickle, 11 June 1932, Malinowski 582.
21 Memo 13 May 1932, Malinowski 582.
22 To Kitteridge, 1 February 1933.
23 Evans-Pritchard to Fortes, 19 August 1934.
24 Oldham to Malinowski, 16 February 1932.
25 Oldham to Thomas, 20 March 1933, Fortes file, Ghana National Archives (hereafter GNA).
26 To Oldham, Toulon, 4 September 1932.

27 Oldham to Thomas, 15 May 1933.
28 Oldham to Thomas, 13 May 1933, Fortes file, GNA.
29 Bottomley to Thomas, 19 May 1933, Fortes file, GNA.
30 Oldham to Thomas, 20 March 1933, 5 April 1933, Fortes file, GNA.
31 5 April 1933, Fortes file, GNA.
32 5 April 1933, Fortes file, GNA.
33 29 March 1933, Fortes file, GNA.
34 On 13 February 1932.
35 Oldham to Thomas, 20 March 1933, 5 April 1933, Fortes file, GNA.
36 19 May 1933, Fortes file, GNA.
37 Bottomley to Thomas, 19 May 1933, Fortes file, GNA.
38 J. Coatman to Oldham, 12 May 1933, Fortes file, GNA.
39 Thomas to Bottomley, 1 January 1933, Fortes file, GNA.
40 Creasey to London, 13 August 1935, Fortes file, GNA (my italics).
41 Thomas, Secretary for Native Affairs, to Governor, 11 April 1936.
42 Hodson to Bottomley, 24 February 1936, Fortes file, GNA.
43 Thomas to Hodson, 22 February 1936, Fortes file, GNA.
44 Thomas to Hodson, 11 April 1936, Fortes file, GNA.
45 Evans-Pritchard writes a note of welcome on 25 July, saying he won't be able to meet them as he is going to North Africa on holiday for several months.
46 Minutes of the 16th meeting of the Executive Committee of the Council of the International African Institute, 12–13 October 1937, Oxford.
47 Mumford to Fortes, 7 October 1937. A fuller version of Fortes' memorandum (the original) is entitled 'Memorandum on the Proposal to establish an Institute of West African Culture at Achimota College, Accra'.
48 Evans-Pritchard to Fortes, 24 March 1937.

4. PERSONAL AND INTELLECTUAL FRIENDSHIPS: FORTES AND EVANS-PRITCHARD

1 See my account of 'British functionalism' (1973).
2 29 August 1932.
3 Evans-Pritchard to Oldham, 6 January 1932 (IAI).
4 Evans-Pritchard to Fortes, undated, Wednesday, Pevensey Bay, 1932(?).
5 Evans-Pritchard to Fortes, 11 (?) January 1953.
6 Evans-Pritchard to Fortes, 29 August 1973; 'Totem and taboo', reprinted, Meyer Fortes, 1987, *Religion, Morality and the Person*, Cambridge.
7 Evans-Pritchard to Fortes, undated (Wednesday, Pevensey Bay 1932) and 24 December 1934.
8 Evans-Pritchard to Fortes, undated (Oxford, 1937), via Gluckman.
9 Evans-Pritchard to Fortes, 8 December 1937, Pevensey Bay.
10 Evans-Pritchard to Fortes, 11 December 1937, Pevensey Bay.
11 Fortes 1936: 590–604; Evans-Pritchard was writing on the theory of

magic, part of which became incorporated in *Witchcraft, Oracles and Magic among the Azande*, part referred to the papers on Tylor and Frazer and on Levy-Bruhl that he had published in Cairo.

12 At the request of C. K. Ogden, he translated B. Petermann's book, *The Gestalt Theory and the Problem of Configuration.*
13 Evans-Pritchard to Fortes, 25 September 1935, en route for Khartoum.
14 Evans-Pritchard to Fortes, 19 August 1934.
15 Evans-Pritchard to Fortes, 18 February, 1941, Malakal, Upper Nile Province, Anglo-Egyptian Sudan.
16 Evans-Pritchard to Fortes, 20 September 1952, Oxford.
17 Letter to Fortes, 15 February 1951.
18 Evans-Pritchard, Cape Town, to Fortes, Cambridge, 12 September 1951.
19 Evans-Pritchard to Fortes, 7 May 1934, Cairo.
20 He recommended Hocart as his successor.
21 Evans-Pritchard to Fortes, 7 May 1934, Cairo.
22 Evans-Pritchard to Fortes, 17 July 1940, Malakal, Sudan.
23 Evans-Pritchard to Fortes, 22 October 1940, Malakal, Sudan.
24 Evans-Pritchard to Fortes, 17 December, 1940. Malakal, Sudan.
25 17 December 1940.
26 Rabinovich and Yaffe 1990.
27 Evans-Pritchard to Fortes, 7 August 1940, Malakal, Sudan.
28 Evans-Pritchard to Fortes, 19 July 1940, Malakal, Sudan.
29 Evans-Pritchard to Fortes, 19 July 1940, Malakal, Sudan. Sir Oswald Mosely was leader of the British Union of Fascists, then under detention. Chamberlain had been the appeasing Prime Minister and Halifax, Simon and Hoare were members of his Cabinet. Coupland was an Oxford imperial historian who had upset some of Evans-Pritchard's plans. Churchill was the head of the wartime coalition which included the Labour party.
30 Evans-Pritchard to Fortes, 30 July 1940, Malakal, Sudan.
31 Evans-Pritchard to Fortes, 18 February 1941, Malakal, Sudan.
32 Evans-Pritchard to Fortes, 5 April 1941, Malakal, Sudan.
33 Evans-Pritchard, Cape Town, to Fortes, Cambridge, 12 September 1951.
34 Evans-Pritchard, Oxford, to Fortes, Cambridge, 28 December 1951.

5. PERSONAL AND INTELLECTUAL ANIMOSITIES: EVANS-PRITCHARD, MALINOWSKI AND OTHERS

1 Evans-Pritchard to Fortes, undated, Wednesday, 1932(?).
2 Evans-Pritchard to Fortes, 7 May 1934, Cairo.
3 Evans-Pritchard to Fortes, 12 October 1940, Malakal, Sudan.
4 Lucy Mair to Fortes, 11 February 1982; Raymond Firth to J. Goody, 26 September 1983.
5 Richards to Malinowski, undated, Thursday (1931).
6 Fortes 1978: 2.

7 Evans-Pritchard to Fortes, 24 December 1934, Pevensey.
8 Lucy Mair to Fortes, 11 February 1982.
9 Evans-Pritchard to Fortes, undated, 1932.
10 Evans-Pritchard to Fortes, Monday, undated, Pevensey Bay (1937).
11 Evans-Pritchard to Meyer Fortes, 19 July 1940, Malakal, Sudan.
12 Evans-Pritchard to Fortes, 12 September 1972.
13 Evans-Pritchard to Fortes, 23 May 1972.
14 Evans-Pritchard to Firth, 15 July 1931, from Khartoum, a copy sent to Fortes.
15 Firth to Fortes. London, 4 November 1982.
16 Richards to Malinowski, 21 September 1931.
17 Richards to Malinowski 21 September 1931.
18 Evans-Pritchard to Fortes, 4 December 1944. However, Radcliffe-Brown had provided courses for colonial administrators in South Africa and Sydney; that was the main economic base for the teaching of the subject.
19 Evans-Pritchard to Fortes, 22 July 1945.
20 Evans-Pritchard to Fortes, 28 June 1945.
21 Evans-Pritchard to Fortes, 22 July 1945.
22 Evans-Pritchard to Fortes, 22 July 1945.
23 Evans-Pritchard to Fortes, 14 December 1944.
24 Evans-Pritchard to Fortes, undated, from Pevensey, 1937(?).
25 Evans-Pritchard to Fortes, 22 July 1945.
26 Evans-Pritchard to Fortes, 24 March 1937, London.
27 Evans-Pritchard to Fortes, 18 February 1941, Malakal, Sudan. This was Nadel's book on the Nuba.
28 Evans-Pritchard to Fortes, 22 July 1945, Cambridge.
29 Evans-Pritchard to Fortes, 29 August 1932.
30 Evans-Pritchard to Fortes, 13 March 1938, Cairo.
31 Evans-Pritchard to Fortes, 19 August 1934.
32 Evans-Pritchard to Fortes, 9 December 1934, London.
33 Evans-Pritchard to Fortes, Monday, undated, Pevensey Bay (1937).
34 Evans-Pritchard to Fortes, Wednesday, undated, Pevensey Bay (1932?).

6. THE OXFORD GROUP

1 As Srinivas put it to me in a letter, the alliance was 'an effort at taking Functionalism away from the meaning which BM gave it to structural-functionalism' (5 October 90).
2 Evans-Pritchard to Fortes, 24 March 1937, London. In the same letter he says he is not going to put in for Johannesburg and that he had supported Driberg for Cambridge but they wanted an older man, Hutton.
3 Evans-Pritchard to Fortes, Tuesday (undated), Oxford (October 1937).
4 Evans-Pritchard to Fortes, Friday (undated), Oxford (1937). The contents of this letter correspond to Fortes' account to me.
5 This view was one expressed by Evans-Pritchard in his correspondence

with Fortes. In fact Radcliffe-Brown submitted their proposal to the Hebdomadal Council at Oxford on 8 March 1940. The plan was for 'sociological research' in Africa. It was entitled 'Memorandum on a plan of research into problems of modern political development in Africa', and proposed to carry out 'sociological research' looking for general principles of changing political systems (based of course on their *African Political Systems* which was about to appear) as they were emerging under British rule and which could be applied 'to current problems of administration *leading to self-government*' [my italics]. In particular they were to deal with the different ways that 'organised' and 'amorphous' (i.e. segmentary, acephalous) societies reacted. After they had formulated their plan, the Government announced that they would establish a large fund for colonial development which would include money for scientific research. Their proposal to the Council suggested that by backing the scheme the University could establish a claim on these funds ('as the London department is no longer functioning and the Cambridge school is concentrating on undergraduate teaching in the main'). In his covering letter Radcliffe-Brown expresses his 'very strong support' but the War-time Research Committee decided it had insufficient funds, although it recommended the proposal to the Council. If he 'had been cleverer or better inclined towards us he would have got the University to continue the scheme ... I much regret to hear that R.-B. did his best to sabotage the scheme ... I suppose he felt you were forced on him in the first place – you were in fact – and that this is his revenge.' (Evans-Pritchard to Fortes, August 1940).

6 14 December 1944.
7 Evans-Pritchard to Fortes, 7 August 1940. Perham was Margery Perham, the historian of the Commonwealth.
8 Evans-Pritchard to Fortes, 18 February 1941.
9 Evans-Pritchard, Oxford, to Fortes, West Africa, 3 October 1945.
10 Evans-Pritchard, Oxford, to Fortes, West Africa, 28 June 1945.
11 Evans-Pritchard to Fortes, 17 December 1940, Malakal, Sudan.
12 Evans-Pritchard, Oxford, to Fortes, Ashanti, 2 June 1945.
13 Evans-Pritchard, Cambridge, to Fortes, West Africa, 22 July 1945.
14 Evans-Pritchard, Natal, to Fortes, Cambridge, 19 August 1951.
15 Evans-Pritchard, Cape Town, to Fortes, Cambridge, 12 September 1951.
16 Firth 1975: 483.
17 Evans-Pritchard to Fortes, 26 July 1946, Cambridge.

7. SOME ACHIEVEMENTS OF ANTHROPOLOGY IN AFRICA

1 See Appendix 2.
2 Fortes 1976: 459.
3 Gellner 1981: 69.
4 Douglas 1980: 29.

5 Evans-Pritchard 1960b: 24.
6 Pocock 1961.
7 Barnes 1955, J. Goody 1957.
8 Edited by M. Banton, 1965. See also my article on 'descent groups' in the *Encyclopedia of the Social Sciences*.
9 Gluckman 1950: 203.
10 Fortes 1954: 316.
11 Fortes 1954: 320.
12 Ware 1978: 23.
13 Radcliffe-Brown and Forde 1950: 2.
14 Werbner 1984: 157.
15 Except in areas that came under Islamic influence when the Arabic script was introduced for the Arabic language, although its use was later broadened to include vernaculars both in East and West Africa.

8. PERSONAL CONTRIBUTIONS

1 A version of this chapter was originally given in Paris where Claude Tardits had asked me to come to give some lectures on the achievements of anthropology in Africa to the 5ème section of the Ecole Practique des Hautes Etudes. I recast it for publication when shortly afterwards I was asked to make a contribution to the *Annual Review of Anthropology*, where it appeared in 1991. I mention these points to explain these egocentric contributions which I include here because they offer one line of development of fieldwork studies. It is not one that all would wish to follow, but it does attempt to pursue in a different way the research of our predecessors that sought to mediate between the general and the particular.
2 For example, I wrote articles on 'Consensus and dissent in Ghana' (1968), 'Rice-burning and the green revolution' (1980) as well as on general impediments to development in Africa as compared to Asia. Much else exists in the unpublished form of talks.
3 I had later the pleasure of acting briefly as his clerk in the reknowned Al-Hajji Baba case in Kumasi in 1957, when the Government tried to expel him from Ghana as an alien.
4 Hart 1985.
5 The Colonial Social Science Research Council, working under the inspired secretaryship of Sally Chilver, was responsible for administering the grants that enabled Lloyd Fallers, Jim and Paula Bohannan, Al and Grace Harris and Bob Armstrong to work, first at Oxford, then in Africa. At the end of the war the Council promoted surveys of research needs in the social sciences in West Africa (undertaken by Raymond Firth), in East Africa (by Isaac Schapera) and Sarawak (by Edmund Leach).
6 J. Goody 1954. I have subsequently published, often in obscure places, a number of contributions to the ethnographic, historical and linguistic study

of the region. I would like to acknowledge the collaboration of a number of scholars working in the lively Institute of African Studies at the University of Ghana, Legon, at that time under the direction of Thomas Hodgkin, especially Kwame Arhin, Ivor Wilks and Nehemiah Levtzion. At the same time I would pay tribute to my long-standing collaborators among the LoDagaa, especially S.W.D.K. Gandah, and among the Gonja, especially the late J. A. Braimah, who became paramount chief of his kingdom and wrote extensively about its history; with Braimah I edited *Salaga: The Struggle for Power* (1967). One of the rewards of working in Africa over this period has been the pleasure of collaborating with Ghanaians such as Kwame Arhin (*Ashanti and the North-West*, 1966), Dougah on Wa (1966), J. A. Braimah on his grandfather, Isanwurfo (1967), K. Gandah on the Bagre (1981) and the memoirs of his own education (*The Silent Rebel*, forthcoming), Mustapha on various translations from the Hausa (1966, etc.). I have said little about these historical papers in this account but they were important in providing a diachronic view of the region as well as in trying to allow for the influences, both stabilising and disruptive, which colonial governments had on the peoples among whom earlier anthropologists were working, whether in Africa, the Americas or in Russia.

7 Lombard 1972: 238.
8 On witchcraft in Africa see Marwick (1965 and 1982).
9 J. Goody 1962: 273–327.
10 J. Goody 1966a.
11 In J. Goody 1971.
12 Fortes on the Tallensi (1945), Leach on the Kachin (1954), and others.
13 See, for example, Leavis 1932 and Watt 1967.
14 J. Goody and Poppi 1994.
15 J. Goody 1991.

9. CONCLUDING REMARKS

1 Boon 1973: 5.
2 Geertz 1966: 2.
3 Geertz 1966: 39–42.
4 Loeb edition 1960: 25.
5 There were of course more conservative trends at the LSE. Among economists Robbins was very influential and he recruited von Hayek to combat more 'liberal' tendencies in the subject.
6 In this final chapter I am much indebted to the remarks of Geoffrey Hawthorn.

APPENDIX I. CHANGING RESEARCH SCHEMES

1 I had considered editing the material on the research projects but concluded that to do so would be to reduce the value of the demonstration.

2 'I may add that I worked out these ideas in full in an essay, which Professor Malinowski induced me to write on some problems of the "functional" method.'

3 'On account of the fact that Government Reports, maps and most of the general works on northern Nigeria deal, in a summary way, chiefly with provinces (e.g. 'Bauchi Province'), I could not make out how far e.g. the following statement on the 'Bauchi-people' really includes the Plateau-tribes. It is necessary to study these people before they become entirely 'hausa-ized' (Morel 1912).'

APPENDIX 2:　TOWARDS THE STUDY OF THE HISTORY OF SOCIAL
ANTHROPOLOGY

1 Kuklick 1991: 25. One problem relates to the category 'anthropology' which Kuklick initially interprets in the current American sense of the term. Early on the analysis relates to social anthropology, archaeology and physical anthropology but in the later discussion the last two branches get quietly dropped.

2 Kuklick 1991: 35.
3 Kuklick 1991: 26.
4 Kuklick 1991: 279 (my italics).
5 Kuklick 1991: 292.
6 Kuklick 1984: 77.
7 Kuklick 1991: 276.
8 Stocking 1984: 114.
9 Stocking 1984: 119.
10 Kuklick 1991: 182.
11 See for example the volume edited by T. Asad (1973).
12 Kuklick 1991: 226.
13 Kuklick 1991: 268–9.
14 Kuklick 1991: 219.
15 Kuklick 1991: 222.
16 Kuklick 1991: 223.
17 Kuklick 1978: 108.
18 Kuklick 1991: 179.
19 Kuklick 1991: 174.
20 Kuklick 1991: 168.
21 Kuklick 1991: 156.
22 Kuklick 1991: 157.
23 Kuklick 1991: 221.
24 Kuklick 1991: 218.
25 Thomas 1983: 41.
26 Kuklick 1991: 86. The Irish too are added.
27 Kuklick 1991: 228.
28 Kuklick 1978: 108.

29 Kuklick 1991: 294.
30 Kuklick 1978: 98.
31 Kuklick 1991: 66.
32 Kuklick 1991: 69.
33 Kuklick 1991: 72.
34 Kuklick 1991: 5.
35 Kuklick 1991: 10.
36 See J. Goody 1956 on the Lobi.
37 Kuklick 1978: 95.
38 Kuklick 1978: 112.
39 Kuklick 1978: 97.
40 Kuklick 1991: 240.
41 Kuklick 1991: 241.
42 Kuklick 1991: 224–5.
43 Kuklick 1991: 225.
44 Kuklick 1991: 275.
45 Kuklick 1991: 279. She refers to those employed by colonial regimes.
46 Kuklick 1991: 76.

References

Aristotle 1960 *Posterior Analytics*. Loeb, London

Arnove, R. F. (ed.) 1980 *Philanthropy and Cultural Imperialism: The Foundations at Home and Abroad*. Boston

Asad, T. (ed.) 1973 *Anthropology and the Colonial Encounter*. London

Baeta, C. G. 1962 *Prophetism in Ghana; A Study of Some 'Spiritual' Churches*. London

Barnes, J. A. 1949 Measures of divorce frequency in simple societies. *Journal of the Royal Anthropological Institute* 79: 37–62

　1955 Seven types of segmentation. *The Rhodes–Livingstone Journal* 17: 1–22

　1962 African models in the New Guinea Highlands. *Man* 62: 5–9

　1967 (2nd edition, 1st edition 1954) *Politics in a Changing Society: A Political History of the Fort Jameson Ngoni*. Manchester.

　1971 *Three Styles in the Study of Kinship*. London

　1979 *Who Should Know What? Social Science, Privacy and Ethics*. Harmondsworth, Middlesex

　1987 Edward Evan Evans-Pritchard. *Proceedings of the British Academy* 73: 447–89

Barth, F. 1987 *Cosmologies in the Making: A Generative Approach to Cultural Variation in Inner New Guinea*. Cambridge

Beattie, J. 1964 *Other Cultures*. London

Becher, T. 1989 *Academic Tribes and Territories: Intellectual Enquiry and the Cultures of Disciplines*. Milton Keynes

Bennett, G. 1960 Paramountcy to partnership: J. H. Oldham and Africa. *Africa* 30: 353–61

Berman, E. H. 1980 Educational colonialism in Africa: the role of American foundations, 1910–1945. In R. F. Arnove (ed.), *Philanthropy and Cultural Imperialism: The Foundations at Home and Abroad*. Boston

Bohannan, P. J. 1957 *Justice and Judgement among the Tiv*. London

　(ed.) 1960 *African Homicide and Suicide*. Princeton

　1963 *Social Anthropology*. New York

Bohannan, P. and Dalton, G. (eds.) 1962 *Markets in Africa*. Evanston, Ill.

Boon, J. A. 1973 Further operations of 'Culture' in anthropology: a synthesis of and for debate. In L. Schneider and C. M. Bonjean (eds.), *The Idea of Culture in the Social Sciences*. Cambridge

Boyer, P. 1994 *The Naturalness of Religious Ideas: A Cognitive Theory of Religion.* Berkeley, Calif.

Braimah, J. A. 1967 *The Two Isanwurfos.* London

Braimah, J. A. and Goody, J. 1967 *Salaga: The Struggle for Power.* London

Brown, R. 1973. Anthropology and colonial rule: Godfrey Wilson and the Rhodes–Livingstone Institute. In T. Asad (ed.), *Anthropology and the Colonial Encounter.* London

　　1979 Passages in the life of a white anthropologist: Max Gluckman in Northern Rhodesia. *Journal of African History* 20: 525–41

Bulmer, M. 1980 The early institutional establishment of social science research: the Local Community Research Committee at the University of Chicago, 1923–1930. *Minerva* 18: 51–110

　　1981 Sociology and political science at Cambridge in the 1920s: an opportunity missed and an opportunity taken. *The Cambridge Review* 27 April 1981: 156–9

　　1982 Support for sociology in the 1920; the Laura Spelman Rockefeller Memorial and the beginnings of modern large-scale sociological research in the University. *The American Sociologist,* 17: 185–92

　　1984 Philanthropic foundations and the development of the social sciences in the early twentieth century: a reply to Donald Fisher. *Sociology* 18: 572–9

Bulmer, M. and J. 1981 Philanthropy and social science in the 1920s; Beardsley Ruml and the Laura Spelman Rockefeller Memorial, 1922–29. *Minerva* 19: 347–407

Busia, K. A. 1951 *The Position of the Chief in the Political System of Modern Ashanti.* London

Caldwell, J. C. 1976 Toward a restatement of demographic transition theory: an investigation of conditions before and at the onset of fertility decline employing primarily African experience and data. *Population and Development Review* 2: 321–66

　　1978 A theory of fertility: from high plateau to destabilization. *Population and Development Review* 4: 553–77

Caldwell, J. C. and P. 1987 The cultural context of high fertility in sub-Saharan Africa. *Population and Development Review* 13: 409–37

Clozel, M. F. J. 1902 *Les Coutumes indigènes de la Côte d' Ivoire.* Paris

Coben, S. 1976 Foundation officials and fellowships: innovation in the patronage of science. *Minerva* 14: 225–40

Cohen, A. 1969 *Custom and Politics in Urban Africa: A Study of Hausa Migrants in Yoruba Towns.* Berkeley, Calif.

Cohen, R. 1961 Marriage instability among the Kanuri of Northern Nigeria. *American Anthropologist* 63: 1231–49

Cohen, R. and Middleton, J. (eds.) 1970 *From Tribe to Nation in Africa: Studies in Incorporation Processes.* Scranton

Delafosse, M. 1912 *Haut-Sénégal-Niger.* Paris

Douglas, M. 1963 *The Lele of the Kasai.* London

1966 *Purity and Danger: An Analysis of Concepts of Pollution and Taboo.* London

1970a *Natural Symbols: Explorations in Cosmology.* London

1970b *Witchcraft, Confessions and Accusations.* London

1975 *Implicit Meanings: Essays in Anthropology.* London

1980 *Evans-Pritchard.* Brighton

Durkheim, E. 1893 *De la Division du Travail* (Engl. transl. 1933). Paris

Durkheim, E. and Mauss, M. 1963 *Primitive Classification* (trans. R. Needham). London

Evans-Pritchard, E. E. 1933–5 The Nuer tribe and clan. *Sudan Notes and Records:* 1–53; 1–57; 37–87

1936 Nuer age-sets. *Sudan Notes and Records:* 233–69

1937 *Witchcraft, Oracles and Magic among the Azande.* Oxford

1937–8 Economic life of the Nuer. *Sudan Notes and Records:* 209–45; 31–77

1940 *The Nuer.* Oxford

1949 *The Sanusi of Cyrenaica.* London

1951 *Social Anthropology.* London

(ed.) 1954 *The Institutions of Primitive Society: A Series of Broadcast Talks.* Oxford

1956 *Nuer Religion.* Oxford

1960a *Kinship and Marriage among the Nuer.* Oxford

1960b Introduction to R. Hertz, *Death* and *The Right Hand* (transl. R. and C. Needham). London

1963 *The Comparative Method in Social Anthropology.* London

1965a *Theories of Primitive Religion.* Oxford

1965b *The Position of Women in Primitive Societies, and Other Essays on Social Anthropology.* London

1973 Genesis of a social anthropologist – an autobiographical note. *The New Diffusionist* 3: 17–23

1981 *A History of Anthropological Thought.* London

Fallers, L. A. 1957 Some determinants of marriage instability in Busoga: a reformulation of Gluckman's thesis. *Africa* 27: 106–21

Firth, R. 1956 A. R. Radcliffe-Brown, 1881–1955. *Proceedings of the British Academy* 42: 287–302

(ed.) 1957 *Man and Culture: An Evaluation of the Work of B. Malinowski.* London

1963 A brief history of the department (1913–1963). In *Department of Anthropology* (a London School of Economics and Political Science prospectus)

1975 Max Gluckman, 1911–1975. *Proceedings of the British Academy* 61: 479–96

Fisher, D. 1978 The Rockefeller Foundation and the development of scientific medicine in Great Britain. *Minerva* 16: 20–41

1983 The role of philanthropic foundations in the reproduction and production of hegemony: Rockefeller foundations and the social sciences. *Sociology* 17: 206–33

Forde, C. D. 1934 *Habitat, Economy and Society: A Geographical Introduction to Ethnology.* London (ed.) 1954 *African Worlds; Studies in the Cosmological Ideas and Social Values of African Peoples*. London

Forde, C. D. and Gluckman, M. (eds.) 1966 *Essays on the Ritual of Social Relations*. Manchester

Fortes, M. 1930. A new application of the theory of neogenesis to the problem of mental testing. (Perceptual tests of 'g'.) PhD thesis, University of London

　1932 Perceptual tests of 'general intelligence' for inter-racial use. *Transactions of the Royal Society of South Africa* 20: 281–99

　1936 Ritual festivals and social cohesion in the hinterland of the Gold Coast. *American Anthropologist* 38: 590–604

　1938 Social and psychological aspects of education in Taleland. *Africa* 11 (4): supplement

　1943 A note on fertility among the Tallensi of the Gold Coast. *Sociological Review* 35: 99–113

　1945 *The Dynamics of Clanship among the Tallensi, Being the First Part of an Analysis of the Social Structure of a Trans-Volta tribe*. London

　1949a *The Web of Kinship among the Tallensi: The Second Part of an Analysis of the Social Structure of a Trans-Volta Tribe*. London

　1949b Time and social structure: an Ashanti case-study. In M. Fortes (ed.), *Social Structure: Essays Presented to A. R. Radcliffe-Brown*. Oxford

　(ed.) 1949c *Social Structure: Essays Presented to A. R. Radcliffe-Brown*. Oxford

　1953 The structure of unilineal descent groups. *American Anthropologist* 55: 17–41

　1954 Mind. In E. E. Evans-Pritchard, Firth, R., Leach E. R., *et al. The Institutions of Primitive Society*. Oxford

　1959 *Oedipus and Job in West African Religions*. Cambridge

　1969 *Kinship and the Social Order: The Legacy of Lewis Henry Morgan*. London

　1970 *Time and Social Structure and Other Essays*. London

　1976 Cyril Daryll Forde, 1902–1973. *Proceedings of the British Academy* 62: 459–83

　1978 An anthropologist's apprenticeship. *Annual Review of Anthropology*. Palo Alto, California

　1987 *Morality, Religion and the Person*. London

Fortes, M. and Evans-Pritchard, E. E. 1940 *African Political Systems*. London

Freud, S. 1913 *Totem and Taboo*. Vienna

Gandah, K. forthcoming *The Silent Rebel*

Geertz, C. 1966 Religion as a cultural system. In M. Banton (ed.), *Anthropological Approaches to the Study of Religion*. London

　1983 Slide show, Evans-Pritchard's African transparencies. *Raritan Quarterly*, Fall: 62–80

Gellner, E. 1981 Introduction to E. E. Evans-Pritchard, *A History of Anthropological Thought* (ed. A. Singer). London

　1988 The stakes in anthropology. *The American Scholar*, Winter: 17–30

Gluckman, M. 1945 African land tenure. *The Rhodes–Livingstone Journal* 3: 1–12

1950 Kinship and marriage among the Lozi of Northern Rhodesia and the Zulu of Natal. In A. R. Radcliffe-Brown and C. D. Forde (eds.), *African Systems of Kinship and Marriage*. London

1954 *Rituals of Rebellion in South-East Africa*. Manchester

1955a *Custom and Conflict in Africa*. Oxford

1955a *The Judicial Process among the Barotse of Northern Rhodesia*. Manchester

1958 *Analysis of a Social Situation in Modern Zululand*, Rhodes–Livingstone Paper, no. 28. Manchester

1963 *Order and Rebellion in Tribal Africa: Collected Essays with an Autobiographical Introduction*. London

1965a *The Ideas in Barotse Jurisprudence*. New Haven

1965b *Politics, Law and Ritual in Tribal Society*. Oxford

Goody, E. N. 1962 Conjugal separation and divorce among the Gonja of northern Ghana. In M. Fortes (ed.), *Marriage in Tribal Societies*. Cambridge

1973 *Contexts of Kinship: An Essay in the Family Sociology of the Gonja of Northern Ghana*. Cambridge

1982a *Parenthood and Social Reproduction: Fostering and Occupational Roles in West Africa*. Cambridge

(ed.) 1982b *From Craft to Industry: The Ethnography of Proto-Industrial Cloth Production*. Cambridge

Goody, J. 1954. *An Ethnography of the Northern Territories of the Gold Coast East of the White Volta*. London (mimeo)

1956a A comparative approach to incest and adultery. *British Journal of Sociology* 7: 286–305

1956b *The Social Organization of the LoWiili*. London

1957 Fields of social control among the LoDagaba. *Journal of the Royal Anthropological Institute* 87: 75–104

1958 The fission of domestic groups among the LoDagaa. In J. Goody (ed.), *The Developmental Cycle in Domestic Groups*. Cambridge

1959 The mother's brother and the sister's son in West Africa. *Journal of the Royal Anthropological Institute* 89: 61–88

1962 *Death, Property and the Ancestors*. Stanford

(ed.), 1966a *Succession to High Office*. Cambridge

1966 Ed. and Introduction: J. C. Dougah, *Wa and its People*, Local Studies Series, 1, Legon, Ghana

1967 Introduction and notes: J. A. Braimah, *The Two Isanwurfos*. London

(ed.) 1968a *Literacy in Traditional Society*. Cambridge

1968b Consensus and dissent in Ghana. *Political Science Quarterly* 83: 337–52

1971 *Technology, Tradition, and the State in Africa*. Oxford

1972 *The Myth of the Bagre*. Oxford

1973 British functionalism. In R. and F. Naroll (eds.), *Main Currents in Cultural Anthropology*. New York

1977a *The Domestication of the Savage Mind*. Cambridge

1977b *Production and Reproduction*. Cambridge

1980 Rice-burning and the Green Revolution in northern Ghana. *Journal of Developmental Studies* 16: 136–55

1982 *Cooking, Cuisine, and Class.* Cambridge

1983a *The Development of Family and Marriage in Europe.* Cambridge

1983b Introduction. Memorial Issue for M. Fortes. *Cambridge Anthropology* 8: 2–3

1984 Under the lineage's shadow. *Proceedings of the British Academy* 70: 189–208

1986 *The Logic of Writing and the Organisation of Society.* Cambridge

1987 *The Interface between the Written and the Oral.* Cambridge

1990 *The Oriental, the Ancient, and the Primitive.* Cambridge

1991 Icônes et iconoclasme en Afrique. *Annales ESC* 1235–51

1993a *The Culture of Flowers.* Cambridge

1993b Meyer Fortes, 1906–1983. *Proceedings of the British Academy* 80: 275–87

Goody, J. and Addo, N. 1977 *Siblings in Ghana.* University of Ghana Population Studies, 7. Legon, Ghana

Goody, J. and Arhin, K. (eds.) 1966 *Ashanti and the North-West.* Legon, Ghana

Goody, J. and Duly, C. 1981 Studies in the use of computers in social anthropology. Report of the Social Science Research Council, London

Goody, J., Duly, C., Beeson, I. and Harrison, G. 1981a On the absence of implicit sex-preferences in Ghana. *Journal of Biological Science* 13: 87–96

1981b Implicit sex-preferences: a comparative study. *Journal of Biological Science* 13: 455–66

Goody, J. and Gandah, K. 1981 *Une Récitation du Bagre.* Paris

Goody, J. and Goody, E. N. 1966 Cross-cousin marriage in northern Ghana. *Man* n.s. 1: 343–55

1967 The circulation of women and children in northern Ghana. *Man* n.s. 2: 226–48

Goody, J. and Mustapha, T. M. 1966 Salaga in 1874. *Research Review*, Institute of African Studies, Legon, Ghana, 2 (2): 23–37

Goody, J. and Poppi, C. 1994 Flowers and bones: approaches to the dead in Italian and Anglo-American cemeteries. *Comparative Studies in Society and History* 36: 146–75

Goody, J. and Tambiah, S. J. 1973 *Bridewealth and Dowry.* Cambridge

Goody, J. and Watt, I. P. 1963 The consequences of literacy. *Comparative Studies in Society and History* 5: 304–45

Greenberg, J. H. 1946 *The Influence of Islam upon a Sudanese Religion.* Monograph of the American Ethnological Society, 10. New York

Hart, K. 1982 *The Political Economy of West African Agriculture.* Cambridge

1985 The social anthropology of West Africa. *Annual Review of Anthropology* 14: 243–72

Hellman, E. 1948 *Rooiyard, a Sociological Survey of an Urban Native Slumyard.* Cape Town

Hertz, R. 1960 *Death* and *The Right Hand* (transl. R. and C. Needham). London

Hill, P. 1963 *Migrant Cocoa-Farmers of Southern Ghana: A Study in Rural Capitalism.* Cambridge

1970 *Studies in Rural Capitalism in West Africa.* Cambridge

1972 *Rural Hausa: A Village and a Setting.* Cambridge

1977 *Population, Prosperity and Poverty: Rural Kano 1900 and 1970.* Cambridge

1982 *Dry Grain Farming Families: Hausaland (Nigeria) and Karnataka (India) Compared.* Cambridge

1986 *Development Economics on Trial: The Anthropological Case for a Prosecution.* Cambridge

Hinde, R. A. 1987 *Individuals, Relationships and Culture: Links between Ethology and the Social Sciences.* Cambridge

Homans, G. C. and Schneider, D. 1955 *Marriage, Authority, and Final Causes: A Study of Unilateral Cross-Cousin Marriage.* Glencoe, Illinois

Jarvie, I. 1964 *The Revolution in Anthropology.* London

Karl, B. and Katz, S. 1987 Foundations and ruling-class elites. *Daedalus* 116 (1): 1–40

Kenyatta, J. 1953 *Facing Mount Kenya: The Tribal Life of Gikuyu.* London

King, K. J. 1969 Africa and the southern states of the United States of America: notes on J. H. Oldham and American negro education for Africans. *Journal of African History* 10: 659–77

Krige, E. J. and J. D. 1943 *The Realm of a Rain Queen.* London

Kuklick, H. 1978 The sins of the fathers: British anthropology and African colonial administration. *Research in the Sociology of Knowledge, Sciences and Art* 1: 93–119

1984 Tribal exemplars: images of political authority in British anthropology, 1885–1945. In G. W. Stocking, Jnr (ed.), *Functionalism Historicized: Essays on British Social Anthropology.* History of Anthropology, 2. Madison, Wis.

1991 *The Savage Within: The Social History of British Anthropology 1885–1945.* Cambridge

Kuper, A. 1973 *Anthropology and Anthropologists: The British School 1922–1972.* London

1982 Lineage theory: a critical retrospect. *Annual Review of Anthropology* 11: 71–95

Kuper, H. 1947 *An African Aristocracy: Rank among the Swazi.* London

Langham, I. 1981 *The Building of British Social Anthropology: W. H. R. Rivers and his Cambridge Disciples in the Development of Kinship Studies, 1898–1931.* Dordrecht

Leach, E. R. 1951 The structural implications of matrilateral cross-cousin marriage. *Journal of the Royal Anthropological Institute* 81: 23–53

1954 *Political Systems of Highland Burma: A Study of Kachin Social Structure.* London

1957 Aspects of bridewealth and marriage stability among the Kachin and Lakher. *Man* 57: 50–5

1958 Magical hair. *Journal of the Royal Anthropological Institute* 88: 147–64

Leavis, Q. D. 1932 *Fiction and the Reading Public.* London

Lewis, I. M. 1961 *A Pastoral Democracy: A Study of Pastoralism and Politics among the Northern Somali of the Horn of Africa*. London
 1962 *Marriage and the Family in Northern Somaliland*, East African Studies, 15. Kampala
 1965 Problems in the comparative study of unilineal descent. In M. Banton (ed.), *The Relevance of Models for Social Anthropology*. London
 1971 *Ecstatic Religion: An Anthropological Study of Spirit Possession and Shamanism*. Harmondsworth, Middlesex
 1976 *Social Anthropology in Perspective: The Relevance of Social Anthropology*. Harmondsworth, Middlesex
 1986 *Religion in Context: Cults and Charisma*. Cambridge
Lienhardt, G. 1961 *Divinity and Experience: The Religion of the Dinka*. Oxford
 1964 *Social Anthropology*. London
Lloyd, P. C. 1962 *Yoruba Land Law*. Cambridge
 1966 *The New Elites of Tropical Africa*. London
Lombard, J. 1972 *L'Anthropologie britannique contemporaine*. Paris
Lorrimer, F. 1954 *Culture and Human Fertility*. UNESCO
Maine, H. S. 1861 *Ancient Law*. London
Mair, L. 1962 *Primitive Government*. Harmondsworth, Middlesex
 1969 *Witchcraft*. London
 1971 *Marriage*. Harmondsworth, Middlesex
Malinowski, B. 1922 *Argonauts of the Western Pacific*. London
 1927a *The Father in Primitive Psychology*. London
 1927b *Sex and Repression in Savage Society*. London
 1929 *The Sexual Life of Savages in North-Western Melanesia*. London
 1929 Practical anthropology. *Africa* 2: 23–39
 1939 The present state of studies in culture contact: some comments on an American approach. *Africa* 12: 27–47
Marwick M. G. 1965 *Sorcery in its Social Setting: A Study of the Northern Rhodesian Cewa*. Manchester
 (ed.) 1982 [1970] *Witchcraft and Sorcery: Selected Readings*. Harmondsworth, Middlesex
Mauss, M. 1924 *Le Don*. Paris
 1954 *The Gift* (transl. I. Cunnison). London
Middleton, J. 1960 *Lugbara Religion: Ritual and Authority among an East African People*. London
 (ed.) 1970 *Black Africa: Its Peoples and Their Cultures Today*. London
Middleton, J. and Tait D. (eds.) 1958 *Tribes without Rulers: Studies in African Segmentary Systems*. London
Migeod, F. W. H. 1908 *The Mende Language*. London
Mitchell, J. C. 1956 *The Yao Village: A Study in the Social Structure of a Nyasaland Tribe*. Manchester
 1959 *The Kalela Dance: Aspects of Social Relationships among Urban Africans in Northern Rhodesia*. Livingstone
 1960 *Tribalism and the Plural Society: An Inaugural Lecture*. London

1961 Social change and the stability of African marriage in Northern Rhodesia. In A. Southall (ed.), *Social Change in Modern Africa*. London

1969 *Social Networks in Urban Situations: Analyses of Personal Relationships in Central African Towns*. Manchester

Morel, E. D. 1912 (2nd edn) *Nigeria: Its Peoples and its Problems*. London

Nadel, S. F. 1942 *A Black Byzantium: The Kingdom of Nupe in Nigeria*. London

1947 *The Nuba: An Anthropological Study of the Hill Tribes in Kordofan*. London

1951 *The Foundations of Social Anthropology*. London

1952 Witchcraft in four African societies: an essay in comparison. *American Anthropologist* 54: 18–29

1954 *Nupe Religion*. London

1957 *The Theory of Social Structure*. London

Panoff, M. 1972 *Bronislaw Malinowski*. Paris

Peel, J. D. Y. 1968 *Aladura: A Religious Movement among the Yoruba*. Oxford

Petermann, B. 1932 *The Gestalt Theory and the Problem of Configuration* (transl. M. Fortes). London

Peters, E. L. 1990 *The Bedouin of Cyrenaica: Studies in Personal and Corporate Power*. London

Pocock, D. F. 1961 *Social Anthropology*. London

Rabinovich, I. and Yaffe, G. 1990 An anthropologist as political officer: Evans-Pritchard, the French and the Alawis. In H. Shamir (ed.), *France and Germany in an Age of Crisis, 1900–1960*. New York

Radcliffe-Brown, A. R. 1922 *The Andaman Islanders*. Cambridge

1924 The mother's brother in South Africa. *South African Journal of Science* 21: 542–55

1935 Patrilineal and matrilineal succession. Reprinted in A. R. Radcliffe-Brown, *Structure and Function in Primitive Society* (1952). London

Radcliffe-Brown, A. R. and Forde, C. D. (eds.) 1950 *African Systems of Kinship and Marriage*. London

Richards, A. I. 1932 *Hunger and Work in a Savage Tribe: A Functional Study of Nutrition among the Southern Bantu*. London

1939 *Land, Labour and Diet in Northern Rhodesia: An Economic Study of the Bemba Tribe*. London

1950 Some types of family structure amongst the central Bantu. In A. R. Radcliffe-Brown and C. D. Forde (eds.) *African Systems of Kinship and Marriage*. London

Rivers, W. H. R. 1914 *Kinship and Social Organisation*. London

Roberts, S. 1979 *Order and Dispute: An Introduction to Legal Anthropology*. Harmondsworth, Middlesex

Schapera, I. 1947 *Migrant Labour and Tribal Life: A Study of Conditions in the Bechuanaland Protectorate*. London

1955 (2nd edition) *A Handbook of Tswana Law*. London

1956 *Government and Politics in Tribal Societies*. London

Schildkrout, E. 1978 *People of the Zongo: The Transformation of Ethnic Identities in Ghana*. Cambridge

Schneider, D. M. 1953 A note on bridewealth and the stability of marriage. *Man* 53: 55–7

Schneider, D. M. and Gough, K. (eds.) 1961 *Matrilineal Kinship*. Berkeley, California

Smith, E. W. 1934 The story of the Institute: the first seven years. *Africa* 7: 1–27

Smith, M. G. 1955 *The Economy of Hausa Communities of Zaria: A Report*. Colonial Social Science Research Council, London

1960 *Government in Zazzau, 1800–1950*. London

1974 *Corporations and Society*. London

1978 *The Affairs of Daura*. Berkeley, California

Spencer, P. 1965 *The Samburu: A Study of Gerontocracy*. London

Stocking, G. W. Jnr. 1983 The ethnographer's magic: fieldwork in British anthropology from Tylor to Malinowski. In G. W. Stocking, Jnr (ed.), *Observers Observed*, History of Anthropology, 1. Madison, Wis.

1984 Radcliffe-Brown and British social anthropology. In G. W. Stocking, Jnr (ed.), *Functionalism Historicized: Essays on British Social Anthropology*, History of Anthropology, 2. Madison, Wis.

1985 Philanthropoids and vanishing cultures: Rockefeller funding and the end of the museum era in Anglo-American anthropology. In G. W. Stocking, Jnr (ed.), *Objects and Others: Essays on Museums and Material Culture*, History of Anthropology, 3. Madison, Wis.

Tait, D. E. 1961 *The Konkomba of Northern Ghana*. London

Thomas, K. 1983 *Man and the Natural World: Changing Attitudes in England 1500–1800*. London

van Gennep, A. 1908 *Rites de Passage*. Paris

Verdon, M. 1981 Kinship, marriage and the family, an operational approach. *American Journal of Sociology* 86: 796–818

Ware, H. 1978 The economic value of children in Asia and Africa; comparative perspectives. *Papers of the East–West Population Institute*, Hawaii

Watson, W. 1958 *Tribal Cohesion in a Money Economy: A Study of the Mambwe People of Northern Rhodesia*. Manchester

Watt, I. P. 1967 *The Rise of the Novel: Studies in Defoe, Richardson, and Fielding*. Berkeley, California

Werbner, R. P. 1984 The Manchester school in south-central Africa. *Annual Review of Anthropology*. Palo Alto, California

Westermann, D. 1921 *Die Kpelle, ein Negerstamm in Liberia*. Göttingen

Wilson, G. and M. 1945 *The Analysis of Social Change based on Observations in Central Africa*. London

Wilson, M. 1951 *Good Company: A Study of Nyakyusa Age-Villages*. London

1957 *Rituals of Kinship among the Nyakyusa*. London

1959a *Communal Rituals of the Nyakyusa*. London

1959b *Divine Kings and the 'Breath of Man'*. Cambridge

1964 *Reaction to Conquest: Effects of Contact with Europeans on the Pondo of South Africa*. London

Index